CHINA CEO

Voices of Experience

FROM

20 INTERNATIONAL BUSINESS LEADERS

CHINA CEO

Voices of Experience

FROM

20 INTERNATIONAL BUSINESS LEADERS

JUAN ANTONIO FERNANDEZ

LAURIE UNDERWOOD

JOHN WILEY & SONS (ASIA) PTE LTD

Published in 2006 by John Wiley & sons (Asia) Pte Ltd
2 Clementi Loop, #02-10, Singapore 129809

Other Wiley Editorial Offices
John Wiley & Sons, Inc., 111 River Street, Hoboken, NJ 07030, USA
John Wiley & Sons Ltd, The Atrium, Southern Gate, Chichester PO19 BSQ, England
John Wiley & Sons (Canada) Ltd, 5353 Dundas Street West, Suite 400, Toronto, Ontario M9B 6H8, Canada
John Wiley & Sons Australia Ltd, 42 McDougall Street, Milton, Queensland 4064, Australia
Wiley-VCH, Boschstrasse 12, D-69469 Weinheim, Germany

Library of Congress Cataloging-in-Publication Data:
ISBN-13 978-0-470-82192-3
ISBN-10 0-470-82192-2

Cover design and page layout by Alicia Beebe

Printed in Singapore by Saik Wah Press Pte Ltd.
10 9 8 7 6 5 4 3 2 1

To my wife, Wu Hanning, for her love and patience and to our son, Simon, for the many happy moments he brings to our marriage.
J.A.F.

I never could have finished this project without the support and love of my family and friends. I am extremely thankful to my husband, Jeffrey Wilson, and our children, Sydney and Schafer, for putting up with more than two years of work on "the book." I am also grateful to my parents Dorothy Staley and Larry Underwood and to my manuscript readers and advisors—Aamir Khan, Madhav Timalsina, Constance Woods, and Cheryl Sheridan—for their honest assessment, steadfast encouragement, and deep friendship.
L.U.

Contents

Foreword
China: A Must-win Market

"China has telescoped into one generation what other countries took centuries to achieve. No country (let alone one of continental proportions) has tried to accomplish so much in such a short time. China's unique attempt to complete two transitions at once—from a command to a market economy and from a rural to an urban society—is without historical precedent."

The World Bank, *China 2020: Development and Challenges in the New Century*

In the late 1990s, it was widely reported that half of the world's cranes were located in a single city: Shanghai. Visitors to that city during those years would have believed it; after all, what other metropolis was being developed faster or further than Shanghai, where the skyline was utterly transformed within the span of one decade? Consider the expansion of the transportation infrastructure alone: since the mid-1990s, China's largest city (population of 20 million, with suburbs) has gained a second international airport, a three-line subway system with 11 additional lines under construction, the Inner and Outer Ring roads, two major elevated freeways, and an elevated mag-lev light rail system. And that says nothing of the rapid morphing of many city neighborhoods, from dark, low-rise concrete homes to glistening apartment buildings, from quiet rice paddies to roaring office parks.

The construction boom in Shanghai is merely the most dramatic example of a vast economic transformation under way throughout China. From its position of international isolation at the end of the Cultural Revolution, the country has risen to assume its current status among the world's largest trading nations. Perhaps most remarkable: while developing nations typically experience periods of boom and bust, China has enjoyed a steady growth-rate above 9% since the 1980s.[1] Wealth has increased so rapidly in China's major cities that the average per capita annual income in, for example, Shanghai in 2003 exceeded US$5,700[2] while China overall averaged US$1,100.[3] Government sources predict that by 2007 per capita gross domestic product (GDP) in Shanghai will reach US$7,900. (When purchasing power parity is factored in, the average income of Shanghai residents already approaches US$15,000.[4])

Outside the largest cities, China's transformation is less dramatic but still sweeping. James D. Wolfensohn, then president of the World Bank Group, visited China in 1995 and again in May 2002. After traveling from the underdeveloped west of the country to the prosperous south and east, and meeting with top leaders—then-President Jiang Zemin and Premier Zhu Rongji—as well as private businesspeople and local families, Wolfensohn declared the progress of China in five years to be "impressive and remarkable." He said, "In a relatively short time, China has emerged as a country of truly global stature, having joined the World Trade Organization [WTO], strengthened ties with ASEAN, and won the right to host the 2008 Olympics. This is a more dynamic, more confident China—and rightly so. The simple fact is that more than 250 million people in the past 20 years have been lifted from poverty here. The problems confronting China have not been totally overcome—far from it—but the magnitude of this achievement in a single generation is such that other countries should learn from it."

The economic development of China is not lost on multinational corporations (MNCs). For companies the world over, the nation is

---

1 Some independent estimates are lower. For the 1980s–1990s, the World Bank reduces the PRC government rate by 1.2 percentage points, while the Organization for Economic Cooperation and Development (OECD) cuts 3.8 percentage points. Even after such adjustments are made, China's economic growth remains impressive.

2 *Shanghai Statistical Yearbook*, 2004.

3 *China Statistical Yearbook*, 2004.

4 USDA Foreign Agricultural Service (www.fas.usda.gov)

increasingly seen as a critical component in their global strategy. The Middle Kingdom (a literal translation of the Mandarin-language country name "Zhong Guo") now reigns as the world's largest destination for foreign direct investment (FDI), attracting nearly US$50 billion in 2002 and overtaking the United States for the first time in history.[5] By 2007, annual FDI into China is expected to reach nearly US$65 billion. The investment inflow has sped China's move toward market capitalism, shifting the composition of the economy away from state-owned enterprises (SOEs) toward private companies and encouraging the influx of foreign participation through joint ventures and wholly foreign-owned enterprises (WFOEs).

Business leaders throughout the West already know that China now offers potentially the most attractive investment environment in the world, serving up a heady mix of consistently healthy GDP growth rates plus newly opened industry sectors, political stability, fast-developing human resources, and exploding consumer wealth.

For a growing number of MNCs, this dramatic and ongoing economic transformation increasingly means one thing: China is now, in the words of one top manager profiled in this book, a "must-win market." The nation is critical both as a manufacturing base for export and as a destination market itself. In the three decades since Deng Xiaoping opened China's borders to international trade, MNCs increasingly have made this region a focal point within their global business strategy. The urgency among global players entering or expanding in the nation has only heightened since the country's 2001 entry into the WTO.

Consider the experiences of the 28 China-based top executives and consultants profiled in this book. From Alcatel to Sony, Bayer to Unilever, the message repeated again and again was this: in the words of Du Pont China President Charles Browne, MNCs now have "a laser light focused on China." Du Pont now receives 5% of its corporate sales from China, but that figure is growing steadily. Browne: "China is one of the few countries nowadays where the economy doesn't show signs of slowing down. It is strategically important for the future because of the growth rate. If you go to

5 A note of caution concerning China surpassing the United States as the top FDI destination in the world: U.S.-bound investments plunged in 2001 and 2002, from previous levels near US$300 billion.

our headquarters and ask which region we are concentrating on, the answer is that we are focused on China, China, China."

Other senior executives expressed equally great dedication to their China operations. Consider that:

- For the Coca-Cola Company, China is now the fastest growing market in consumption volume worldwide. In 2005, China was Coke's fifth-largest market in terms of consumption volume, behind the U.S., Mexico, Brazil, and Japan; by 2008, China will likely rank third. Says Coca-Cola China president Paul Etchells: "The business climate [in China] is much more positive—economic growth here is much higher—than in most other places in the world. So we are getting better growth here than in most other places. ... China is very, very important to the Coca-Cola Company."
- For Siemens, China is now the number 3 market worldwide after the U.S. and Europe, and will likely move to number 1 by 2010. China president and CEO Dr. Ernst Behrens says, "The China market is right at the center of Siemens. The growth potential of the China market is significantly higher than that of the more saturated European or U.S. markets."
- China is a "must-win" market for Unilever, according to Unilever China chairman Alan Brown. Brown calls the country Unilever's "strategic focal point" and its primary growth market. "Any consumer goods company with global aspirations would say China is of the highest long-term strategic priority."

The central message from our 28 top executives and consultants in China was simple and clear: China is a country that international companies cannot ignore. Since you probably can't beat it, you're better off joining it. Chances are that most of your competitors are in China already and, perhaps even more important, the nation is now producing new international competitors as domestic Chinese firms develop and expand globally. Sooner or later, you will find that China is changing the rules of the business game no matter what your industry is or where your main target markets are located. It is best to learn the new rules of the game, rather than find yourself relegated to the sidelines.

Introduction
Opportunity and Challenge

"Nowhere in the world is there a market like this—nowhere. To me, the 21st century will be the Chinese century. China will change the economic balance of the world."

Guy McLeod, President, Airbus China

Deng Xiaoping declared on June 29, 1985 that, "[China's reform] is a great experiment that is not described in books." Ironically, it is this "great experiment" statement that has formed the impetus for this book. As Deng so aptly stated, the economic transition now under way in China is unprecedented. Any business executive who frequents China today will agree that the nation is pioneering its own path in the transformation from a planned economy to one that embraces market capitalism—albeit a form with Chinese characteristics. The prevailing characteristic of this journey is uncertainty: uncharted territory, false starts, trial and error.

In the pages that follow, it is our goal as authors to prove the last half of Deng's statement wrong: we have in fact written a book describing the "great experiment." In *China CEO: Voices of Experience from 20 International Business Leaders*, we detail the chaotic, confusing, but highly compelling Chinese business environment, as seen from the eyes of the CEOs and country managers leading the China operations of multinational companies. It is our hope that you will learn as much from these top executives as we did in the course of writing this book.

"

The purpose of this book is to identify and address the primary challenges facing the presidents and managing directors of multinational companies operating in today's China."

The authors,
China CEO

We began our research with a series of in-depth meetings with 20 U.S., European, and Japanese top executives managing China operations for Fortune 500 companies. We matched the first-hand insights and strategies gleaned from these interviews against the assessments of eight China-based expert consultants from broader disciplines—human resources, law, strategy, and family counseling. Our interviewees hail from a wide spectrum of fields and specialties, and our discussions with them cover a broad range of topics.

What surprised us while analyzing our interview transcripts was the high degree of agreement among interviewees on the ideal basic characteristics and skills deemed critical for international (non-Chinese) managers in China. Despite vast differences in the backgrounds of our profiled executives—they work in 20 distinct industries—a rough consensus quickly emerged.

Voices of Experience

The purpose of this book is to identify and address the primary challenges facing the presidents and managing directors of MNCs operating in today's China. Our interviewees were chosen from a wide range of fields—from cars to cosmetics, software to supermarkets—but each had to meet a set of criteria: each one is the top executive for a successful MNC in China. The companies profiled employ a combined three million people worldwide, including 126,200 in China (125,000 Chinese nationals and 1,200 expatriates). Together, these enterprises have amassed 512 years of operating experience in China, for an average of 26 years per company. Three of the profiled companies were operating in China before the communist "liberation": Standard Chartered was established in the Middle Kingdom when it was under the rule of the last emperor (ousted in 1912), while Unilever set up in 1923 and Coca-Cola in 1927. Five other companies have been in the country for more than 20 years, since the very beginning of Deng Xiaoping's reforms.

The professional experience of the 20 individual senior executives we profile is in some ways even more impressive. This group of China hands[1] has a combined total of 466 years of work experience in their companies, including 294 years spent overseas and 105 years spent in China. If we were to create a composite "average" interviewee, he (all of our profiled senior executives are men) would be aged in his early fifties, and would have enjoyed a long and very stable career with the same company (23 years is the average), including 15 years of international experience and five years in China. The basic job description is extremely broad, typically characterized as "oversees operations in China." Specific responsibilities, of course, vary widely; however, each position includes a mix of directing all aspects of the company's current work, leading future growth in China (or Greater China or North Asia), and serving as the company's key representative in external interactions with government, business partners, and customers, as well as internally with global headquarters and local employees. (For a listing of all featured interviewees, see "Who Is in This Book?", below.)

Challenges of China: Leading the Blind Through a Minefield

For all of its allure to multinational companies, China offers international investors at least as much risk as it does promise. All MNCs in China suffer, at least to some extent, in the struggle to straddle two business environments and two social and political systems. So many China ventures fail that not even the fastest growing international firm in China would dare refer to the country as an "easy win." The tension between the foreign motivation to enter this market and China's desire to protect itself is an old, old story spanning many centuries. (Accounts of European traders entering China date back at least to Marco Polo's journeys to Asia in the 13th century.) All of which brings us to the challenges of managing operations in China.

1 "China hand" is a common expression among managers of multinationals to indicate those with ample China experience.

Who Is in This Book?

TOP EXECUTIVES INTERVIEWED
(in alphabetical order)

Dr. Ernst H. Behrens, *president & CEO, Siemens Ltd., China**

Mr. Dominique de Boisseson, *chairman & CEO, Alcatel China Investment Co.*

Mr. Alan Brown, *chairman, Unilever China*

Mr. Charles G. Browne, *president, Du Pont China Holding Co. Ltd.**

Mr. David Chang, *CEO, Philips (China) Investment Co., Ltd.*

Mr. Jean-Luc Chereau, *president, Carrefour China*

Dr. Gary Dirks, *group vice president, president, & chief executive, British Petroleum (BP) China*

Mr. Paul Etchells, *president, Coca-Cola China Beverages Ltd.*

Mr. Paolo Gasparrini, *president & managing director, L'Oréal China*

Mr. Seiichi Kawasaki, *director & president, Sony (China) Ltd.*

Mr. Guy McLeod, *president, Airbus China, Ltd.**

Mr. Philip Murtaugh, *chairman & CEO, General Motors China Group**

Mr. Ekkehard Rathgeber, *president, Bertelsmann Direct Group Asia**

Mr. Volkmar Ruebel, *general manager, Hilton Shanghai*

Mr. Steve Schneider, *chairman & CEO, General Electric China**

Mr. Christopher Shaw, *president, Eli Lilly China**

Dr. Elmar Stachels, *CEO, Bayer Greater China**

Mr. Jun Tang, *president, Microsoft (China) Co., Ltd.**

Mr. Stanley Y. F. Wong, *chief executive, China, Standard Chartered Bank**

Mr. Kenneth C. H. Yu, *managing director, 3M China Ltd.*

INTERVIEWEES HAILED FROM THE FOLLOWING MNCs
(in alphabetical order, by region)

EUROPE		UNITED STATES
Airbus	L'Oréal	3M
Alcatel	Philips	Coca-Cola
Bayer	Siemens	Du Pont
Bertelsmann	Standard Chartered	Eli Lilly
British Petroleum	Unilever	General Electric
Carrefour	**JAPAN**	General Motors
Hilton	Sony	Microsoft

PROFESSIONAL SERVICE EXPERTS INTERVIEWED
(in alphabetical order)

Mr. Jack Chang, *chairman, Quality Brand Protection Committee (QBPC) of the China Association of Enterprises With Foreign Investment*

Mr. Norman P. Givant, *Shanghai office managing partner, China Practice Group, Freshfields Bruckhaus Deringer law offices*

Ms. Victoria Hine, *founding director, LifeLine Shanghai**

Dr. Bryan H. Huang, *senior vice president & president Greater China, BearingPoint**

Mr. Simon Keeley, *head of the Hewitt Asia Leadership Center (HALC), Hewitt Associates China*

Mr. Gordon Orr, *director, Shanghai offices, McKinsey & Company*

Ms. Helen Tantau, *senior client partner, Korn/Ferry International (China) Ltd.*

Mr. John P. Wong, *senior vice president and managing director Greater China, The Boston Consulting Group*

*Note: Careers advance and business scenarios change quickly in China. Several of our interviewees (marked with *) changed position, moved company, or retired between the time of our interview and the final editing of this book. For example, Christopher Shaw held the above title from 2001 to 2005 but, as we went to press, accepted an assignment in the Lilly U.S. corporate office. All information and quotes from each interviewee were updated and cleared just before the book went to press.

When multinationals begin operating in China, their interaction with Chinese counterparts—officials, clients, customers—often suffers from a degree of disconnect. The mismatch is like a pair of dancers in which the male partner is moving quickly and the female partner is dancing slowly. Only as the dancers deepen their understanding of each other can they begin to move gracefully and in synch. For MNCs, learning to synchronize operations with the pace of the Chinese business environment is a difficult lesson.

Our profiled legal expert, Norman Givant, Shanghai office managing partner in the China Practice Group of Freshfields Bruckhaus Deringer, sums up the needs of many international companies new to China: "Many of our clients first coming to China have very little understanding of this environment—economic, political, social, and psychological. They frequently make the mistake we all do: presuming that this place is just like home, that people think like you do back in Peoria [Illinois]. You have different cultural mores, different values, different methods of interaction. ... I use the metaphor that we are like a guide-dog leading the blind through a minefield. ... There are many potential problems in investing in a foreign country, especially one that has a socialist or communist tradition, like mainland China."

In the chapters that follow, our expert interviewees offer their frank assessment of how to handle the biggest of the challenges faced in China. The 20 CEOs and eight expert consultants interviewed share their struggles and answer the following questions:

- What skills do I need to manage business operations in China today?
- Should I adapt my management style to China?
- How can I recruit and retain top-grade professional personnel in China's highly competitive market?
- What is the secret to forming successful joint venture (JV) or business partnerships?
- How should I establish effective communication with corporate headquarters?
- How can my company attract China's newly demanding and fickle consumers?
- How should I prepare to fight China's rising domestic competitors in my field?

Methodology

It is a chilly April morning at one of Shanghai's most prestigious shopping-and-office complexes, the glittering Plaza 66 on Nanjing Road. On the 17th floor, we are ushered into a small meeting room in the well-appointed offices of General Electric China. After a few moments spent setting up our digital recorder, camera, and laptop, the chairman and CEO, Steve Schneider, bursts into the room. We quickly get down to business. He has read the outline of the book and the interview questions (see the appendix to this book); he confirms the data we have collected on GE's operations in China. A formal air settles as the interview begins. Should we go through the questions one by one, he asks, or make the discussion more conversational? We mention the format we followed last week while interviewing Philip Murtaugh, chairman and CEO of GM China. Suddenly, the atmosphere changes. "Phil is in this book, too?" Schneider asks with a laugh. Then he adds, "Will you tell me how *he* answered the questions?"

We were asked this question recurrently in the course of researching *China CEO: Voices of Experience from 20 International Business Leaders*. As our featured executives looked over the roster of fellow interviewees, many asked what their peers had told us. They wondered what the others had advised on maintaining good relations with the government, for example, or on adapting their management style to match Chinese business culture. It is exactly this curiosity that we hope to spark in our readers.

Our research method was to go directly to the source, by interviewing 20 American, European, and Japanese top executives from Fortune 500 corporations operating successfully in China, plus eight respected, high-profile consultants expert at assisting international clients to thrive in China.

During the interviews, we followed a structured question-and-answer format. Each session was conducted by the authors along with a research assistant. We took detailed notes as well as recording each interview, then drafted a full transcript. After each transcription was checked and confirmed by the authors and our research assistant, we began compiling interviewee answers into key topics. This provided the basis for our chapters.

The result is a collection of first-hand, battlefield-tested insights on leading the China operations of a multinational company. The advice and strategies outlined in the following chapters focus on two main themes: maximizing the opportunities and overcoming the challenges inevitable in the business environment of China today.

- What is the best strategy for safeguarding intellectual property rights?
- How can my company form good relations with the Chinese government?
- How can I ensure that I—and my spouse or partner and children—lead a satisfying life in China?

> *We are like a guide-dog leading the blind through a minefield. ... There are many potential problems in investing in a foreign country, especially one that has a socialist or communist tradition, like mainland China."*
>
> **Norman Givant**, Shanghai Office Managing Partner, China Practice Group, Freshfields Bruckhaus Deringer

What Will I Learn From This Book?

When we began this project, our main objective was simply to share the learnings we have gleaned in our respective careers as a professor of management and business journalist. During our collective 22 years in Greater China, we have worked directly with international businesspeople, listening to, reporting on, and assessing their problems, frustrations, and achievements.

The list of the most common challenges identified to us by international executives in China forms the basis for the chapters of this book:

Chapter 1: **Qualities of a Successful International Manager in China**
Chapter 2: **Managing Chinese Employees**
Chapter 3: **Working With Business Partners**
Chapter 4: **Communicating With Headquarters**
Chapter 5: **Facing Competitors**
Chapter 6: **Battling Intellectual Property Rights Infringers**
Chapter 7: **Winning Over Chinese Consumers**
Chapter 8: **Negotiating With the Chinese Government**
Chapter 9: **Living in China**

In organizing the specific chapters of this book, we have developed a simple model illustrating the different relationships that top executives must manage in China: internal relations, external relations, and personal relations. The book is structured according to this basic framework, with one chapter dedicated to each of the topics listed.

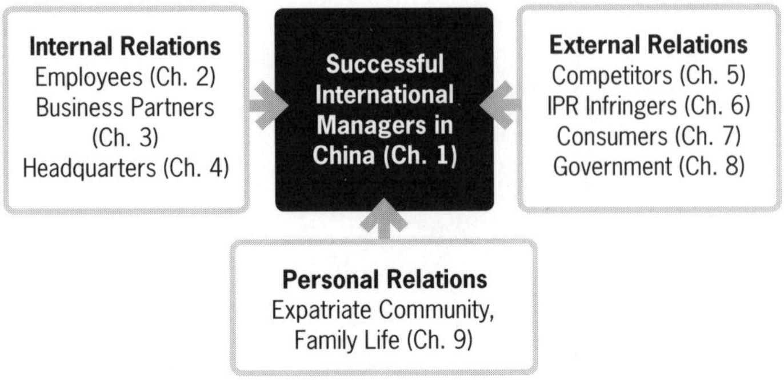

The book pivots around the figure of the international manager in China, our protagonist. This manager occupies the central position in the model, and each chapter outlines his dealings with a key internal or external group (employees, partners, headquarters, etc.).

One final point: Before we begin sharing the insights of our interviewees, we must introduce the concept of *guanxi*, or relationships developed based on obligation and favor swapping. Throughout our interviews with our top executives and China-based consultants, *guanxi*, or "Chinese-style networking," was identified as one of the most important aspects of doing business in China. The concept emerged as such a strong central message that relationships became a central theme of the book. (For a full explanation, see "*Guanxi* Defined" (Parts I and II) in Chapters 1 and 8.)

We conclude this Introduction with a Chinese saying that sums up the essence of *guanxi*: "When I make things difficult for you, I also make things difficult for myself." Stated in the positive, the saying reads: "When I make things easy for you, I also make things easy for me." Let this idiom serve as our first lesson of successful management in China. Many more lessons will follow. Enjoy!

Chapter 1

Qualities of a Successful International Manager in China

"If I had to focus on any one message [for incoming managers], I would emphasize that relationships are very important. ... It is really about people—relationships between people and the confidence they have in each other. China is even more that way than in Europe or in the States."

Dr. Gary Dirks, President and CEO, British Petroleum China

Introduction

One of our primary goals in researching this book was to identify the critical success qualities (CSQs) necessary in an international (non-Chinese citizen) manager who operates successfully in China. Our method for researching this was simple: we asked each of our 20 China-based top executive interviewees, "What qualities would you look for in finding a successor to your current position?" Their answers form the basis for this chapter.

Interviewee Credentials

Before we share our findings on the essential qualities for a successful international manager in China, we wish to share a word on our interviewees—the 20 top executives for China operations profiled in this book. We want you to be sure of their credentials for determining what kind of expatriate manager survives best in China. We set several strict criteria before seeking interviews. Each interviewee must represent the top level of management for his company in China, be based full-time in China (rather than commuting from Hong Kong, for example), and have been working in China for more than a year. Nearly all the interviewees far exceeded these requirements. The record for time spent abroad goes to Volkmar Ruebel, general manager of Hilton Hotels, Shanghai, who as this book goes to press boasts 41 years of international experience, 37 years in the same company, and 11 years in China. Also having a decade of China experience under their belts are Philip Murtaugh, chairman and CEO of General Motors China, Dr. Gary Dirks, group vice president and chief executive of British Petroleum China, and Paolo Gasparrini, president and managing director of L'Oréal China.

Our interviewees have witnessed tremendous changes during their time in China. Many describe the dramatic physical transformation in the urban centers. In the plush lounge of the 42-storey Hilton Shanghai—a building now surrounded by high-rises—general manager Volkmar Ruebel describes his first night in the city. "I arrived in Shanghai on New Year's Eve 1995. The city was dark. There were no lights. There were very few high buildings. ... That changed very quickly." Others describe the transformation in the business climate. When Dr. Ernst Behrens arrived in Beijing for Siemens in 1981, he lived in a small room in a rundown domestic hotel near Tiananmen Square—one of the few hotels designated by the Chinese government for foreign visitors. Because Siemens policy restricted Behrens from bringing his family to China, he spent three years living for 10 weeks at a time in China, followed by 10 days in Hong Kong. Today, such restrictions—both governmental and corporate—have all but disappeared. At the time of writing this book, 63,000 expatriate professionals and their families live in Shanghai alone, served by 25 international schools.

Paolo Gasparrini (now L'Oréal president and managing director for China) describes arriving from Hong Kong in February 1996, carrying a briefcase of cosmetic products. Although he also brought with him seven years of experience as president of L'Oréal Brazil, the difference in China was that he had to launch the company on his own, virtually from scratch. "There was nothing here; it was starting from zero," he recalls. Back then L'Oréal's presence in China consisted of a handful of makeup counters in Shanghai and Beijing displaying Maybelline or Lancôme products. Initially, Gasparrini did not even have permission to rent office space. Instead, he and his sole employee, a communications director, traveled to Shanghai and Beijing each week from Hong Kong. Today, L'Oréal has invested US$150 million in its operations in China, which now include the manufacture, distribution, and sale of 12 international mega-brands and two local brands that the company acquired in 2003 and 2004. A large chunk of L'Oréal's production in China is exported to Japan, South Korea, and other markets in Asia.

Any international manager in China quickly realizes that this is a country in the midst of a transformation that is both fast-moving and far-reaching, a shift that is not only redirecting the economy but also changing social and cultural norms. Factors including ongoing economic reform, regulatory changes triggered by accession into the WTO, increased consumer wealth, and growing international exposure, even preparations for the 2008 Olympic Games, are all bringing about significant and sometimes surprising changes. It is from the perspective of having survived (and thrived) in this environment that the executives we interviewed offer advice on what it takes to lead a winning business operation in China now.

> *"When expatriates come to China, local people expect them to bring something—in terms of knowledge or skill—that they need but that is not available here. There is a strong expectation that the expatriate will do that."*
>
> **Simon Keeley,**
> Head of the Hewitt Asia Leadership Center (HALC), Hewitt Associates

The Right Stuff for China?

During our interviews, the question of what characteristics our executives would look for in a successor sparked a rich mixture of responses. We have organized these responses into three categories based loosely on the logical sequence followed in considering the qualifications of a potential manager:

Level 1: Professional Qualities
Level 2: Personal Global Qualities
Level 3: Personal China-specific Qualities

This concept of levels conveys the idea that an international manager, especially one destined for China, must first demonstrate rock-solid professional qualifications, then show the ability to work in an international environment, and then prove able to handle specific challenges posed by China's business environment. We illustrate the progression of necessary qualifications in Figure 1.1.

FIGURE 1.1
Critical Success Qualities for International Managers in China

Level 1 CSQs: Professional Qualities

Not surprisingly, the first set of qualities our interviewees named as critical in selecting an international manager for China are professional prerequisites. Our interviewees identified two types of professional requirements they would insist upon for a candidate filling their current position of heading China operations for a multinational company:

- Technical and company expertise
- International experience

See Figure 1.2.

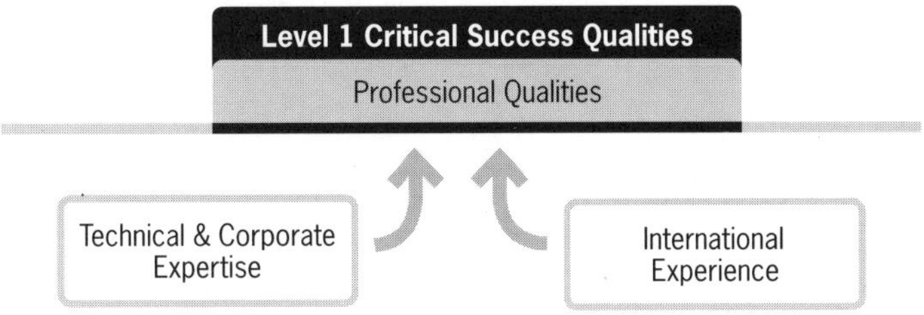

FIGURE 1.2 *Level 1 Critical Success Qualities*

Professional Quality #1: Technical and Corporate Expertise

A look at the careers of our 20 successful top executives in China themselves reinforces the idea that rock-solid technical expertise and rich management experience are a critical starting point for evaluating a candidate for an overseas senior management position. As a group, our interviewees have spent an average of 23 years working their way up in the same company. This gives them an extraordinarily broad and deep knowledge of their industries and of the company they are to represent abroad.

One of the first points made by our profiled consultants is that in today's China, expectations of expatriate managers are sky-high among the employees, business partners, and officials with whom they will be working. As China's own workforce rapidly gains ability in the international business arena, the demands on foreign nationals working in China are quickly rising. Human resources

TIP **Select people with a rock-solid professional background and an excellent knowledge of the company. Send your best personnel to China.**

(HR) expert Simon Keeley of Hewitt Associates explains that the bar is rising for expatriate managers and technical experts. "When expatriates come to China, the local people expect them to bring something—in terms of knowledge or skill—that they need but that is not available here. There is a strong expectation that the expatriate will do that." Keeley warns that foreign managers or specialists who fail to gain recognition for the expertise they bring to the China operations will likely quickly run into trouble.

As a result, Keeley says, foreign companies are increasingly raising the requirements for those being sent to China. "Now companies are paying more attention to [expat selection], probably because they take China as a very important part of their global strategy." He adds that companies are much more selective today than in the 1990s. He points to a client company that recently transferred eight top-performing professionals from their home country to China. "This company knows China is an important part of its worldwide strategy and is sending its best people here. I think more companies will do this."

The second type of professional skill our China hands deemed necessary in China is the ability to manage difficulty. Serving as president, CEO, or country manager in a foreign environment requires handling different levels of responsibility simultaneously. First, they must oversee all the standard duties typically performed by a top-level manager back in the home country: managing relations externally (with officials, business partners, customers) and internally (with superiors, staff members). Second, when posted abroad, expatriates must manage these same relationships while facing significant obstacles separating them from each of these

FIGURE 1.3 *Senior Manager Working in Home Country*

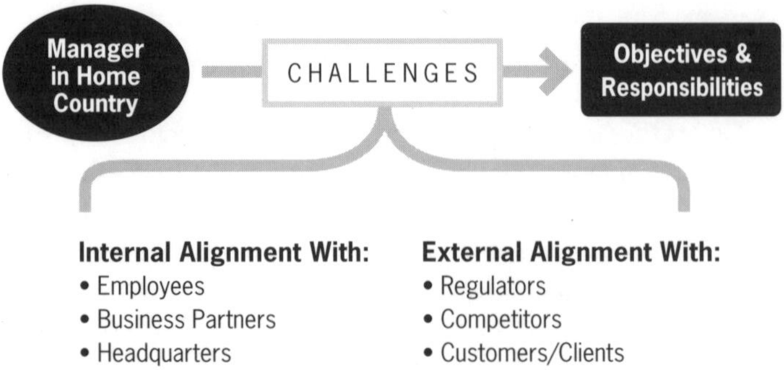

critical groups. For example, when interacting with the corporate headquarters, the China-based manager suddenly faces geographic distances, time differences, and vast gaps in knowledge caused by working on the other side of the planet from one's boss. The opportunity is ripe for misunderstandings, delays, and other forms of disconnect. Meanwhile, when the manager works with business partners and employees (who will mostly be Chinese nationals), he or she suddenly faces vast cultural differences and a language barrier. The chances are high for conflicting expectations, differing standards, and clashing operating styles.

Figures 1.3 and 1.4 show the added layer of complexity inherent in most overseas management postings.

This new "distance" between the international manager and the different groups with which he or she must align makes virtually all aspects of the manager's work more challenging.

Finally, our interviewees mentioned several other reasons why professional savvy can make or break a manager working abroad. First, a foreign manager will likely be working with a smaller, less experienced support team than would exist back home. Second, he or she will be confronted with problems and challenges that don't exist in the home country. Third, the international manager will personally represent the MNC in many instances in the host country, which means that he or she must exude water-tight professionalism, integrity, confidence, and industry expertise when meeting with government officials, business partners, competitors, customers, and employees.

The underlying message to employers is: send your best personnel to China.

> *"We have very few first-time expats in China. ... Our expats almost always have at least 10 years' experience."*
>
> **Alan Brown,** Chairman, Unilever China

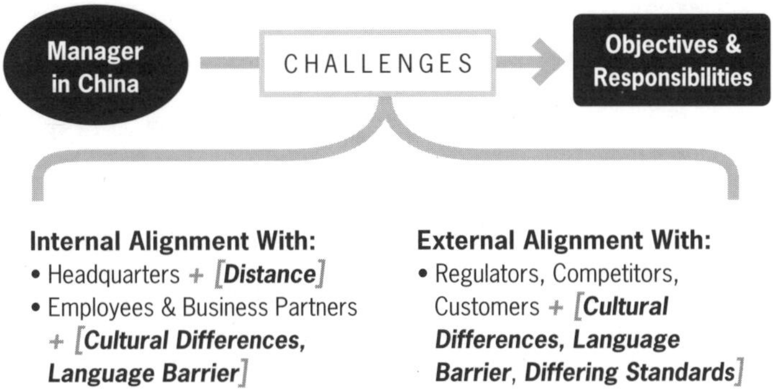

FIGURE 1.4 *Senior Manager Posted in China*

"

The first international posting cannot be in China. You must choose someone who already has the skills to run this position. It must be someone with the necessary calm and balance to face all kinds of different things."

Paolo Gasparrini,
President and Managing Director, L'Oréal China

Professional Quality #2: International Experience

The second message heard from our interviewees was that the best preparation for an expatriate manager heading overseas was, well, previous experience in managing business operations overseas. In other words, many of our interviewees said they would make "prior overseas experience" a prerequisite when placing an international manager in China. Simply put: a posting in China becomes vastly more manageable after an assignment in either another Asian location or another developing market, or both. The 20 senior executives profiled had spent an average of 10 years in upper management positions overseas before coming to China. Many had completed three or four assignments abroad before taking their current posting. Unilever China chairman Alan Brown's viewpoint is typical: "We have very few first-time expats in China. ... Our expats almost always have at least 10 years' experience."

A case-in-point for experienced expatriate managers is Bayer Greater China CEO Dr. Elmar Stachels. Although Stachels had to modify his management style with each of his overseas assignments—from Germany to Iran, Mexico, and now China—he says the adaptation process becomes faster and smoother with each new posting. "The biggest challenge probably comes when you first go outside [your home country] and take over a foreign assignment," he says. Most challenging is the initial shock of adapting to the business culture during the first overseas posting, a process Stachels calls becoming "a member of a new community." Having made the transformation once, it was easier with the next posting. Using his own experience as a guide, he now deems international experience as "very important" for expatriate executives in China.

At BP China, president and CEO Dr. Gary Dirks says the following of his expatriate managers in China: "Most of them were expatriates with experience in other places already. We don't bring people here as their first expatriate posting." Dirks favors those with not only overseas experience, but experience in a developing country. "In that way, they had some exposure to the fact that it is a different place and you've got to live in a very different way. They need to be able to demonstrate they can work in a non-Anglo culture."

"The first international posting cannot be in China," agrees L'Oréal China president and managing director Paolo Gasparrini. "You must choose someone who already has the skills to run this position. It must be someone with the necessary calm and balance to face all kinds of different things." He stresses that managers in China will need to be able to solve problems on their own, without relying too much on headquarters. Once the right person is found, he urges the company to keep him or her in China for a significant period of time in order to gain expertise. "You cannot stay only two years [in China]; you need more time. China is so big and so diverse; it's not a quick study. You need more time in [order to] ... get to know the people, know the risks."

TIP **A posting in China becomes vastly more manageable after an assignment in either another Asian location or another developing market, or both.**

Most interviewees stressed that if you are coming from a Western culture vastly different from that of China, taking at least one "easier" overseas posting helps smooth the transition. "My recommendation is to try to have an international expatriate assignment before coming to China," says Carrefour's Jean-Luc Chereau. His own career took him from his native France to Spain, then Brazil, Taiwan, and now China—a pattern of moving systematically toward increasingly foreign business cultures. In particular, many of our interviewees recommended working in Taiwan or Hong Kong as a gateway into Greater China.

Level 2 CSQs: Personal Global Qualities

In many ways, professional skills are the easiest qualifications to assess when selecting a manager to send to China, our interviewees stressed. More difficult for employers to assess, they said, is the host of personal qualities needed to succeed in the Middle Kingdom. We divided the personal qualifications they named into two types: Global Qualities and China-specific Qualities.

We first share the Global Qualities named by our interviewees. There was a general consensus among them that expatriate managers must display two characteristics in order to succeed on any overseas assignment. These Global Qualities are:

- Multicultural mindset
- Commitment to learn

See Figure 1.5.

FIGURE 1.5
Level 2 Critical Success Qualities

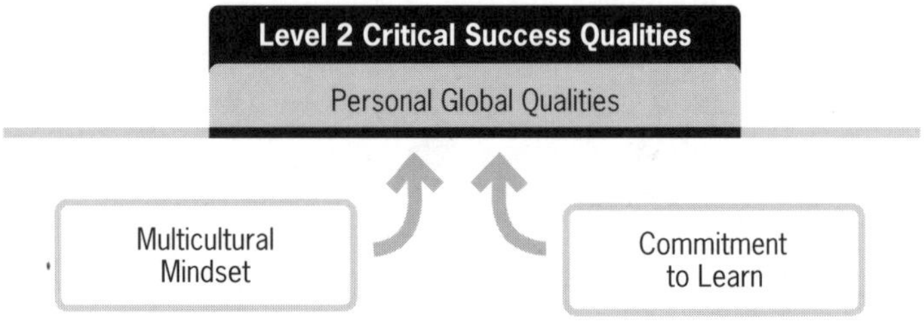

Global Quality #1: Multicultural Mindset

In describing the personal qualities necessary to manage in China, the first characteristic many of our interviewees mentioned was a willingness to recognize the limitations of one's own cultural norms and to accept and adapt to the culture of the host country. We termed this characteristic "multicultural mindset."

Coca-Cola China president Paul Etchells nominates this mindset as a first step in considering a candidate for a China assignment. "The most important thing is that you actually like being here and like working with the Chinese—and that you are able to make the cultural adjustments necessary," he says. "If you are having trouble dealing with China and with the Chinese, then [your business] is unlikely to be a success."

The biggest mistake foreign managers typically make, Etchells says, is in failing to adapt to the business practices of the host country. Learning when and how to meld into the new business culture seems an obvious point, but our interviewees agreed that this problem is both prevalent and difficult to overcome. "It is a big mistake to come in with preconceived ideas—thinking that your industry is necessarily going to operate as it does in some other market you are familiar with," says Etchells. Newcomers to any foreign environment, he says, often discover major differences, such as finding that the role of government is different, the competitive environment is different, or the industry cost structure is different.

TIP When selecting an executive for an overseas posting, look for someone with an adventurous spirit, a sense of humor, and an open mind.

"Flexible," "open," and "adaptable" were the most often-used adjectives in describing the critical personality traits of an overseas business leader. Philips China CEO David Chang explains that not only must foreign managers accept elements of the new business culture, but also (especially in an emerging market such as China) they must constantly shift to keep pace with that culture as it further develops and changes. "First, you need an open mindset," Chang says. "This is a changing world. Anyone who does not accept different ways of working won't succeed. You need to be able to detect and understand changes."

Such a malleable mindset, it seems, is most often a personality trait rather than an acquired skill. "The first important thing is to find someone with a certain personality. My belief is: if you pick the wrong person, no matter how much training you give, it won't work," says Ekkehard Rathgeber, president of Bertelsmann Direct

The Need to Adapt

When does an international manager's overly rigid mindset harm China operations? Microsoft's Jun Tang describes a recent case in which a Western manager insisted on leaving the office of his China-based facility nightly at 6 PM, just as he had in the United States. The policy caused friction because he also requested that Chinese staff finish projects according to deadlines, which entailed them working overtime. In China, it is important for a leader to show that he or she is part of a team, Tang stresses. "There is a saying in China: 'Together we share happiness, together we bear pain.'" In this instance, Tang believes the U.S. manager should have followed the local practice, which is for executives to keep similar hours to their professional staff. "The number 1 mistake [newcomers] make is trying to apply their way of running a business to the local culture without any understanding of the basic local business philosophy," he says.

> "
> *My belief is: if you pick the wrong person, no matter how much training you give, it won't work. You need to find a person who is very determined and can handle the ambiguity you find every day [in China]. ... You must be very open to new things, excited by new things—not someone who wants to preserve his own culture and identity."*
>
> **Ekkehard Rathgeber,** President, Bertelsmann Direct Group Asia

Group Asia. "You need to find a person who is very determined and can handle the ambiguity you find every day [in China]. You must have an adventurous spirit. You must take things in a humorous way, not too personally. You must be very open to new things, excited by new things—not someone who wants to preserve his own culture and identity."

After 10 years of placing executives into China-based firms, Shanghai-based Senior Client Partner Helen Tantau of Korn/Ferry agrees that the quality most necessary for expatriate executives is adaptability. "China is a very ambiguous place, in terms of the bureaucracy and the way rules change from today to tomorrow. You have no control over it." Tantau says foreign managers must be flexible and "more responsive to their environment" than they would be at home in the U.S. or Europe.

A word of caution, however: Our China hands stress that adaptation and flexibility do not simply mean "going native." "Multicultural mindset" does not mean giving up the home-country business culture and adopting local business customs. In fact, a careful balance must be struck in knowing which aspects of the business operations to maintain according to home or global norms and which aspects to adapt.

Global Quality #2: Commitment to Learn

Our interviewees stressed that, in order to succeed, international managers must go a step further than merely showing an openness to and acceptance of the host-country culture; they also need to display a commitment to spending time and energy learning about the host-country culture, and especially its business practices and norms. Many of our profiled top executives added that a working knowledge of the local language is extremely beneficial, but less critical.

Du Pont China president Charles Browne puts it this way: "You should try to understand the [foreign] culture and the language. Sometimes you get so tied up by the numbers and the projects that you lose sight of that. It is your understanding of customers and employees that really matters. Don't ignore that."

How much cultural knowledge is enough to lead a business

venture? In the case of China, 3M's Kenneth Yu stresses that quality is more important than quantity. "You don't need to know the names of all the different family relationships in Chinese—you don't need to go that deep," he says. "But you *do* need to understand Chinese values." In Yu's view, understanding Chinese values requires two types of commitment. The first is substantial time spent living and working in China. Says Yu, "Among the experienced China hands I have known, there is one common denominator: they all have lived in China for some years—not one or two years." The second type of commitment is a continuous connection with the country. Yu stresses that Chinese culture, and especially business norms, are now changing very quickly. What was true in a certain field as recently as one or two years ago is very possibly no longer valid now.

Other top executives warn against a mistake commonly made by long-time foreign residents of Asia: believing that understanding the business culture in Japan, Hong Kong, or Taiwan translates into understanding the culture in China. Standard Chartered China CEO Stanley Wong warns against thinking of China as being "just like Hong Kong 20 years ago."

"You should try to understand the [foreign] culture and the language. Sometimes you get so tied up by the numbers and the projects that you lose sight of that. It is your understanding of customers and employees that really matters. Don't ignore that."

Charles Browne,
President,
Du Pont China

Listening is Key

Interviewees also recommended listening as the best way to learn about the key elements of Chinese business culture. In other words, they recommend seeking out input—from employees, JV partners, government officials, clients—and then acting on it. This advice may seem to be common sense, but our interviewees say it is not second nature for many top executives. After all, listening implies a humble, receptive attitude—which goes against the grain of many incoming Western managers.

TIP **Learn from those around you. Listen to your employees, JV partners, clients, and customers.**

"You have to listen. Don't come with preconceived ideas about the best way to approach the market, the best way to approach the customers, how to do business," says Du Pont China president Charles Browne. "The customs, small things, are different. You can make terrible mistakes if you don't pay enough attention," he says. "The first thing you have to do is to listen and try to understand your customers and employees. Once you have that, you can begin to develop your strategies and plans."

"

Leadership in China means not forcing your point of view—not saying, 'I am the expert, I know everything. We do it this way worldwide.'"

Dr. Elmar Stachels, CEO, Bayer China

Listening, learning, and understanding is a process that managers must undergo in China, says Bayer Greater China CEO Dr. Elmar Stachels. "As much as possible, [incoming foreign managers] should listen in the first phase and not try to do it exactly in the way they learned at headquarters."

At Carrefour China, company president Jean-Luc Chereau says that listening must become an integral part of an expatriate manager's leadership style. Not only will the manager learn a great deal, but he or she will earn the trust and goodwill of partners, officials, and employees. "If you don't have the quality of listening to people, trying to understand the differences between them, you cannot manage," he says. "To succeed in Asia, especially in China, you need to listen to people. If you don't do it, it can be a disaster."

Level 3 CSQs: Personal China-specific Qualities

After detailing the general personal qualities useful to top-level managers heading abroad, we asked our interviewees to delve more deeply into the specific qualities necessary for succeeding in China's business environment. Below are five qualities the experts identified as specifically necessary to succeed in today's China.

Interestingly, we found that the main qualities named as being critical in China seem to be opposed. Our senior executives recommend humility but also strength, patience but also speed. As is apparent in the discussion below, these experts stress that the business environment in China requires a mix of different skills and characteristics, plus the understanding of when—and when not—to display certain qualities. The fifth "must-have" skill—*guanxi*-building—we discuss separately in the final section of this chapter.

- Humility and strength
- Patience and speed
- *Guanxi*-building (networking)

See Figure 1.6.

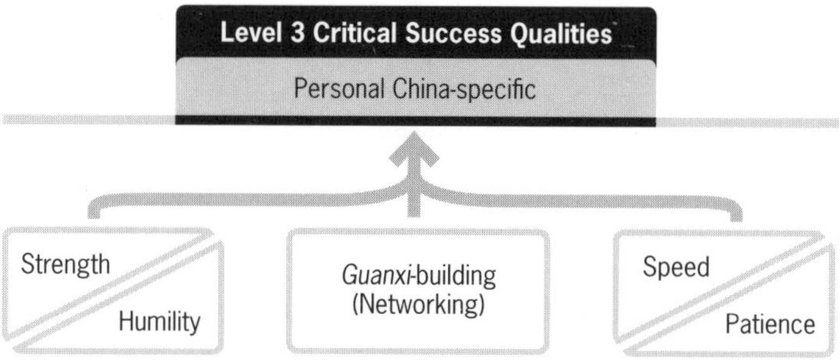

FIGURE 1.6
Level 3 Critical Success Qualities

China-specific Quality #1: Humility

Humility and patience? Is the message from our top executives beginning to sound as if all foreign managers should take the vows of monkhood? (Fear not. None of our interviewees mentioned a need for poverty or chastity.) The basic message to newcomers is that, in China, aggressive leadership styles built on arrogance or patronizing attitudes can (and do) cause failure.

TIP Be humble and avoid using an authoritarian style. Influencing and coaching is the way to get the best out of your Chinese employees.

The worst strategy for an incoming manager to follow is to begin an overseas assignment by laying down the law, especially an imported law. "Leadership in China means not forcing your point of view—not saying, 'I am the expert, I know everything. We do it this way worldwide'," says Elmar Stachels of Bayer China. He adds, "The main reason some [expatriates in China] are not very successful is that they act in their usual way, or the headquarters way. They just want to teach their own ways to their peers and subordinates in China. This can be a mistake."

One of the first lessons GE's Steve Schneider learned when he came to Asia in 1987 (working first in Japan) was to tone down his U.S.-style management approach. "I grew up in the U.S. system: things were black and white, arrogance was popular back then, 'take no prisoners' was popular back then. Everything was win-only, not win-win," Schneider says. Since taking a position at GE China in 1999, he has adopted a far more humble management style. "It isn't a directive style; it's more of an influencing or coaching style. That's the way you get the best out of people."

Showing respect for colleagues, employees, clients, and friends in China, as well as admitting areas where your own knowledge

TIP Be unyielding in defending core corporate values and culture.

is lacking, can be a powerful tool in establishing goodwill. "People who arrive here and say: 'I already understand everything about China'—this can be a disaster," says Paolo Gasparrini of L'Oréal. "You have to find a way to integrate with the people, to understand what is China, what is the culture, what do people expect from you and from the employer, and what they expect of themselves."

To illustrate the positive power of humility in China, Microsoft China president Jun Tang uses the example of an expatriate manager seeking to make drastic changes in a company of 300 employees in China. "There is no way to change 300 people. If you could change 300 people, you could change all of China," Tang says. But if the manager presents himself humbly—as a part of the team—he can establish grassroots support for his proposal. Step 1 is to show sincerity in learning about the new culture and environment, then establishing credibility as a team member, Tang says. "If I were [perceived as] an outsider, every decision I made would be analyzed by the employees [of Microsoft]," Tang says. "But if I am a part of them, I am sure every decision I made could be accepted by most of the people."

One surprising message is that even incoming Asian or Asian-savvy managers are advised to adopt a more humble attitude than is the regional norm, says Taiwan native David Chang of Philips. Although the Taiwanese generally are schooled in Confucian ethics, which stress humility, Chang tells Taiwanese managers to adopt an even more self-deprecating attitude in China; otherwise they may offend a Chinese client, colleague, employee, or official. Chang is especially careful not to injure national pride when making any kind of criticism of China or the Chinese system, which could inadvertently embarrass a Chinese colleague. While Western and Taiwanese businesspeople are used to challenging each other in the course of doing business and often view contradictions as valued input, the Chinese still tend to view challenges, criticism, or contradictions as a loss of face.

Chang is especially careful not to criticize Chinese business practices for not following international standards or norms. He warns international managers to remember that when business policies in China seem impractical or inefficient, there may be social or political reasons. For example, in solving a certain business problem, the first priority for the Chinese government may be to protect national pride rather than to settle the business dispute. "National pride must be well considered," says Chang. "From that point of view, you should be humble. Otherwise, you will easily tend to think, 'We think rationally. This is common sense.' The [Chinese side] may agree with your suggestion, but it may still not match their priorities."

> "*If you simply adapt yourself to the local habits, then you lose a lot of advantages. You end up with something you didn't want."*
>
> **Ekkehard Rathgeber**, President, Bertelsmann Direct Group Asia

China-specific Quality #2: Strength

It will be a sometimes maddening characteristic of this book that as soon as we present a piece of advice, we contradict it. The following is just such an example.

In the same breath that our experts recommended humility and acceptance of different points of view in China, they followed up with opposing advice: being strong, at least in terms of sticking to principles and rigidly maintaining the key aspects of the MNC's corporate culture. In other words, it is a mistake to go too far in adapting to the host-country's business practices. The trick is to find the correct balance between melding with some aspect of the host-country business environment and maintaining the key tenets of the original corporate culture.

Ekkehard Rathgeber of Bertelsmann explains it well: being too flexible can be as problematic as being too rigid. "If you simply adapt yourself to the local habits, then you lose a lot of advantages. You end up with something you didn't want," he says. He recommends two ways of finding the correct level of adaptation versus firmness: first, choose your battles (insist on only truly necessary changes); and second, work patiently. "In the beginning, when you come [to China], you have culture shock," he says. "You think, 'I have to teach people how to do business in a proper way.' But you have to encourage people not only to do certain things but to understand why it makes sense to do those things." In other words, rather than simply installing new corporate policies, international managers should instill a new corporate culture.

As a rule of thumb, HR specialist Simon Keeley of Hewitt advises international managers to err on the side of maintaining

"When people have just arrived, they want to change things. But making quick moves in the wrong way isn't the right thing to do. You need to have patience, patience, patience. It is one of the clichés you hear in China, but it is true. You need to make a long-term strategy and stick to it."

Guy McLeod, President, Airbus China

corporate or international practices. "For a company to be successful, it should place the company culture first, and then address the national culture [of the host country]," he says. But he also stresses that the process of introducing a foreign corporate culture must be undertaken with sensitivity and patience.

Balancing corporate standards against host-country practices is one of the challenges Kenneth Yu, a 36-year veteran of 3M in Asia, has undertaken for the MNC. After completing a three-year assignment in the global headquarters in the U.S., he moved on to overseeing operations in Taiwan, then China. Yu, now the company's managing director for China, stresses that certain of 3M's global management practices have been introduced unchanged in China—for example, corporate ethical standards, or procedures related to the development and promotion of employees. "Our core values do not change," he says.

When advising her corporate clientele on managing in China, Korn/Ferry Senior Client Partner Helen Tantau delivers a similar message: "You shouldn't manage your business in a completely different way just because this is China." The ultimate goal, she says, is to combine aspects of Chinese business culture with home-country practices—a trick that Chinese domestic firms are learning quickly these days.

Microsoft China president Jun Tang also emphasizes the need to stick firmly to corporate policy in some aspects. Although intimately familiar with Chinese culture (Tang was born and raised in China, becoming a U.S. citizen as an adult), he insists on transporting certain elements of corporate culture directly from the global headquarters in Seattle. "I never compromise on the core values of integrity, passion, respect," he says.

In some cases, maintaining Microsoft corporate policy has forced Tang to take a tough stance in China. For example, he maintains a firm policy with employees of "one serious mistake, you're out." Says Tang, "I have fired a lot of people. I cannot compromise."

China-specific Quality #3: Patience

The single most-repeated word when our interviewees described what makes or breaks an international manager in China was "patience." It seems that a calm, steady, long-term approach is critical to many aspects of a manager's work in China—from winning approval from officials to negotiating with suppliers, cooperating with joint venture partners, and building demand among consumers.

TIP Be patient; use a step-by-step approach in China, not a Big Bang approach.

The first test of one's patience, China hands explain, is to accept that gaining a thorough understanding of the business environment in China will take time. "It is extremely difficult for someone to drop into China, spend a few weeks or months here, then attempt to define a strategy," says Alan Brown of Unilever. "It is extremely difficult and not practical." Brown stresses that newcomers need time to "get the feel for the technicalities and practicalities of operations." Until then, decision-making is often guesswork—a dangerous scenario.

Jean-Luc Chereau, president of Carrefour China, explains that the first piece of advice he would give a newcomer would be: practice patience. "If [a new manager] comes from Europe, I will show him the difference between Europe and Asia. I will tell him to be patient. 'Don't think that in one week, one month, or even one year you can understand China very well.'" Chereau says newcomers should generally reduce their expectations not only in terms of how fast they can make changes, but also how far they can go. "You must be patient and modest. You can learn from [the Chinese] how to do business better in China. You can bring something new, something different, but don't think that you can completely change people's style of doing business."

A similar point is made by Airbus China president Guy McLeod: "When people have just arrived, they want to change things. But making quick moves in the wrong way isn't the right thing to do," he says. "You need to have patience, patience, patience. It is one of the clichés you hear in China, but it is true. You need to make a long-term strategy and stick to it."

Even when changes must be made, Elmar Stachels of Bayer advises moving slowly. "You have to be persistent in pursuing your target and objectives, but you also need patience—step-by-step, not a Big Bang approach."

Impatience can pose a far deeper problem than simply rubbing

TIP Be flexible and quick. Stay well informed; the business environment in China is in constant and rapid flux.

Chinese colleagues and clients the wrong way. Our interviewees comment that many MNCs' business plans show an element of expecting too much too soon. Short-term thinking and unrealistic expectations can undermine an entire business plan. Volkmar Ruebel, general manager of the Shanghai Hilton, has seen many foreign managers suffer from such an ailment. "The most commonly made mistake for people coming into Shanghai is that they've got to get rich quick," he says. Many managers forget that their own companies were built up over time back home, and somehow expect instant results in China. "The philosophy is to invest [in China] and in five years' time you have your money back. That's not realistic."

Ruebel espouses a slow and steady approach. "Don't jump into full speed and make changes in 24 hours. [Chinese employees] will not accept that," he says. "They want to understand you first. They want to see what you can do. Prove your professionalism, show them you are an expert in the field, let people see how good you are, and then slowly change things, if necessary." He advises incoming managers to listen and learn, then act. "Watch first. Understand the people a little bit—how they work, what they do. It's better to go a bit slower than too fast."

The tendency to rush can be especially prevalent among American and European expatriates. "Sometimes my Western colleagues, especially new heads, tend to be not patient enough—especially when they are under pressure from their superiors to get things done in China," says Kenneth Yu of 3M. As an example, he describes a common response from headquarters in the U.S. when they hear that China operations are understaffed. "U.S. executives typically advise simply hiring more people, not realizing that the employment process is very complex in China. It's not just [a matter of] hiring the right people, but also training, educating, and developing them."

Another area rife for misunderstanding: measuring business results in China by U.S. standards. Yu says that American executives—and Wall Street analysts—place much pressure on performing, or achieving an impressive and steadily climbing growth rate. "There is no shortcut to success. For our friends from the U.S. in particular, this is where the cultural clash comes in," he says. "Wall Street likes to see results, likes to see numbers they can measure, one quarter against the same quarter last year. But if you are developing something from scratch, you don't do that. It could be very dangerous." Yu says that many companies suffer under the pressure to double revenue yearly—an unrealistic mandate.

> *"The pace of change is so fast [in China] relative to a lot of other places that, unless it is well articulated as an evolution, the corporate headquarters often find it hard to understand why the company had Strategy A in China and now has Strategy B."*
>
> **Gordon Orr**, Director, Shanghai offices, McKinsey & Company

One of the ironies of working in China is that managers need patience, but they also need to survive in a fast-paced, highly competitive market. L'Oréal's Paolo Gasparrini explains this dichotomy. "Our business is developing very fast; we want to take market share. We are not here to be patient," he says. But foreign managers must understand that acting too aggressively will sometimes move the company backward, not forward, he says. The trick is knowing when to push, and how far. As an example, he points to the need for patience when negotiating in China. "You need to be patient for some things. If you apply too much pressure, you won't get what you need—you need to be sensitive," he says. In a negotiation, showing impatience is the kiss of death. Once the other side senses your urgency, this shifts the power balance in their favor. They can then take advantage of your neediness by raising the stakes.

China-specific Quality #4: Speed

While patience is a necessary survival skill when managing a business venture in China, the ability to adapt quickly to change is equally important. In other words, some aspects of an MNC's business operations need to simmer away slowly, while other aspects progress at a fast boil not seen in developed and mature markets.

It is safe to say that virtually nowhere in the world is the business environment changing more rapidly than it is now in China's urban centers. Fast and dramatic change—in regulations, in competition, in consumer tastes—is a fact of life when doing business in China. Interviewees explained that while the aspects critical to your particular industry may not change according to the schedule you would like, it is certain that some aspect of your business will be in a state of flux at any given time, from the status of your business partners to the expectations of customers and clients.

Siemens China president and CEO Ernst Behrens explains the situation for international managers in this way: "The recent change in this country is enormous, and the [implications of] reform are also enormous." Although China started from a "very low economic level," standards are catching up quickly now in many aspects. One example of speediness in China: when new regulations are released, they often go into effect within a month—far sooner than in Europe. In addition, the release does not mean the law is final. Says Behrens, "Usually [the promulgation of a law] is followed by some adaptations." He adds that

Guanxi Defined: Part I

What exactly is *guanxi*? In Mandarin, *guan* means "gate" and *xi* means "links." The concept can thus be defined as a gateway or connection between two people created by a link of mutual obligation to each other. *Guanxi* exists between families because of blood ties, between classmates or workmates because of a shared history, or between business acquaintances after building up a relationship through assisting one another. It is business *guanxi* that we focus on in this book.

While business networking takes place directly or indirectly in cultures worldwide, it is used more often, within a wider scope, and is generally given more importance in China. In addition, while Western businesspeople are pressured to keep their personal and professional lives separate, the lines between family, friends, and work are far blurrier in China.

In practice, business *guanxi* works like this: When Person A "builds *guanxi*" with Person B (by providing favors or assistance), A gains a surplus that can be cashed in with B later. In this way, *guanxi* serves as a form of "social currency" with both sides keeping track (loosely) of favors given and favors owed. For example, let's say you befriended a fellow executive at an EMBA course, and that person helped you to find difficult-to-get information for an assignment. Several months later, it would not be unusual for you to hear from that EMBA acquaintance seeking help in finding a summer internship for his nephew. While such a scenario could easily these post-promulgation changes to new laws "could have a great impact on your operation."

It is not surprising that having to cope with constant, sometimes drastic, change is one difficulty that sends clients to McKinsey & Company in China. Gordon Orr, a director in the company's Shanghai office, says new developments in the operating environment are a key source of misunderstandings between the China offices and corporate headquarters of his MNC clients. Says Orr: "The pace of change is so fast relative to a lot of other places that, unless it is well articulated as an evolution, the corporate headquarters often find it hard to understand why the company had Strategy A in China and now has Strategy B."

happen in the West, the concept of favors given and debts owed is far stronger in China.

At this point, readers may be wondering if *guanxi* is simply a nice way of saying "corruption." The answer is, no. *Guanxi* is not inherently unethical, as is sometimes assumed by Westerners. The *guanxi* system does not, for example, mean that companies can do whatever they like after bribing or striking under-the-table deals. It does, however, mean that business partners often develop deeper and closer relationships than is standard in the West. It means that the international manager often finds himself operating in a friendly and personal (rather than professional) capacity in the normal course of doing business.

In many cases, *guanxi* played a more critical role a generation ago, when the Chinese faced limited access to resources, information, and influence. For example, when opening a new office in the early 1980s, it might take many months to get a phone line installed—unless you had *guanxi* with an official at the government-run telephone company. Today, our interviewees say such backdoor connections are less often necessary, especially in China's business-friendly urban centers.

Certainly, "exchanges of favors" can and do cross into the realm of illegal favors, but this type of negative *guanxi* is not the topic of our discussion. (For more information on the dark side of *guanxi*, see the box "*Guanxi* Defined: Part II" in Chapter 8.)

Before we explain the final critical success quality deemed necessary for an international manager in China, we summarize in Figure 1.7 the qualities discussed so far.

In describing the critical success qualities of our ideal international manager, we have saved the most complex, but potentially the most important, quality for last: *guanxi*-building. The importance of *guanxi* (Chinese-style networking) is a key theme throughout this book, central to the advice given on a range of topics from how to manage Chinese employees, to how to negotiate with business partners, to how to work with government officials. In fact, the concept of building and maintaining *guanxi* is one of the core messages of this book.

FIGURE 1.7
Critical Success Qualities of an International Manager in China

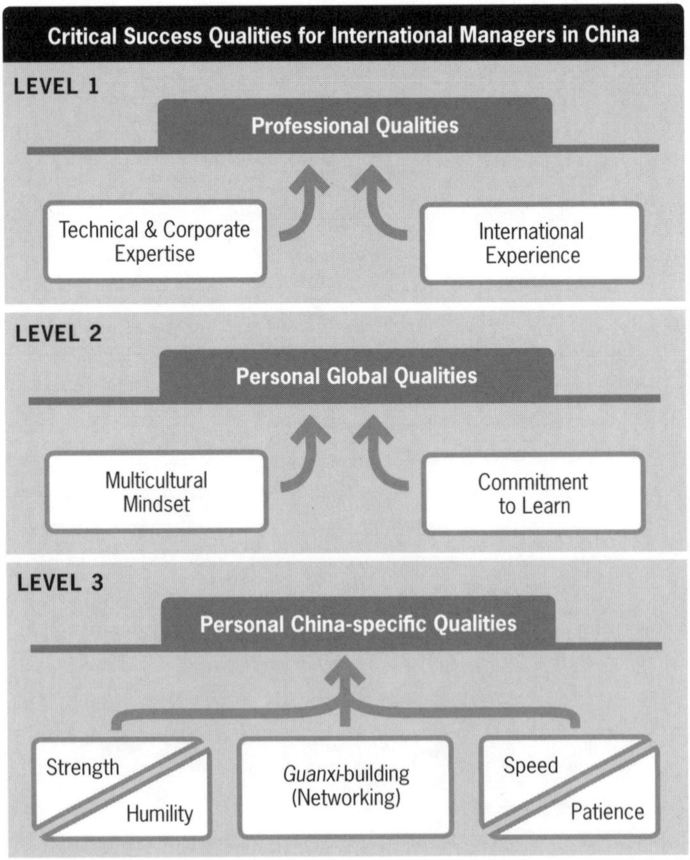

China-specific Quality #5: *Guanxi*-building Skills

As we mentioned in the Introduction, the concept of *guanxi* will be a recurrent theme throughout the coming chapters. The importance of forming and maintaining strong, close relationships was repeatedly mentioned by our interviewees as a key quality necessary in international managers in China, critical to many aspects of their work. (For a full explanation of the concept, see the box "*Guanxi* Defined: Part I" in this chapter, and "*Guanxi* Defined: Part II" in Chapter 8.)

TIP **Build your *guanxi* not only internally (with subordinates, peers, and superiors) but also externally (with clients, suppliers, and government officials). A strong *guanxi* network is a fundamental element in your success in China.**

As readers will find in the chapters that follow, international managers in China generally must spend more time and energy in building and maintaining close, positive relationships with those they work with than would be necessary in their home countries. *Guanxi* must be created with employees, business partners and suppliers, government officials, and customers. While good relations with these stakeholders is, of course, also necessary in Western business environments, far more importance is generally placed on relationships in China.

BP China president Dr. Gary Dirks explains the need for *guanxi*-building skills in this way: "The style of operating here versus in Europe is a bit different, but mostly in degree not in kind. In the trading business, it can be very personal. It is really about people—relationships between people and the confidence they have in each other. China is even more that way than in Europe or in the States." Dirks says this concept makes business decision-making far more complex, because one must think not only of the company's interests but also of the interests of all parties with whom the company has *guanxi*. This requires that expatriate managers develop new sensitivities to the impact of business decisions on a wide range of individual stakeholders. "If I had to focus on any one message [for an incoming manager], I would emphasize that relationships are very important," says Dirks.

At Siemens China, country president and CEO Ernst Behrens stresses that while China is changing rapidly, the *guanxi* system remains embedded to a large degree. "We always talk about the enormous changes in China. Maybe processes have changed. People have not changed. The underlying *guanxi* culture—networking—is still there." He says while China's business environment has developed and internationalized since WTO accession in 2001, and trade regulations are becoming "more and more familiar to us," this has not lessened the importance of *guanxi*. "Networking and relationships still play an extremely important role. Personal connections are still very important."

Thus, the fine art of relationship-building will be a useful, even critical skill, for incoming managers. Unfortunately, it is one of the trickiest skills to learn, requiring expatriates to carefully balance East and West, building positive relations while maintaining the codes of conduct required by their corporations.

Conclusion

Chapter 1 has introduced the key professional and personal qualities that our China experts named as necessary for managing operations for an international company in China. After analyzing the rich descriptions shared by our interviewees, we organized their responses into three levels of critical success qualities—namely, professional qualities, personal global qualities, and personal China-specific qualities. The concept of levels implies a certain career progression in which solid professional qualities form the foundation. From that foundation, a candidate manager for any overseas assignment must also show personal qualities, including a "multicultural mindset" and a commitment to learn. Finally, interviewees described China-specific personal qualities, such as humility and strength, patience and speed, plus *guanxi*-building, or Chinese-style networking.

SUMMARY OF TIPS

CRITICAL SUCCESS QUALITIES FOR EXPATRIATE MANAGERS IN CHINA

LEVEL 1: PROFESSIONAL QUALITIES

1. Technical and Corporate Expertise

Select people with a rock-solid professional background and an excellent knowledge of the company. Send your best personnel to China.

2. International Experience

A posting in China becomes vastly more manageable after an assignment in either another Asian location or another developing market, or both.

LEVEL 2: PERSONAL GLOBAL QUALITIES

1. Multicultural Mindset

When selecting an executive for an overseas posting, look for someone with an adventurous spirit, a sense of humor, and an open mind.

2. Commitment to Learn

Learn from those around you. Listen to your employees, JV partners, clients, and customers.

LEVEL 3: PERSONAL CHINA-SPECIFIC QUALITIES

1. Humility

Be humble and avoid using an authoritarian style. Influencing and coaching is the way to get the best out of your Chinese employees.

2. Strength

Be unyielding in defending core corporate values and culture.

3. Patience

Be patient; use a step-by-step approach in China, not a Big Bang approach.

4. Speed

Be flexible and quick. Stay well informed; the business environment in China is in constant and rapid flux.

5. *Guanxi*-building

Build your *guanxi* not only internally (with subordinates, peers, and superiors) but also externally (with clients, suppliers, and government officials). A strong *guanxi* network is a fundamental element in your success in China.

Chapter 2
Managing Chinese Employees

"The Chinese—and Asians generally—enter into employment with a different understanding than we have in Europe. For us, the company certainly is important, but mainly as an employment base. To the Chinese, the company is more like a family. The idea is, 'I am giving myself to Siemens. Now you have to take care of me.'"

Dr. Ernst Behrens, President, Siemens China

Introduction

In the nine years that Dominique de Boisseson has headed up Alcatel's China operations, the eight years that Seiichi Kawasaki has led Sony's ventures in China, and the seven years that Steve Schneider has overseen General Electric China, one challenge has consistently plagued each man despite the vast differences in the industries they serve. In fact, this same problem vexes each of the 20 top executives we profile and was named as the number 1 client concern by six of the eight professional consultants we interviewed.

What was this pervasive problem? When we asked our 20 top executive interviewees to name the most difficult challenge they face in leading China operations, the most common answer (by far) was: "human resources issues." Among the HR headaches named, the most prevalent problem was lack of white-collar staff. Because recruitment and retention of adequate personnel troubled virtually all of our profiled China hands, in this chapter we have focused on facing and overcoming these difficulties.

While it was expected that HR problems would be a primary concern for international managers in China, we were surprised to find that nearly all interviewees listed it as a *major* concern. As we researched, however, we found that our interviewees' concerns mirror a larger trend. Consider that the 2005 Business Climate Survey, a poll of 450 member companies of the American Chambers of Commerce in Beijing (AmCham-China) and Shanghai (AmCham Shanghai), listed "management level human resources" as the number 1 Top Business Challenge—above bureaucracy, unclear regulations, and difficulty enforcing contract terms.

One telling example of the importance of HR issues in our profiled companies: many of our top executive interviewees are far more directly involved in handling day-to-day HR issues than are their counterparts in the West or Japan. Consider the recruiting strategy of GE China. The company has made it a duty of its top-echelon managers to make regular recruitment visits to Chinese universities. The 10 top managers nationwide have each been designated one of China's 10 best-ranked universities to visit several times a year to promote the company to promising students. GE China chairman and CEO Steve Schneider describes the program in this way: "Each one of the GE China business leaders 'owns' a university. That's where we drive the recruiting." He himself speaks at Fudan University in Shanghai roughly every six weeks. More proof of the high priority given to recruitment: Schneider personally interviews all new hires above the mid-management level. "I interview anyone in a leadership role," he says. "That's how much buy-in we have in the leadership team."

Staff retention, too, often involves the top executive. L'Oréal China's president and managing director Paolo Gasparrini says that working to prevent turnover is a significant part of his job, both in meeting directly with key personnel to gauge their job satisfaction and in training middle managers to keep their staff members happy and committed. "The [general manager] has to be involved [in retention efforts], and also the division manager," says Gasparrini. "I spend a lot of time trying to make my managers sensitive to the fact that people are very important. Every time we lose someone we neglected, this is a very big problem. I discuss it with everyone."

Because many of our interviewees were directly involved in solving retention and recruitment issues, our interviews provided a rich—and vast—collection of advice. In describing their HR strategies, our China experts again raised the topic of *guanxi* (relationships) as a central theme. The starting point for overcoming HR difficulties often lay in forming a positive, effective employer–employee relationship. This seems straightforward, except that the Chinese ideal for boss–staff relations differs significantly from the Western ideal. This difference is covered in Section III of this chapter.

The Problem: China's White-collar Workforce Shortage

Before we get to the bad news on the workforce shortfall in China, we will set the scene with some good news. After all, a promising employment pool—from unskilled laborers to management-level professionals—is a primary reason why China is a major investment destination for so many MNCs. International managers stressed four reasons for long-term optimism concerning China's workforce.

First is the overall quality of the professional workforce. Airbus China president Guy McLeod is typical in his assessment. "There is an incredibly capable workforce here. It's not like some other places in the world where people are uneducated," he says. In fact, McLeod advises foreign managers to leave many aspects of their work to local staff. "The key is being able to delegate. You have to be able to trust your subordinates. Local Chinese can do the job a lot better than anyone coming in. Let them do their job." He stresses that the Airbus China management team consists of three vice presidents, two of whom are Chinese nationals. "We have the best team we have ever had," McLeod says. "They know the system here and in Europe. They are very high-quality people."

The second bit of good news: internationally renowned MNCs still enjoy "pull" when recruiting in China. British Petroleum, for example, finds strong interest among the Chinese workforce, based largely on its reputation and its position as a global player. When recruiting, company president and CEO for China Dr. Gary Dirks plays up BP's position as a global industry leader. "I think a lot of [Chinese] staff feel good about being a part of a very big multinational," he says. One of the biggest draws for MNCs: Chinese professionals hunger for opportunities for training and work experience abroad. BP has now sent 25 Chinese management and technical specialists to positions outside of China, mainly in the U.S. and the U.K.

The third reason for optimism is that the scramble for experienced professionals in China has eased a bit since the late 1990s, consultants and foreign managers agreed. During those years, John Wong, The Boston Consulting Group's (BCG's) managing director for Greater China, was seeing annual turnover of 75–80% among clients in volatile industries such as retail. Between 2003 and 2005, turnover rates of 20–30% among white-collar employees were more standard in many industries (figures used by BCG and Hewitt Associates). Wong names two factors slowing the job-hopping rate. First, professionals in China can no longer expect to make a 20% salary jump with every new job, as was common in the late 1990s. Since then, Wong says, many MNCs have ceased luring talent away purely through salary increases. (Hewitt Associates does stress that in certain "hot" areas, such as the industrial parks of Suzhou, or hot industries, such as sales and marketing or research and development, salary boosts were a major factor in job-hopping during 2005.)

> *"There is an incredibly capable workforce here. ... The key is being able to delegate. You have to be able to trust your subordinates. Local Chinese can do the job a lot better than anyone coming in. Let them do their job."*
>
> **Guy McLeod**, President, Airbus China

Then too, the gap between talent demand and supply is beginning to narrow in some fields. John Wong points out that those who graduated from university after China's economic reforms kicked into high gear in the mid-1980s are now in their mid-thirties, with 18 years of experience in a market-oriented economy. Thus, while there used to be a noted gulf in seasoned middle management-level personnel in modern industries, the gap is beginning to close.

Korn/Ferry Senior Client Partner Helen Tantau agrees that local professionals are rapidly gaining in skills and expertise. "The local supply of management is a lot stronger than it used to be." However, she says, supply still lies far below the burgeoning demand. "China's employment market has never been as hot as it is right now," she says, adding that companies are seeing "lots of people movement."

Offering hope for employers, though, is the good reputation China is earning as a career destination for expatriates. Recruitment specialists say that enticing Westerners or non-Chinese Asians for positions in China is now relatively easy, since China is a "hot" market in the international business arena. As Tantau puts it, within circles of Western professionals willing to work overseas, "Everyone wants to come to China now."

The Bad News

But there is also some bad news for MNCs recruiting in China. There are four components to the professional staff shortage:

- Fierce competition from international and domestic firms
- Fast growth rate of competing China-based MNCs
- Lack of Chinese middle managers
- High expectations of Chinese employees (leading to frequent job-hopping)

Figure 2.1 represents how these four factors create the shortage of skilled personnel facing many international managers in China.

FIGURE 2.1
Components of the Professional Staff Shortage

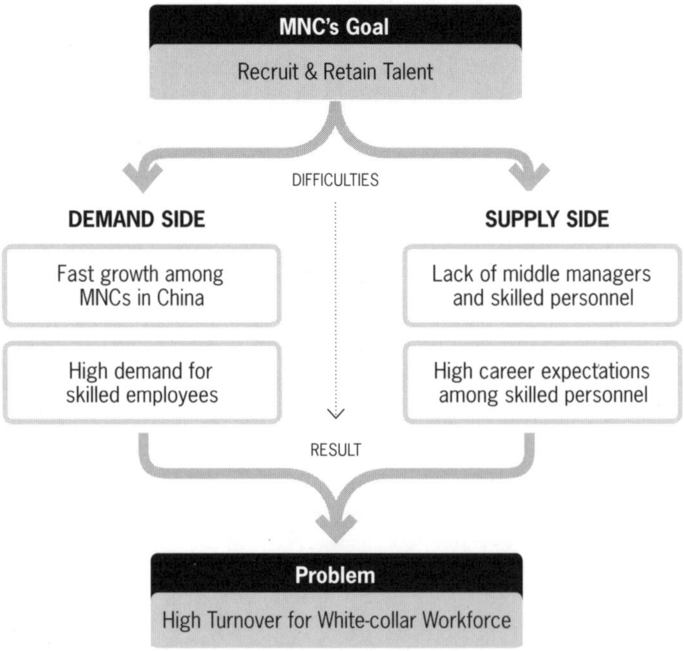

More Demand Than Supply

Gone are the days when international employers were rare and highly sought-after as employers, especially in China's urban centers. Most MNCs operating today face far more competition when recruiting than they did a decade ago, both from incoming international firms (especially from now booming smaller-sized firms) and from newly internationalized Chinese firms. "Chinese companies have now started taking people from multinationals," says Simon Keeley of HR consultants Hewitt Associates. Helen Tantau of Korn/Ferry agrees, stressing that a growing number of domestic companies, private or state-owned, are not only becoming more professional and internationalized but also profitable.

Dr. Ernst Behrens, president and CEO of Siemens China, describes the current atmosphere. "Retention of well-performing staff is our greatest concern. Especially in the high-tech sector, we are fighting the war for talent every day," he says. In China's current business environment, Siemens' reputation for high standards and its policy of thorough staff training has become a disadvantage in that the company is now a major target for headhunters. "People often stay two or three years with Siemens to add the name of this well-respected company to their CV, then look for a better-paying job," says Behrens. He says that other MNCs are also feeling the pinch as employees bounce between them.

A similar frustration is described by GE China's Steve Schneider. "We MNCs [in China] all kind of laugh because we have become the target not only of other MNCs but also of Chinese companies. There's such a need for great talent. Executive recruiters are very popular right now." At GE, turnover is particularly problematic among sales, marketing, and management personnel. "GE is a huge target for headhunters," Schneider says.

In fact, many Chinese companies now enjoy some significant advantages over MNCs in recruitment and retention. Many can offer perks more easily than can international companies. For example, some state-owned enterprises can provide a top manager with housing that would cost a foreign-based company far more to obtain.

One sign of growing professionalism among domestic

> *We MNCs [in China] all kind of laugh because we have become the target not only of other MNCs but also of Chinese companies. There's such a need for great talent. Executive recruiters are very popular right now."*
>
> **Steve Schneider,** Chairman and CEO, General Electric China

companies: more local firms are hiring international consultants to help them upgrade. Korn/Ferry's Helen Tantau describes her local company clients as sophisticated and demanding. "Chinese companies are willing to pay, but they want the best—McKinsey, BearingPoint. They are very difficult to serve," she says. Our interviewees at China offices of McKinsey & Company, BCG, and BearingPoint report that 50–85% of their clients are now Chinese firms.

The upshot of this highly competitive employment field is that retention of key personnel is the top concern faced by the 20 international managers we interviewed. "Many organizations are now reporting a talent shortage; they cannot get the people they need," says Hewitt Associates' Simon Keeley. While the degree of shortfall varies from industry to industry, and is more acute at higher management levels, Keeley stresses that well-qualified Chinese executives are in demand across the spectrum. "Skills are scarce. The good people can move around," he says.

Clients of John Wong at BCG also struggle to retain qualified personnel. Wong stresses that star employees in China tend to be especially valuable. "Good guys here make a huge difference because the market is still relatively inefficient and undeveloped," he explains. He says that a single excellent manager in the U.S., for example, may make only a small overall impact on a large company's business successes. However, a single talented manager in China often has a much larger impact on business outcomes. "In the U.S., there are many systems in place that mitigate the advantage gained from one single person. But in China, there is a lot of inefficiency. So if you have a guy who is really good, he can have a huge impact on your business," he says. Companies work hardest at retaining effective players in key positions such as head of sales, head of marketing, and head of HR.

Fast-growth Mode

For MNCs in labor-intensive industries in China, the biggest problem is simply ramping up their hiring to a scale that matches the company's growth pace. For low-skilled positions, there is generally no shortage of personnel. Recruitment problems focus more on creating a workable system to manage the scale of hiring and training.

Siemens China receives 4,000 electronic applications each month for various positions. (The China operations of Siemens employ 25,300 people nationwide, 99% of whom are Chinese nationals.) "The greatest challenge is how to filter the right ones out," says Dr. Ernst Behrens. Although many applicants are not qualified, and are simply mass-emailing their resumes out, Behrens insists that his HR department screens each application. "It's a very tedious, time-consuming process. But [if you don't], you may miss a good person."

One method Siemens uses to cope with its recruitment rush, ironically, is to slow down. Behrens explains that when he took his current position in China in 1997, Siemens was growing "extremely fast." Behrens found himself rushing to keep pace. Eventually, he realized that slowing the hiring pace and solidifying standards helped to recruit and retain consistently high-quality personnel. He says, "If you want to keep the best in the company, you have to give them other top-quality people to work with."

At Coca-Cola China, Paul Etchells says the company's "biggest barrier" to growth is not hiring fast enough. In 2003, the company indirectly hired 1,000 new salespeople—a massive undertaking in recruitment, hiring, and training. This influx created another concern: developing a management team to oversee the new hires.

In 2003, Du Pont saw a 20% increase in total employees, to 3,065 persons (98% of whom are Chinese nationals). Du Pont China president Charles Browne also struggles to hire and train fast enough to match the company's pace of growth. Says Browne, "That is one of the difficult issues—just getting those numbers into the company."

Gone Missing: Middle Managers

A more prevalent problem among interviewees is a dearth in semi-skilled and professional staff in China. One reason for this lack is historical. China's 45-65-year-olds make up the "lost generation" who saw their education interrupted or aborted during the Cultural Revolution (1966–76). In contrast, most 30-somethings enjoyed a stable education and have gained work experience in the new market-oriented economy. The result is a workforce with a serious generation gap.

"There are huge numbers of graduates each year, but there is a middle management level that you need," says John Wong, managing director Greater China for BCG. He says those who began work in the SOE system "don't have the same management perspective." The result: for the moment, mid-level management talent is "very scarce." Wong points to a typical problem experienced by his MNC clients. If a company wants to hire a team of sales reps, it often struggles to find middle managers to oversee them.

Helen Tantau of Korn/Ferry agrees that many of China's over-45-year-old white-collar professionals who have spent long periods of time in Chinese organizations would not adapt easily

A Word About Women in the Workforce

One point that may surprise international employers concerns female executives. Our interviewees tell that, in some key ways, Chinese women today are more strongly encouraged to focus on their careers than are their counterparts in the West. One reason is that women received equal rights and held equal responsibilities under the "Women hold up half the sky" philosophy of Communist rule. Also important today is the one-child policy, which means that Chinese mothers necessarily spend less time on child-care than do their peers elsewhere. Perhaps most importantly, the tradition of grandparents caring for young children remains strong. In fact, new mothers are often expected to contribute income to the extended family by returning to work quickly. It is quite common for mothers to work in an urban center, leaving their children with relatives located elsewhere. During the week, they focus their energies on work, spending time with their child on weekends and holidays.

to working for an MNC. Not only is there a language barrier for most, but also a "huge cultural difference," she says.

For these reasons, specialized positions are also difficult to fill in China, especially in professions that were undeveloped under the state-run system. For example, BP China's Dr. Gary Dirks has trouble finding HR managers. Unilever China chairman Alan Brown tells of a frustrating recent search for a marketing director: "In the whole of China, we found eight [candidates] who could speak English and were worthy of the title." And among these, three candidates were former Procter & Gamble (P&G) employees, while another three were formerly with Unilever. "That proves just how small the market is," says Brown.

> *"There are huge numbers of graduates each year, but there is a middle management level that you need."*
>
> **John Wong**, Managing Director Greater China, The Boston Consulting Group

The upshot is that those Chinese professionals with both experience and professional skills are extremely sought-after. Says Du Pont China's Charles Browne, "There is really high-quality talent in the market. The difficulty is that all businesses—including the top Chinese companies—are recruiting from the same pool." Du Pont faces "heated competition" for qualified scientists, engineers, researchers, and other personnel with international experience and English-language skills.

Consultants stress that the problem is temporary, and should ease as younger professionals gain expertise. Already the workforce includes 20- to 30-year-old professionals well trained in the new international, market-oriented economy, and this group grows with every university graduation ceremony. "The university system in China is turning out a lot of smart people," says BP's Gary Dirks. "They work very hard and are very interested in personal development."

High Expectations

Another factor boosting the pace of staff turnover in China is the deeply ingrained culture of pursuing professional advancement. Christopher Shaw, president of Eli Lilly China, describes the career expectations of Chinese professionals as "much higher here than in many other countries." For many, career ambitions are fueled by pressure from their family and from society. "People are driven by their parents' expectations, and the possible implications of the one-child policy." Shaw is referring to the fact that many young-generation Chinese have been prepped from childhood to compete—first in the academic realm, then in the business arena. As only children, they tend to face intense pressure to perform from parents, relatives, and teachers. As adults, they continue to prove themselves to their family and peers. "They feel the strong need to develop and progress," says Shaw. Such ambition means employers must work hard to keep top talent satisfied that their careers are advancing quickly enough.

Frustratingly, the brightest and best-trained are often the quickest to leave. GM China chairman and CEO Philip Murtaugh says he battles a degree of excessive ambition among his most talented personnel. "One of my frustrations is that when you hire smart people who graduated from Tsinghua University or Jiaotong University, they come to your desk and say, 'In three years, I want your job'," he says. "It took me 25 years to get here. There is such a thing as learning the business, and you don't do that in three years."

CASE STUDY

CHINESE FAST-TRACKERS

Dominique de Boisseson, chairman and CEO of Alcatel China, advises international managers to accept that, in China, a certain percentage of extremely ambitious personnel will leave. "People learn very quickly, but we also lose them," he says. Seven years ago, Alcatel hired and trained a team of Chinese lawyers. Today, every one of them has left the company to work in a large company as general counsel. One of these attorneys, aged 28, took extra holidays in order to attend, at his own expense, an executive training program at the Harvard Business School. When de Boisseson asked him why he was ready to invest so much money, the lawyer replied: "I am 28. It is time to build my worldwide network." De Boisseson says that young Chinese professionals have "unbelievable" ambition. "You cannot keep those people more than a few years, but it is still acceptable as they are strong contributors while they are with us."

The Solution: HR Best Practices

Given the tight employment market (for professionals) and other challenges, to what extent must an MNC adapt its HR policy for its China operations? This is a question each of our 20 international managers considered upon taking up the position as head of China operations, and it is also a common question that MNC clients ask of our profiled HR consultants. The overriding response during our interviews may bring a sigh of relief to readers; most of our interviewees recommended keeping international HR principles and policies largely intact.

GE China's Steve Schneider stressed that the company has retained most of its HR policies in China, making only minor adaptations in order to meet the requirements of the PRC Labor Law or local governmental restrictions. The challenge, he says, is that there are often differences between central government-initiated regulations and those initiated by local-level governments (city or province). Regulatory inconsistency means that GE offers slightly different benefit policies in different places. "From Sichuan to Guangdong to Shanghai to Tianjin, all those areas have slightly different policies and procedures," Schneider says.

Still, MNCs can largely count on using their standard international HR practices in China. At McKinsey & Company's Shanghai offices, director Gordon Orr generally advises his MNC clients to retain their global HR standards in China, rather than adapting them for this market. First, this helps to merge China operations with global operations. Second, using international-standard policies in hiring, training, and promoting is a key selling point for MNCs in recruiting; Chinese professionals are attracted by companies offering a truly international work environment because learning such standards will help to advance their careers. For example, concepts such as formal performance reviews, performance-based (rather than seniority-based) bonuses and promotions, employee training programs, and emphasis on developing a corporate culture are not common among traditional Chinese companies and are a selling point to ambitious Chinese professionals. "Credibility in attracting and

> "*One of my frustrations is that when you hire smart people who graduated from Tsinghua University or Jiaotong University, they come to your desk and say, 'In three years, I want your job.' It took me 25 years to get here. There is such a thing as learning the business, and you don't do that in three years.*"
>
> **Philip Murtaugh**, Chairman and CEO, General Motors China

retaining talent depends on using global standards," he says. "Compromising too much and assuming you have to do everything from scratch is not the right starting premise." In fact, Orr recommends considering carefully before adapting any aspect of corporate HR policies for China. "You should challenge what you are changing," he warns. Specifically, he says, policies on job rotations inside and outside China should remain the same as those used elsewhere worldwide, giving domestic employees a chance to work at stints abroad.

At Alcatel China, chairman and CEO Dominique de Boisseson has also transferred global corporate HR practices with little adaptation. "If we want to succeed in China, we must make sure the Chinese employees have a worldwide view and use best practices," he says. Global policies are generally embraced by younger-generation employees, who are mostly eager to work under international standards, he says, while older staff "behave more in the old way" and have difficulty adapting.

BP China has also imported its HR policies with virtually no change. Its top executive, Dr. Gary Dirks, says: "The HR tools we use in China are the same we use anywhere. We apply them exactly the same way. Some of them are translated into Chinese. That's all."

At the same time, no international top executive we interviewed was able to simply transplant each and every HR policy to China without some degree of alteration. And even those policies that were merely "translated" had to be thoroughly introduced to the Chinese workforce (often to employees who were not familiar with the concepts), and then carefully implemented. As a result, none of our interviewees considered the establishment or implementation of HR policies easy in China. Unilever's Alan Brown uses this description to explain how he has adapted his management style. "To use an analogy, it is like golf: you need different clubs for different situations. What is important in China is that one tends to need a greater range of clubs than in most other environments. One needs a management style that can be adapted to different circumstances."

In the following section, we use recommendations from our

experts to create a full "bag of clubs" which managers can use to tackle specific HR challenges in China. Below are the strategies gleaned from our roster of China hands in addressing:

- Compensation
- Recruitment
- Retention
- Promotion

HR Strategy #1: The Right Compensation

The first point stressed by our international managers in China is that recruitment and retention should not hinge on offering a high salary. "Retaining people isn't a matter of money. If somebody wants to leave and you offer her more money, it's too late," says Airbus China president Guy McLeod. Instead, he says, employees are ultimately swayed by less mercenary reasons. "Employees should enjoy what they are doing, like working for the management, be interested in the business, feel trusted, feel proud of the company, feel a part of the success."

General Motors China follows a strategy of setting compensation within industry standards, but stresses other aspects to recruit and retain staff. "We don't offer the highest wages. If you look at our compensation, you will find it's not the most competitive," says Philip Murtaugh. He focuses his HR strategy on empowering key staff to directly influence their own career paths.

Having made these points, however, the international managers also stressed that compensation must match current industry pay scales. Chinese professionals tend to be extremely well-versed on the going salary rates in their field. And rates are rising quickly, especially in regions where foreign direct investment is pouring in. Not only are salaries rising, but benefits are expanding as well. Korn/Ferry Senior Client Partner Helen Tantau says it is possible for Chinese professionals in their thirties to be not only well-paid according to market rates, but also rewarded with stock options and a housing loan.

TIP **Performance-based pay may initially be a hard sell, but is often welcomed by young and ambitious Chinese professionals.**

The compensation issue which MNC employers struggle with most is introducing performance-based pay. The problem stems from a cultural difference, since many Chinese managers are used to a seniority-based pay system. Philip Murtaugh met with such a conflict when GM China sought to introduce its Chinese JV partner to the bonus system the company uses globally. The issue proved a "big challenge," Murtaugh says. "Chinese usually evaluate [bonuses] based on educational background and professional rating, whether you are an engineer or a senior economist. All things related to the bonus have nothing to do with performance," he says. After considerable effort, he was able to introduce a performance-based bonus system. "In Shanghai GM, we have completely adopted the American way," he says.

CASE STUDY

LAUNCHING PERFORMANCE-BASED PAY AT HILTON HOTELS, CHINA

It is possible to launch a performance-based pay system in China, says Hilton Shanghai's general manager Volkmar Ruebel. Ruebel should know. When he took his current post in 1995, he inherited the hotel's traditional salary system which was determined by a rigid, 12-layer hierarchical employment grid. All employees received pre-set salary increases yearly, in lock-step across the board. Within six months, Ruebel had gutted and rebuilt the system, reclassifying each employee in terms of competence, productivity, and contribution toward achieving the hotel's objectives. The new plan recommended firing 190 persons deemed redundant, while promoting 160 persons who were found to be underpaid. Savings from the staff cuts were passed on to those promoted.

The revision process caused several days of heated discussion, but all of Ruebel's managers eventually agreed to the plan. Then came the hardest part—selling it to the employee union. To Ruebel's surprise, union officials approved the scheme within 30 minutes. "They accepted based on the basic principle of allowing people who have knowledge and competence to advance over seniority," he says.

HR Strategy #2: Recruit Smart

TIP **While retaining people is not just a matter of money, managers in China must constantly track fast-rising salary standards in order to stay competitive.**

Despite offering the right compensation and bonus pay schemes, many of our interviewees face trouble recruiting fast enough to match company growth-rate goals in China. Below are strategies for large-scale hiring and training drives. The main message heard in overcoming the professional workforce shortfall was this: if you can't find them, make them.

Several of our interviewees have adopted a policy in China of hiring younger staff than they would elsewhere, then offering more training and guidance early on. At Coca-Cola China, company president Paul Etchells says the lack of English-language ability among professionals aged 40-plus has forced him to hire 20- and 30-somethings into higher positions than is the corporate standard elsewhere. "It is difficult for us to hire people who don't speak English. That forces us to go for a younger crowd," he says.

Other international managers use the same strategy to jump the language barrier. "A very good trend in China is that the new generation speaks more and more English," says Jean-Luc Chereau, president of Carrefour China. When he arrived in Shanghai in 1999, lack of English ability was "a big problem." Says Chereau, "The official language of Carrefour is English. It was very difficult, at the store level, for the store manager to communicate with people." Today, however, 20% of his personnel speak "very good" English.

Many international managers commented on the ability—and ambition—of China's younger-generation professionals. Volkmar Ruebel says this of Chinese aged in their twenties and thirties: "Young people are eager, want to show off, have energy and want to learn," he says. "I get 100% support. They don't let you down."

Hiring younger personnel does require that managers develop a more hands-on approach. Says Kenneth Yu of 3M China: "We sometimes do a little bit more telling than advising [in China]." In contrast, Yu managed in a less hands-on manner in Taiwan, where many of his staff had international experience and expertise. He stresses that the situation in China is changing; during the past decade, Chinese employees have become more proactive, more confident, and more competent.

At Alcatel China, chairman and CEO Dominique de Boisseson has also noted a transformation among Chinese white-collar workers. When he arrived in China in 1997, he found vast differences between the management team he had left behind in France and the one he formed in China. "My management style is to delegate as much as possible and to trust people. My team in Paris was perfect. If anyone needed me, they would come and ask for support. Once a month or every two weeks, I talked with them about details," he says. "But in China, that was impossible initially because the employees were far too junior."

De Boisseson also stresses that while his local management team started from a position of inexperience, they progressed extremely quickly. "[At the beginning] I was working day and night, on weekends. Everything was up to me—nobody knew how to solve a problem," he says. "Customers asked to talk to me directly because people did not know how to deal with them." Thus, his first task was to build a team of domestic managers. He quickly formed a group he describes as young and inexperienced but "very good and very reliable people—diligent and very dedicated." With this team in place, Alcatel quadrupled China sales between 1997 and 2001.

Philips China's David Chang experienced a similar development after moving to China from Taiwan in 2002. Back in Taipei, Chang generally gave minimal instructions to management staff, allowing them to sort out details on their own. In China, such arms-length methods didn't work. "I thought I could just tell [a manager] to do something and it would happen," he says. "Here, if you give an assignment, you have to describe it to the last detail to make sure there is complete understanding." Chang says guidance is particularly important if staff members are to solicit cooperation and support from personnel in other departments. Chinese employees tend to be uncomfortable whenever the hierarchy of a work group becomes unclear. Says Chang, "It will not be enough to simply say, 'Please organize cross-functional support.' You have to bring the relevant people together in front of you and say exactly the same thing in front of all of them. And after that, you still need very strong follow-up."

When training new hires, McKinsey & Company's Director in Shanghai Gordon Orr recommends expanding orientation to begin at a more basic level than what is used elsewhere—for example introducing the fundamentals of the company's operational scope, corporate culture, company history, and mission statement. He also advises covering the basic international business practices used by the firm. "It is almost like offering a mini-MBA to get people aligned from Day 1 on what it is they are joining," Orr says.

TIP **Lack of competent staff can hinder growth. Smart companies hire and train in advance more people than they currently need, in order to build a reserve.**

For companies facing a severe workforce shortage that impacts their growth plans in China, Charles Browne suggests the strategy used at Du Pont. For skilled positions, new hires need six months of training before becoming truly productive—a time lag that "restricts growth," Browne says. His solution, initiated in 2000, is to hire and train more people than are immediately needed, as a reserve. "We go out and select people, and put them into jobs a little bit before we run into a crisis and *have* to have them," he says. Such advance hiring is not undertaken elsewhere within Du Pont's global operations. "This is unique from the other parts in the world. We bring in a large quantity of people because of our growth," Browne says.

HR Strategy #3: To Retain, Train

In tackling employee retention, one of the clearest messages voiced by our international managers is that the way to stop turnover is to offer professional training. Simon Keeley of Hewitt Associates explains the mindset of Chinese professionals in this way: "Chinese employees are incredibly hungry for learning, for development. They are very entrepreneurial."

In the annual employee survey conducted by Bayer China for its global annual report, employees are asked why they joined the company in the first place. The answer most often given by Chinese personnel is: professional development. China CEO for Bayer Dr. Elmar Stachels says that retaining top staff in China

TIP Companies unable to recruit professional staff hire young staff and develop extra training programs. Offer new employees a "mini MBA" to get them up to speed with international standards and practices.

depends on making personnel confident that staying with the company will increase their professional worth.

Hilton Shanghai general manager Volkmar Ruebel says the top motivators for keeping local "team members" (employees) always involve professional development. First, employees must feel certain that supervisors have their best professional interests at heart. Second, they must believe they will learn and grow at your company. Third, they must feel that the company provides opportunities for advancement.

Du Pont China president Charles Browne stresses that Chinese employees tend to be more motivated by educational perks than are Western staff. "[Chinese professionals] expect the company to give them opportunities for continuous growth and development, not only career-wise but also intellectually," he says. "This has to do with the long tradition of valuing education in China. If you fail on that one, it's a deal-breaker."

Microsoft China also places a clear emphasis on training as a means to hire and keep personnel. "Opportunities are the first motivation for people to stay, more so than money," says the company's China president Jun Tang. Although many of his employees could make a similar salary elsewhere, he says they stay with Microsoft because "they are happy with the culture, the environment, and most importantly, the career opportunities." When recruiting new hires or persuading a star player to stay on, Tang heavily stresses career development via professional training. "I always ask people to ask themselves, after being with Microsoft for three years, will you increase your market value? Every year, you should ask yourself: 'Did I earn a reputation, gain experience, gain new skills compared to last year?'"

Microsoft China uses an "open policy internally" in which information on a range of training courses is posted on the corporate intranet. All employee training courses are free, but employees must qualify for certain classes. Training sessions typically cover topics such as sales and marketing techniques, presentation skills, management philosophy, effective teamwork, and business strategy.

Several of our interviewees have made large-scale investments in employee training in China. GE opened its second-largest training center outside its New Jersey headquarters in 2003 with the 42,000-square-foot Global Resources Center in Shanghai. The center offers R&D, sourcing, and training courses for employees as well as for government officials and GE customers.

Carrefour China has also invested heavily in employee training. In 2000, the company opened the Carrefour Chinese Institute in Shanghai to offer executive staff a range of professional development courses taught by invited professors from area universities. Since then, the company has established four additional training centers—in Beijing, Chengdu, Wuhai, and Guangzhou. "Chinese love to receive training, no matter what their professional level," says Carrefour China president Jean-Luc Chereau.

Other popular training programs offered to Chinese employees cover practical topics such as presentation skills, business writing, or foreign-language classes. Eli Lilly's Christopher Shaw says the language classes he offers on company premises are well worth the investment, "This is something our employees value and something we value. We want to keep people and we want to promote people. It is very important. When they join my company, they say: 'Eli Lilly is looking out for my future.'"

“

This [company-sponsored language class] is something our employees value and something we value. ... When they join my company, they say: 'Eli Lilly is looking out for my future.'"

Christopher Shaw,
President, Eli Lilly China

Overseas Training

Although many companies in China are now using training as a means for recruiting and retaining top personnel, MNCs enjoy a distinct advantage over local companies in that they can offer star players a chance to learn international practices and standards.

One reason why employees join Du Pont, says the company's top executive in China Charles Browne, is to learn how MNCs do business. This desire for international training gives Du Pont an edge over domestic companies competing for the same personnel. In fact, one of the most tantalizing carrots MNCs can dangle in front of qualified Chinese personnel is the possibility of overseas training or an overseas work stint.

At the Hilton Shanghai, all employees know that two or three persons per year are sent to hotel management training at Cornell University in the U.S. The policy has helped general manager Volkmar Ruebel retain some of the most talented personnel in

TIP Chinese employees tend to place a higher value on company-sponsored training than do counterparts elsewhere, making training programs a key retention "weapon."

his hotel. "I haven't lost a single person I have sent to Cornell. They all come back and stay with us," he says.

Troubles With Training

The most common problem faced by China-based MNCs when offering training programs is "train and run." Several interviewees acknowledged the risk of investing in a promising Chinese staff member, only to watch him jump to a competitor. Dr. Ernst Behrens, Siemens China president and CEO, says Chinese professionals tend to take an "opportunistic" view of employment, displaying "a mindset more similar to Americans than Europeans." He says, "Chinese employees work hard and are engaged but at the same time constantly screen the market for other opportunities and move jobs rather frequently. This is different to the German or the Japanese attitude of expecting very long-time employment with one company." Behrens says one of the biggest challenges in personnel education in China is to make employees understand and accept that Siemens expects to receive something in return for the "often very expensive" training that is provided. "Many Chinese employees believe that a company such as Siemens is obligated to offer training opportunities for the personal benefit of the employee," he says. "I try to explain that we have to enhance the performance of the company through training of our employees." Behrens says staff members sometimes return from a training course and immediately ask when they can expect to attend the next, more advanced training. "This is a frustrating moment because it is obvious that there is little appreciation for what the company has just provided and there seems to be little understanding that this investment has now to earn its returns through enhanced, and hopefully higher, performance of the employee. Siemens must see that the course was worthwhile for the company, not just the person."

Such differences in thinking between Siemens management and personnel reflect a common West–East gap, as well as a generational gap; young-generation Chinese tend to be far less loyal to a company than are older professionals.

The final section of this chapter discusses how Chinese tend to consider the company they work for as a kind of family, in which a supervisor takes care of his or her individual employees in return for their loyalty.

In order to manage what can become unrealistic demands for training courses, Christopher Shaw of Eli Lilly says it is important to communicate the benefit of such programs to employees. Personnel should be told clearly how the classes taken can benefit their careers. Shaw tells how he heightened employee satisfaction with a recent marketing course; participants were specifically shown how the class could be used in their jobs. "[The course] goes on their resumes and helps their marketing career," he points out.

TIP **MNCs can use the promise of sending Chinese professionals on overseas work assignment or training sessions as an extremely valuable perk.**

HR Strategy #4: Offer a Fast Track

After professional training, the second-most important "hook" for hiring and keeping Chinese professionals is rapid career advancement. Recruitment professional Helen Tantau knows this first-hand. She is finding that in China a primary reason for job-hopping is the perception that one's career is advancing too slowly. "The hardest thing to manage in this market is the high expectation of the [Chinese] employees," she says. "People expect to be developed very quickly."

The annual employee satisfaction survey conducted by BP China shows the importance of a fast track. Company president and CEO Dr. Gary Dirks explains: "When we ask [Chinese employees] 'What do you want?', the answer is, absolutely, career development. These people want to do interesting and exciting things, big projects."

How should companies in China tailor career management to retain top talent? The first rule is to communicate clearly all opportunities for advancement. Carrefour China's Jean-Luc Chereau says that internal promotion opportunities are his main defense against turnover. He stresses opportunities for advancement to employees at all levels, so that every cashier knows that they could become a store manager.

Client multinationals of The Boston Consulting Group are advised to ensure that Chinese employees do not perceive a glass

"

[Chinese professionals] come to foreign companies with very different expectations from what they expect at Chinese companies. They expect to be trained and developed. If you cannot help them to grow, you are going to lose them."

Helen Tantau, Senior Client Partner, Korn/Ferry

ceiling through which only expatriates can penetrate. Company managing director for Greater China John Wong says that some Chinese professionals avoid international firms for this reason.

At the same time, MNCs benefit from having a reputation for promoting personnel faster than do Chinese firms. That means local staff are likely to expect rapid advancement. "They come to foreign companies with very different expectations from what they expect at Chinese companies. They expect to be trained and developed. If you cannot help them to grow, you are going to lose them," says Helen Tantau. With this in mind, she advises international managers to consider ratcheting up the promotion speed they would normally use back home. "You may be promoting people faster than you are ready to," she says.

At GE China, Steve Schneider has built a fast track using "stretch assignments"—promoting individuals into positions they are "clearly not completely ready for." Such leaps force key staffers to "really accelerate their growth," says Schneider. His own career path has been dotted with stretch assignments. "You are forced to do things you are uncomfortable with, forced out of your comfort zone. You either grow rapidly, or not. And you discover that quickly." This tool is especially effective in China, he says, because people tend to be highly motivated to advance their careers. Schneider's goal is to "keep [employees] focused and growing, and to provide a great place to participate."

Another method GE China uses to avoid disappointing staff members is to promote realistic advancement expectations. "Part of retention begins on Day 1 with managing expectations," says Steve Schneider. "A lot of folks [in China] have the desire to move to the president level in a short time." He says a certain percentage of his employees simply have impossible expectations for how fast and how far they will advance. He recommends accepting the fact that some employees will go, letting them go, and focusing on the rest. "There are those folks who leave because they don't get what they want, and that is probably okay," he says.

Schneider says that companies can expect "cycles" of turnover whenever the pace of promotion slows. In other words, a general economic slowdown or a deceleration in GE's plans for expansion can trigger employee flight. "Retention will become a concern again if we slow our growth down and people aren't moving fast enough," Schneider says.

At Du Pont China, the company fights turnover and keeps employee career advancement goals realistic through a "target development" scheme used worldwide. Under the system, employees meet with a supervisor to draft a five-year career plan, including listing specific steps necessary to reach those goals: training, work experience, and stepping-stone positions.

TIP **Career opportunities are the first motivation for Chinese employees to stay. You may need to promote people faster in China than you would elsewhere.**

Promotion Problems: Loss of Face

One problem international managers run into in China is that promoting one person in an organization can cause those not promoted to "lose face". While personnel in the West may also react with resentment when overlooked for an advancement, such resentments often run far deeper in China, even leading key personnel to resign. "Because relationships are very important, every time you promote one person, you involve face. You may risk losing others. In a way, people measure themselves in comparison with others, which is culturally correct here, especially in the context of an increasingly competitive market," says Paolo Gasparrini of L'Oréal China.

To prevent a slew of unwanted resignations after a promotion, Gasparrini recommends finding a way to give face to those not promoted. One method is to combine several promotions to be offered simultaneously, so that other key players advance at the same time. "Be ready to open other new positions. If you aren't fast enough, this is a problem," says Gasparrini. He also trains middle managers to help in the effort to prevent staff turnover by meeting often with their subordinates to gauge worker satisfaction and to make improvements.

Creative Job Titles

Another variation on the theme of frequent promotions is to create more layers of positions than exist in an MNC in other countries. In this way, key personnel can be given new titles with every "mini-promotion."

"

Part of retention begins on Day 1 with managing expectations. A lot of folks [in China] have the desire to move to the president level in a short time."

Steve Schneider, Chairman and CEO, General Electric China

In general, job titles tend to be far more important to Chinese employees than they are to Western counterparts. Bryan Huang of BearingPoint explains that the job titles presented on one's business card are critical for Chinese, as they clearly define a person's status, role, and rank. Problems arise because, first, Western companies tend to place less emphasis on titles and rank, and second, the standard titles chosen by MNCs may be misunderstood by Chinese employees. Says Huang, "Problems sometimes arise in global organizations that use strictly monitored titles, because in China [a title such as] 'division manager' may sound quite unimpressive to Chinese ears." For example, the title "China HR Manager" may be a standard title in a global organization in which "director" is reserved for regional-level managers. But the term "manager" may turn off many talented HR executives. Huang says a typical reaction among Chinese is: "How can I face my friends when they are all directors and I am just a manager? We went to the same university and I work as hard as they do." In order to retain people, Huang urges employers to offer good career opportunities, an attractive work environment, and titles that portray a "very good social position."

In fact, many MNCs struggle with the pressure on the one hand to meet the demands of Chinese personnel for titles that accurately portray their level of responsibility within Chinese business circles, and on the other hand to maintain the standardized titles the corporation uses globally. Korn/Ferry's Helen Tantau offers a creative solution to the title issue: many companies create internal and external titles. This allows personnel to use standard titles when working with colleagues outside China, but to use separate China-specific titles within the country. Since individual name-cards are printed in English and Chinese, another option is to use a standard corporate-wide title on the English side, but an adapted title on the Chinese side. For example, an employee could be "PR Department Manager" in English but "Director of Public Communications" in Chinese.

Flexibility in titles also gives international managers a method for offering mini-promotions, in which the English title remains the same but the Chinese title is upgraded. Tantau says that many large-scale MNCs cannot do this, but smaller companies can.

The final section of this chapter offers perhaps the most important HR strategy of all: establishing good employer–employee *guanxi* (relations). As our international managers explained, forming and maintaining strong, positive, and close-knitted relationships with your staff can prove extremely influential in finding and keeping Chinese professionals.

Figure 2.2 illustrates how HR best-practice strategies, including employer–employee relations, help to solve the serious problem of white-collar workforce turnover in China.

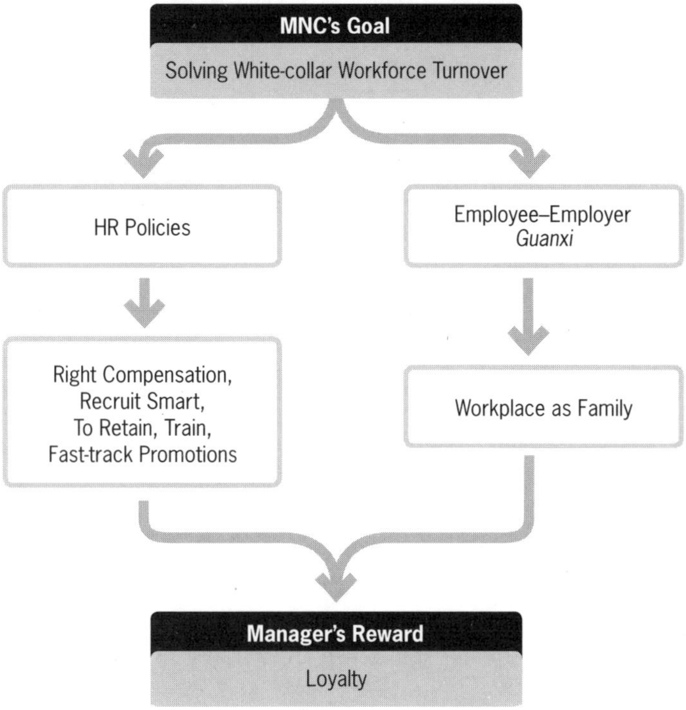

FIGURE 2.2 *Solving White-collar Workforce Turnover*

TIP Be aware of loss of face if one team member is promoted but another is not. Objective promotion rules, and personal attention to them, will ease the problem.

Best HR Defense: Building Employer–Employee *Guanxi*

We conclude this chapter by introducing another surprising contradiction that exists in today's business environment in China. Despite all that we have just described concerning the highly ambitious nature of Chinese professionals—and the consequent struggles that MNCs face in retaining skilled staff—a somewhat contradictory characteristic is also prevalent in China: Chinese employees tend to be more loyal to the companies they work for than their counterparts in the West.

The 20 top executives we interviewed found that two opposing motivating forces exist within the Chinese workforce: the tendency to job-hop, and the tendency to form a deep commitment to one's employer. The key ingredient in creating a committed and loyal staff, the interviewees agreed, is strong employer–employee *guanxi*.

In many ways, we have saved the most important retention tool for last. In analyzing the HR advice given by our China experts, one theme emerged again and again: the basis for reducing turnover (and overcoming other HR difficulties) lies in forming and maintaining a positive and effective employer–employee relationship. And the first step toward accomplishing this is to understand the difference between the Western and Chinese definitions of an ideal working relationship with one's boss.

In general, Chinese tend to form a much closer relationship to their employer (the individual supervisor, not the company) than do Westerners. In China, staff members expect more from their supervisors—in terms of training, career management, professional development, and even assistance with personal problems. In return, supervisors expect more from their staff—in terms of respect, loyalty and commitment. Both sides tend to blur professional and personal lines, seeking a level of dedication that extends beyond the Western standard. For example, a Chinese supervisor may expect long hours of overtime work from his closest staff, without apology or special compensation. Meanwhile, a Chinese employee may ask for help from a supervisor (or from the supervisor's spouse or cousin or classmate) in assisting a friend to secure a bank loan, obtain a travel visa, or apply to a foreign university. (Such personal requests from professional contacts are examples of the *guanxi* system in action.)

Gaining a full understanding of the Chinese definition of good employer–employee *guanxi* is critical because, in many cases, achieving this ideal was used as a means for solving the most common HR problems plaguing MNC executives in China.

TIP The hardest thing to manage is Chinese employees' high career expectations. Focus on your top talent and high potentials. Show them a clear career path with no glass ceiling for Chinese professionals. Remember that job titles are extremely important.

Positive Workplace *Guanxi*

We begin this section of the chapter by detailing what we do *not* mean by employer–employee *guanxi*. We are not discussing how an employer can abuse his or her power with respect to employees, or how employees curry favor with superiors in return for career advancement. Of course, this behavior does happen in China (as it does worldwide), but it is not the norm and it is not the focus of our discussion. Instead, we review the methods outlined by the 28 top executives and consultants we interviewed as the methods they use to develop positive and effective inter-workplace *guanxi*. It is this body of insight and advice that we share here.

The best way to explain positive inter-workplace *guanxi* is through the definition most used by interviewees: in China, we heard repeatedly, the workplace is "like a family." After nearly a decade in China, Dr. Ernst Behrens, top executive at Siemens China, explains the thinking of his local personnel in this way: "The Chinese, and Asians generally, enter into employment with a different understanding than we have in Europe. For us, the company certainly is important, but to the Chinese, the company is more like a family. The idea is, 'I am giving myself to Siemens. Now you have to take care of me.'" This contrasts sharply with the Western standard in which professional and personal lines are clearly drawn. The idea that employers and employees work

TIP **Chinese employees have to feel that their supervisor supports and looks after them. They must feel that their workplace is a second family.**

together from 8 AM to 5 PM, exchanging competence for pay—but not exceeding defined boundaries—is not standard in China.

Dr. Bryan Huang, BearingPoint senior vice president and China president, clarifies how the Chinese and Western standards differ concerning appropriate workplace relationships. A Chinese national who spent 19 years working in Europe, the U.S., and Japan before returning to China in 2001, Huang understands the contrast between East and West. "In Chinese culture, management relationships are much more personal than in Western culture," he says. This personalization adds another layer of responsibility for managers. "People [in China] will work hard for the company because they like working for [their supervisor], because of their personal relationship with that person. This requires a very different management style. You need not only to care about the employees' work, but also care about their families and other personal issues."

Workplace as Family

Successfully creating a family environment for employees is the reason the Shanghai Hilton has not lost a single departmental head in the past 11 years, says top executive Volkmar Ruebel. "You've got to create a paternalistic or patriarchal style and allow people to trust you," he says. "[Chinese employees] have to feel that you like them; they have to feel that you look after them. When they work, it is like they are in a second family. And when they have that feeling, they will follow you. They will endure hardship if necessary, even when the business is not good."

In China, the workplace serves as a form of social network, explains Microsoft China's Jun Tang. Tang says that while Americans tend to consider the companies they work for primarily as "a place to make a living," many Chinese form a deeper connection. In fact, the workplace often serves as a social unit. "In China, the company is as important as the family," Tang says. "When you have a problem, you can talk to your company management. If you are unhappy, you can discuss it with colleagues." As an example, he points out that many people celebrate their birthdays not with family but with co-workers. With this in mind, Tang recommends that China-based managers create a close intra-office atmosphere by facilitating social interaction through gatherings and outings.

> "*People [in China] will work hard for the company because they like working for [their supervisor], because of their personal relationship with that person. This requires a very different management style. You need not only to care about the employees' work, but also care about their families and other personal issues.*"
>
> **Bryan Huang**, Senior Vice President and China President, BearingPoint

Manager's Reward: Loyalty

The workplace-as-family ideal requires that the top executive takes on a more complex role in the company. In order to build positive employee relations, a manager must not only win respect and confidence as a leader; he or she must also win trust and appreciation as a mentor and guardian. Dominique de Boisseson, of Alcatel China, explains it this way, "[Chinese] employees like to have a good relationship with the boss. You need to make sure you are not only a boss, but also a friend and a teacher."

Another way of explaining the local mindset is this: in China, people work for a person, not for a company. This idea was repeated by several interviewees. "In China, [employee] loyalty is often more directly to the immediate supervisor. This one concept changes the way people work," says Paolo Gasparrini, of L'Oréal China. "In a Chinese company, everything is relationships—even more so than in other countries. So, if your direct boss doesn't like you, doesn't respect you, doesn't give you face, you will lose your attachment to the company and sooner or later, you will write your resignation letter."

When a manager is liked and trusted by Chinese employees, the reward is often a deeply loyal staff. This creates the close-knit workplace relations seen at many local companies, especially among private companies, which are often family-owned. "Loyalty is much stronger in a Chinese company [than at Western companies]," says Helen Tantau of Korn/Ferry. "There is a lot of team spirit and a feeling of community."

This community environment places a new layer of responsibility on a manager, explains Tantau. It means that the boss's role is more critical to the organization, as he or she provides

TIP In China, people work for a person, not for a company. Thus, when a manager leaves a company, their staff members will sometimes quit as well, either to stay with their previous supervisor or to avoid working with a new supervisor.

not only business leadership but also guidance and motivation. "For a lot of new companies, the personality of the boss really becomes the company culture," Tantau says.

Given this mindset, Ekkehard Rathgeber, head of Bertelsmann Direct Asia, says it can be difficult for Western managers to develop a corporate structure that remains intact even if an individual supervisor is replaced. "People listen to the individual, not to the position," Rathgeber says. As a result of such thinking, if a department head leaves, it can mean that the entire department must be rebuilt. Another result: the mindset of "once a boss, always a boss" still prevails. In other words, an employee who once worked under a certain supervisor generally will continue to treat the former boss as a superior even if both parties change posts and rank.

For international managers, Bryan Huang advises that forming a close relationship with Chinese employees can be extremely useful in bridging the culture gap. "Inter-cultural trust is very difficult because the language difference can cause a lot of misunderstandings," he says. He adds that once a close relationship has been built with a foreign manager, Chinese employees are often as loyal as they would be to a Chinese boss.

One common illustration of Chinese-style employee loyalty: when professionals do leave a company, especially a domestic company, many avoid joining a direct competitor because such a move would be considered an act of disrespect or even betrayal. When a person does leave, he or she often shifts into a different field. (The international managers interviewed stressed that jumping ship does happen, but it happens less frequently and less blatantly than in the West.)

Another variation on this theme: if a manager or division head leaves, his or her personnel will sometimes quit as well, either in order to continue working for that person or simply to avoid working with a new supervisor. "If a manager who is very well-regarded leaves, you may expect those working under him to leave, too," says Simon Keeley of Hewitt Associates.

Such customs make firing, promoting, or transferring problematic. L'Oréal's Paolo Gasparrini says that when a supervisor is promoted, his former team of employees goes through a "moment of loss" which can trigger a flurry of resignations. When Gasparrini recently transferred one department head to a new division, he did a lot of groundwork first in order to avoid losing key employees who worked under that person. "I had to work on a lot of things before [making the transfer]—invite people for dinner and lunch," he says. "Chinese don't like you changing the boss. It is quite a delicate situation."

> *"[Chinese] employees like to have a good relationship with the boss. You need to make sure you are not only a boss, but also a friend and a teacher."*
>
> **Dominique de Boisseson**, Chairman and CEO, Alcatel China

Conclusion

The biggest single problem experienced by our interviewees across a wide spectrum of industries was the lack of white-collar employees. On the one hand, China is seeing fast growth and high demand for professional staff among both international and domestic firms. On the other hand, the workforce suffers from a gap in mid-level managers because the 45-and-older generation suffered from a disrupted education and work experience during the Cultural Revolution. In addition, China's professionals today hold extremely high expectations for a fast-track career. All this adds up to difficulties for international managers in recruiting and retaining managers and technical specialists.

Below is a summary of the strategies our profiled top executives offer in addressing workforce shortages. The central message from our interviewees was this: good *guanxi* between employers and employees can be an extremely useful tool in slowing the high turnover rate and creating a positive, effective work environment.

SUMMARY OF TIPS

MANAGING CHINESE EMPLOYEES

1. The Right Compensation

Performance-based pay may initially be a hard sell, but is often welcomed by young and ambitious Chinese professionals.

While retaining people is not just a matter of money, managers in China must constantly track fast-rising salary standards in order to stay competitive.

2. Recruit Smart

Lack of competent staff can hinder growth. Smart companies hire and train in advance more people than they currently need, in order to build a reserve.

3. To Retain, Train

Companies unable to recruit professional staff hire young staff and develop extra training programs. Offer new employees a "mini MBA" to get them up to speed with international standards and practices.

Chinese employees tend to place a higher value on company-sponsored training than do counterparts elsewhere, making training programs a key retention "weapon."

MNCs can use the promise of sending Chinese professionals on overseas work assignment or training sessions as an extremely valuable perk.

4. Offer a Fast Track

Career opportunities are the first motivation for Chinese employees to stay. You may need to promote people faster in China than you would elsewhere.

5. Promotion Problems: Loss of Face

Be aware of loss of face if one team member is promoted but another is not. Objective promotion rules, and personal attention to them, will ease the problem.

The hardest thing to manage is Chinese employees' high career expectations. Focus on your top talent and high potentials. Show them a clear career path with no glass ceiling for Chinese professionals. Remember that job titles are extremely important.

6. Building Employer–Employee *Guanxi*

Chinese employees have to feel that their supervisor supports and looks after them. They must feel that their workplace is a second family.

In China, people work for a person, not for a company. Thus, when a manager leaves a company, their staff members will sometimes quit as well, either to stay with their previous supervisor or to avoid working with a new supervisor.

Chapter 3
Working With Business Partners

"In choosing a JV partner, some people may want [first] to make sure the partner has business experience. But if I am the person choosing, trust is very important. This basically means that we can share the same vision. Character is very important—more than business experience. A JV is like a marriage."

Seiichi Kawasaki, Director and President, Sony China

Introduction

One of the very first questions almost all MNCs must ask when entering the China market is: should we operate as a joint venture with a Chinese partner firm, or as an independent, wholly owned foreign enterprise?

The question is a relatively new one for foreign managers; up until the mid-1990s most foreign companies in many sectors were forced to form joint ventures in order to operate in China. In fact, from the economic opening of the mid-1980s through the early 1990s, the Chinese government often chose JV partners for foreign investors. This frequently meant being paired with an outdated, loss-making SOE, sometimes with no understanding of your industry.

One famous (or infamous) case matched Pepsi with the Sichuan Radio & Television Industrial Co. (SRTIC), a provincial government-run broadcasting company with zero experience in the packaged beverage business. This mismatch, formed in 1993, resulted in one of the best-known and longest-running legal battles among foreign–Chinese ventures. After the JV began making money, differences emerged between the partners. In mid-2002, Pepsi charged SRTIC with misuse of funds and breach of contract for planning to launch a competing drink product. That August, Pepsi enlisted a Swedish arbitrator to try and dissolve the partnership. This bid was rejected in 2003, but the saga did not end. The Chinese partner filed a counter-suit against Pepsi for "violating commercial secrets." It was not until 2005 that the Stockholm-based Arbitration Board of Commercial Council legitimized the "divorce" of the partnership.

Happily, such high-profile mis-matches are rare among joint ventures. In fact, our interviewees generally agreed that JV partnerships can be extremely valuable to MNCs entering China. The most-cited benefit of working via joint venture is that the domestic partner can assist greatly in negotiating PRC government entities. Local companies also offer newcomers a head start when launching in China, bringing valuable insight into local customs and understanding of the business environment, as well as providing established operations, a ready-made workforce, and access to existing clients and customers. General Motors China's Philip Murtaugh, who oversees five JVs and two WFOEs, is a satisfied international partner. "[Our] JVs have been very successful. Our JV partners have made valuable contributions," he says. "I wouldn't set up a wholly owned company even if the laws were to change."

Regulations in Flux

MNCs operating in China today generally have much more freedom concerning partnerships than they did in the mid-1990s. The PRC government continues to designate certain industries as sensitive, and to require that foreign enterprises in these sectors operate via JV. But even in protected sectors, investors are now far more likely to be allowed to choose their JV partners themselves. In addition, China's accession in the WTO in December 2001 opened a host of industries to direct foreign investment, many with a grace period that ended in December 2004 and nearly all ending by 2007. The result: regulations are now in flux, and can vary from sector to sector and even from region to region within the country.

Thus, the first task for any newcomer is to fully investigate how the regulations pertain to your sector, your company, and the region of China you seek to enter. What was true six months ago may no longer be valid today.

Foreign managers in the growing number of sectors with the freedom to choose to JV or not to JV can then begin assessing whether a partnership would help or harm their operations in China. The 28 foreign managers and consultants we interviewed make strong cases both for and against partnering with local companies. In both cases, they are speaking from experience: nearly all of the top executives profiled in this book oversee both JVs and WFOEs in China. At the time of this writing, only two companies did not operate JVs in China: Eli Lilly China and Standard Chartered China. All told, the 20 multinational companies featured in this book operate 152 JVs and 91 WFOEs. The record for the most joint ventures goes to Coca-Cola China

TIP The first task for any newcomer is to fully investigate how the regulations pertain to your sector, your company, and the region of China you seek to enter. What was true six months ago may no longer be valid today.

with 24 JVs, followed closely by the China operations of British Petroleum, Philips, and Carrefour, with 22, 20, and 19 JVs, respectively.

In the coming pages, we present the advice given by our expert interviewees on the three steps of forming a joint venture: deciding whether or not to tie the knot, choosing the right partner, and maintaining the relationship. We conclude Chapter 3 with a special emphasis on maintaining positive relations with Chinese business partners. Thus, the section on "Managing the Partner-to-Partner Relationship" in this chapter will be useful for international managers working not only with JV companies but with Chinese partners of any type—distributors, upstream or downstream suppliers, or colleagues and peers in business alliances or cooperative agreements. The chapter follows the pattern outlined in the decision-tree diagram set out in Figure 3.1.

Stay Single or Marry (to JV, or Not to JV)?

If your company does have a choice concerning partnering, the first rule in deciding which route to take is: don't rush. So says General Electric China's Steve Schneider. He advises foreign companies entering China first to spend time understanding the business environment. "If you don't know the market, it won't make a bit of difference whether you operate as a JV or WFOE," he says. "The reason we've been pretty successful [in China] is that we spend a tremendous amount of time understanding our customers before we commit anything." Only after clarifying the areas in which your company may be weak can you determine whether or not a joint venture is the best choice. GE operates 12 JVs and 24 WFOEs in China. In determining which method to adopt, Schneider keeps in mind the three factors he considers responsible for the fact that each of GE's divisions is profitable: understanding the market, controlling costs, and building cost-effective facilities.

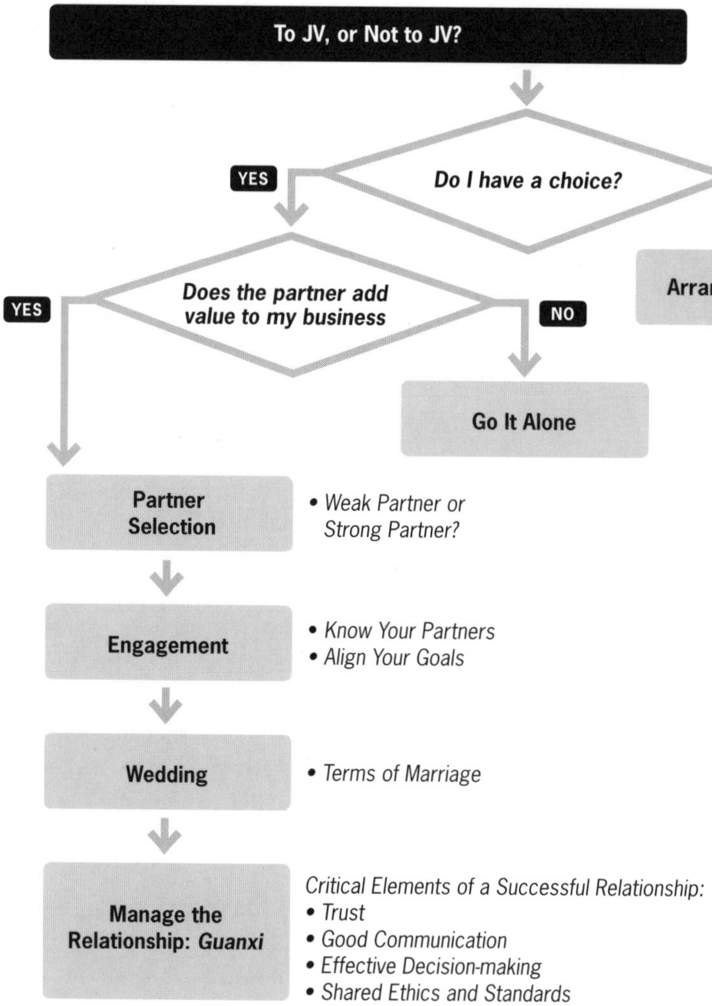

FIGURE 3.1
To JV, or Not to JV?

Another test for whether a JV makes sense for an MNC is the scale of the planned China operations. BP China's Dr. Gary Dirks, who leads 22 JVs and one WFOE, explains how he determines whether or not to form a partnership. "It all depends on the complexity of the [operations] and how it fits into the notion of national interest or provincial interest. For something that is deeply fundamental, with far-reaching consequences, I still feel much better having a Chinese partner." Of BP's large-scale chemical complex in Shanghai, he says: "Frankly, I wouldn't even conceive doing a project of that scale and of that complexity without a Chinese partner." The domestic partner company, which owns 50% of the venture, helps in handling special interest groups, working with PRC government officials, and providing insight into the market and the industrial environment in Shanghai. For such a massive project, Dirks says, "You just need a Chinese partner."

But smaller-scale ventures, he says, are often best undertaken alone. For example, BP China prefers to operate its LPG terminal and distribution points as independent entities that are managed directly by BP's global operations. For LPG operations, he says, "I would choose 100% owned by us every time. It's so much simpler and so much easier to be on our own. There is nothing a partner could offer strategically to assist in that activity."

Unilever China's Alan Brown uses a simpler method of determining whether or not to form a joint venture. "If you are working in a highly regulated industry, then JV partners are almost essential," he says. "If you are working in a highly *de*regulated industry, they can be a damn nuisance."

One helpful characteristic of today's business environment is that many MNCs can now alter the structure of their existing partnerships. International managers advise monitoring regulatory changes constantly to see if you can, and should, adapt your business structure.

A look at Alcatel China illustrates the value of adaptability. One of the first foreign investors to enter China after its economic reforms, ITT (acquired by Alcatel in 1986) began negotiating with the Chinese central government in 1977. Six years later, the company won approval to form one of the earliest foreign–Chinese JVs: Shanghai Bell, minority owned. Today, Alcatel has regrouped the majority of its operations into a company limited by shares, Alcatel Shanghai Bell, in which it owns 50% +1 shares. Ten-year China veteran Dominique de Boisseson says Alcatel's primary strategy is: be adaptable. In some instances, companies still face stiff restrictions. For example, one interviewee explained that for his operations in central China, his company was forced to form a JV with a government-recommended partner. "The government said, 'You either choose this company or forget it'," the CEO says. "The location wasn't ideal, the partner wasn't ideal, but that was the only chance. We accepted the JV; otherwise, we would have lost the market."

But Alcatel has been able to restructure its operations in China. The company has switched at least one JV to a WFOE and another JV to a company limited by shares. The new structure better suits the telecom business, says de Boisseson. "Before, all the decisions in the JV had to go to the board. It was far too slow, especially for fast-moving products, as they are out of the market in one year. If we lose time, we lose the market."

The overriding advice from our interviewees on JVs is that international managers should assess each China venture case by case against current regulations. In addition, China operations should be reviewed regularly, and perhaps restructured, as regulations are constantly changing.

> "*If you are working in a highly regulated industry, then JV partners are almost essential. If you are working in a highly* deregulated *industry, they can be a damn nuisance.*"
>
> **Alan Brown**, Chairman, Unilever China

The Case Against JVs

The general consensus among international managers interviewed is this: if you can avoid forming a JV, do so. Nine of the 20 international managers interviewed directly advised foreign managers that it is better to go it alone. General business trends bear out this sentiment; the 2005 Business Climate Survey, taken by the American Chambers of Commerce in Beijing and Shanghai, found that the number of chamber member companies with JVs fell from 78% of polled companies in 1999 to 27% in 2005, while the number of companies formed as WFOEs went from 33% to 60% during that period.

The viewpoint on JVs of Kenneth Yu, of 3M China, is typical: "As a rule of thumb, if you have enough knowledge locally, if you have the distribution or can develop distribution, if you have adequate resources, then do it on your own." 3M managers can speak on JVs from experience; in 1984, the company launched the first wholly foreign-owned company in China to be located outside a special economic zone. Today, 3M operates nine WFOEs and one JV in China.

The downside to operating as a WFOE, Yu explains, is that

the foreign company must "start from scratch," which is often problematic in China. "If you team with a JV company with distribution and an existing operations base, you get started right away," he says. But the benefits of a JV are often eventually overshadowed by the problems, he adds. "In a WFOE, you call the shots. In a JV, it takes longer to get things done." Then, too, foreign companies typically must share technology with their local partner, which may raise intellectual property rights (IPR) concerns. And when the JV does well, of course, profits are also shared.

> *If you team with a JV company with distribution and an existing operations base, you get started right away. [On the other hand], in a WFOE, you call the shots. In a JV, it takes longer to get things done."*
>
> **Kenneth Yu**, Managing Director, 3M China

Other concerns are summed up by Bertelsmann Direct Group Asia's Ekkehard Rathgeber, who oversees two JVs and four WFOEs in China. "Given the choice, I would always go for a WFOE, never ever for a JV," he says. First, he says, MNCs with joint ventures tend to "waste a lot of time in the process of negotiating with the JV partner." Rathgeber says that contracts with JV partners inevitably leave many issues to be ironed out after the two sides have begun working together. "The minute you start working together, especially if you work with an SOE, you spend so much time educating people on thinking differently," he says. "This is time you would rather spend on operations."

Another common problem occurs when MNCs overestimate the abilities of their domestic partner. Many foreign newcomers hold unrealistic expectations of their Chinese partner's skill at speeding up bureaucratic processes or providing insight into the market. Says Rathgeber: "I'm not saying JVs are never successful. But if you don't have to do it, don't."

For many international managers, forming a partnership with a Chinese firm may sometimes represent less freedom and flexibility. L'Oréal shifted from a JV to independent companies three years after its entry into China. The company's Paolo Gasparrini sums up the benefits of operating WFOEs: "You can create your own culture. You can make decisions 100% on your own."

China-based consultants also tend to advise MNCs against joint ventures when possible. Explains Norman Givant, office managing partner at Freshfields Bruckhaus Deringer law offices in Shanghai, "There are other structures available which, over the long term, may offer better operating ability and fewer headaches." Of particular concern to his clients is the potential risk incurred when a multinational shares its technology and intellectual property with JV partners.

The central message among China hands is that WFOEs are often simpler, faster, and more efficient. GE China's Steve Schneider summarizes the feeling of many international business executives in China, when he says: "We are not against JVs—some of the JVs have been among our most successful operations. But we love WFOEs because they give us control."

TIP Avoid JVs unless you are required to form one or are certain of the benefits. WFOEs are generally simpler, faster, and more efficient to operate.

The Case For JVs

Despite the clear consensus among our interviewees to avoid joint ventures when possible, and the well-documented shift among foreign investors in China toward forming wholly owned companies, most interviewees said that instances still exist when a partnership is the preferred *modus operandi*. In fact, some of our interviewees said they will stick with JVs even if WFOEs are allowed in their sector.

The most important benefit of a Chinese partner company mentioned by the China hands profiled here is: skill in negotiating with Chinese government entities. The basic trade-off in forming a joint venture is summed up well by David Chang, CEO of Philips China: "When you are deciding between a JV and WFOE, the WFOE is faster. But if you are a WFOE, you need to find a way to build the networks and get the benefits of connections with the local governments." Philips has established 17 of its 34 China companies as JVs, in part because working with the Chinese government entities is critical to success.

Coca-Cola China has established all of its manufacturing and distribution operations—27 companies—as JVs. (These joint ventures are formed through Coca-Cola's bottlers, rather than directly through Coca-Cola.) As of late 2005, the beverage industry had not been formally opened to WFOEs, but Coca-Cola's Paul Etchells says even if the regulations are eventually loosened, Coke will likely continue to operate via partnerships. "It is fanciful to think we are going to convert all those JVs into

> *"If we were doing it now from scratch, we would still take local partners. The Coke business is a local business. We need a local partner. ... They smooth the way to getting things done with the local government. They get rid of some of the red tape."*
>
> **Paul Etchells**, President, Coca-Cola China

WFOEs. We're not," he says. Despite initially having been forced to form JVs, Etchells says business operations have worked well. "If we were doing it now from scratch, we would still take local partners," he says. "The Coke business is a local business. We need a local partner." Connection with local authorities is one of the key contributions from Coca-Cola's partners.

Like executives at other MNCs, Etchells says the main benefit of his local partners is their expertise in maneuvering through the Chinese bureaucracy: "They smooth the way to getting things done with the local government. They get rid of some of the red tape."

Carrefour China's Jean-Luc Chereau also says that operating as an independent company in China would be "impossible," mainly because local partners provide assistance in working with officials. Retail was a protected industry in China until December 2004, and as of late 2005 relatively few entrants had been approved into the field. Chereau says he will likely continue to operate 19 of his 20 China subsidiaries as JVs even after regulations allow him to switch to WFOEs.

Guy McLeod, of Airbus China, says his company's two Chinese JV partners handle purchasing—an extremely challenging sector for foreign companies to manage efficiently. "Many people think it is a lot easier to work as a wholly-owned company. For us, we want to work with a Chinese partner," says McLeod. "When we look at the JVs we have, we are very happy."

Seiichi Kawasaki, of Sony China, says JVs provide a necessary channel for newcomers who are "not very familiar with local issues." Sony operates three joint ventures and three independent companies in China. "JVs have many positive factors, while the wholly owned companies have some negative factors," he says. "By combining both types of management, we try to maximize the total benefits."

One caveat: for MNCs bringing a new product or service to China—such as Coke—a domestic partner, although valuable in other ways, typically can offer little in the way of market expertise. "I don't know that local partners bring much in terms of understanding the market," says Paul Etchells. He explains that, in many areas of China, the soft-drinks market was very small before

Coke entered. "So, the assistance that the local partner has given us concerning the local market has been pretty minimal."

The bottom line from our interviewees is that a mix of WFOEs and JVs often presents the best option in China. Charles Browne, of Du Pont China, says that while his company is shifting toward more WFOEs as regulations liberalize (Du Pont operates seven joint ventures, 15 wholly owned companies), he still expects to maintain several JVs. "We have several outstanding, excellent partners that we have developed through the years. We could change to WFOEs, but we continue to work with JVs because they add value to the relationship and we continue to grow," he says.

TIP **Use JVs when the local partner offers connections with authorities and market knowledge that a WFOE would be unable to achieve on its own.**

Partner Selection, Partnership Terms

If you have decided to (or must) form a joint venture in China, the challenge is to find the perfect partner. As Sony China's Seiichi Kawasaki points out, a JV is like a marriage: selecting the right mate is the most important step.

The advice of our international manager interviewees on finding the ideal match can be boiled down to five messages:

- Choose a weak, silent partner, or
- Choose an active, value-added partner
- Know your partner
- Align your goals
- Set the correct "marriage" terms

The process of forming a JV begins by determining which type of partner best suits your needs in China. Our profiled top executives described two ideals: (a) a weak, silent partner that won't interfere with operations; or (b) a stronger, more active company that brings to the venture valuable government-relations savvy, business connections, and/or industry knowledge. Our interviewees were divided on which type makes the best Chinese JV partner, but the tide seems to be turning away from weak partners toward stronger, value-adding ones.

Finally, a word on the importance of financial health in potential partners: one difference in searching for a JV partner in China is that the criterion of financial strength (or at least financial stability) is not generally considered to be as important as it would be in a developed economy. In China, other qualities are very often more important—and more available. Even so, several interviewees did warn against working with a partner that is in serious financial trouble. They also stressed that MNCs can and should demand to see full financial records of any potential partner.

Strategy #1: Choose a Weak, Silent Partner

From the mid-1980s to the mid-1990s, when most foreign enterprises were forced into JVs, international managers assumed that their Chinese partner could not contribute much to the partnership. Thus, the best match was a company that would at least not hinder business operations.

One option was to form a short-term partnership that could be dissolved after its initial mission was accomplished. This was the *modus operandi* used by L'Oréal's Paolo Gasparrini in setting up operations in China in 1997. L'Oréal formed a partnership giving 5% ownership to the Suzhou Medical Hospital. Gasparrini says the hospital was "not an active business partner" but did allow L'Oréal to "understand China better" and to acquire some useful relevant expertise (medical information on the characteristics of Chinese skin). After three years, L'Oréal bought back its 5% shares, the JV was dissolved, and both partners had accomplished their goals. Gasparrini sums up the situation this way: while foreign companies entering China in the early 1990s tended to "feel more secure with a JV," such a need is diminishing now. Today, he says, MNCs generally benefit from operating independently.

Other MNCs have maintained long-running partnerships in which the domestic company is not directly involved in the JV business. The Shanghai Hilton, for example, operates with a local partner that owns the property but does not interfere with day-to-day operations. Hotel general manager Volkmar Ruebel says the primary means of communication is via a monthly report issued to the property owners. Only rarely does the Chinese partner want to approve decisions. "The owner trusts us as an international company; we are the custodian of the property," says Ruebel. "It is relatively smooth. We don't have any operating problems." He

CASE STUDY

UNILEVER SWITCHES JV STRATEGIES

Unilever China's Alan Brown says one reason his company initially struggled behind competitor Procter & Gamble in China is that P&G chose JV partners that allowed the former to manage the business, while Unilever chose JV partners that wanted to retain strong management control. "P&G was right, because they got stronger [after forming JVs]. You want to manage your own destiny," says Brown.

Brown says Unilever suffered with the "impediment" of not having management control until 1999, when the company was able to alter the structure of its JVs. But by then, P&G enjoyed a nine-year head-start.

How did strong partners hinder Unilever's growth? Brown gives an example: soon after Unilever formed a JV with a Chinese toothpaste producer in 1994, the partnership struck discord. When Unilever requested that its partner remove an ingredient from the toothpaste formula, the partner refused. The dispute continued through 1999. Brown says Unilever's first mistake was not realizing when it bought the brand that the product contained this ingredient. The second mistake was not immediately realizing that the Chinese partner company was a major supplier of the component in question, and was thus unwilling to remove it. But its third mistake was forming a partnership that gave Unilever little clout against a large, well-established Chinese company with strong-willed management. "We basically lost five years arguing with the JV partner about the formulation," Brown says.

The disagreement was finally resolved in 1999 when Unilever restructured several of its JVs as companies limited by shares. The move allowed Unilever to "get management control" of its joint ventures in China, says Brown. Eventually, when the legal environment liberalized, Unilever bought out the former partner and turned the company into a WFOE.

> “
> ***In China, when we establish a new JV, we share the investment but never the management. You cannot have two bosses.”***
>
> **Jean-Luc Chereau**, President, Carrefour China

adds that the partnership gives Hilton “relatively strong autonomy in the way we deal with personnel and quality standards.”

Carrefour China’s Jean-Luc Chereau also partly attributes the successes of the hypermarket chain to its policy of choosing relatively passive local partners. The company entered China in 1995 and now operates 19 JVs and one WFOE. Chereau oversees local ventures according to Carrefour’s corporate-wide policies—some of which have evolved over 40 years of trial and error. During the chain’s first 20 years of international operation, Chereau says, Carrefour “made a lot of mistakes” in selecting business partners. In the last 20 years, the company has followed a policy of not “sharing” the management with a local partner. “In China, when we establish a new JV, we share the investment but never the management,” he says. “You cannot have two bosses.” Even weak partners can bring value to the JV, insists Chereau, who demands several characteristics from the Chinese side, “First, all of our partners in China must have a long-term view. If they just buy shares and sell them within two years, what’s the use? Second, the company must have some cash. Third, the company must have a very good network at local level. To succeed in Shanghai, your partner should be Shanghainese. To succeed in Guangzhou, your partner should be Cantonese.”

(*Note:* In December 2004, WTO-related regulations opened up the retail sector and many aspects of distribution to WFOEs. Despite the fact that relatively few MNCs were approved to enter these sectors during 2005, and many were frustrated by the government’s slow approval pace and confusing procedures, retail and distribution are two of the most promising sectors formerly closed to direct foreign investment.)

Strategy #2: Choose an Active, Value-added Partner

Not all MNCs seek meek and mild local partners. In recent years, more MNCs are forming partnerships with active domestic companies that bring real value to the partnership.

A look at the JVs formed by Bayer China illustrates this trend. Company CEO Dr. Elmar Stachels says that in years past, Bayer had little choice but to form JVs with government-selected partners. "The contribution of this partner to us was very often just the land and the building—no real contribution to marketing, services, technology, or production," he says.

Today, Bayer selects its partners according to its own criteria and standards. "We not only look at the activities, assets, and performance of a company, but also at the management, the people," says Stachels. He points out that, in recent years, Bayer has begun recruiting management personnel for the holding company directly from the top executives of its Chinese JVs. Thus, if the management of a potential partner company does not impress Bayer, Stachels keeps looking. Also, following deregulation, Bayer has recently (for many reasons) restructured some of its JVs into WFOEs.

TIP **When regulations force you to form a JV in which the partnership adds limited value to the business, choose a weak partner that you can easily control.**

At British Petroleum China, which operates 22 joint ventures, Dr. Gary Dirks looks for JV partners that truly contribute toward the corporate goals. "No matter where you go in the world, the key to success for partnerships is the alignment of your strategic interests, your ability to maintain the alignment over a significant period of time, and making sure your partner can contribute to those strategic interests. If both parties are perceived to be contributing as well as expected, then it can go very well."

Dirks rejects the JV model based on a say-nothing, do-nothing Chinese partner. "Where you tend to have problems is when there is a perception on the Chinese partner's side that their contribution ends the day the JV is formed—you contribute your technology and your know-how and the Chinese partner just sits around."

Today, companies that do form JVs advise looking for partners that offer these benefits: skill at negotiating with the Chinese government, business connections, insight into the local business culture and environment, an established workforce and operations, or a strong existing client base.

Our interviewees explained that many Chinese partners can offer real value to a JV. Thus, if you are going to form a partnership, it is possible—and often beneficial—to demand that the local company contribute toward your goals.

TIP Companies that choose to form a JV today can look for Chinese partners that can contribute toward the company goals by bringing insight into the local business environment, established operations, a strong client base, and skill at negotiating with the government.

Strategy #3: Know Your Partner

No matter what type of partner an MNC is seeking, it is critical to fully assess potential partners before committing. International managers warn that while MNCs often face pressure to establish in China quickly, spending more time up-front can help to avoid serious trouble later. Says GE's Steve Schneider: "Part of the learning I would offer for folks coming in [to China] and setting up JVs is: spend a tremendous amount of time getting to know your partner first. It's better than any due diligence on the financial records."

Charles Browne of Du Pont China gives similar advice. "The key for a successful JV is that you spend a lot of time in partner selection," he says. "Some companies rushed in and picked what was available without doing enough research about the value of the partner—whether their interests are aligned with yours, what they can contribute to the JV. We put a lot of time in partner selection to make sure the values are there."

Knowing your partner entails reviewing detailed information and records, making site visits to see the operations and facilities first-hand, and spending time gathering impressions from industry insiders.

Strategy #4: Align Your Goals

International managers warn that many JVs fail because they fall victim to the Chinese idiom, "same bed, different dreams," which refers to a husband and wife with divergent hopes and ambitions. Du Pont's Charles Browne says that many failed JVs are victims of "split vision" between partners—for example, if the MNC's primary objective is to build market share for its goods within China, but the domestic partner expects to focus on overseas sales. Browne has seen several of Du Pont's China ventures end in failure. "In many cases, the major reason was that we had different interests and different ways of doing business," he says.

Most problems that arise are innocent misunderstandings

rather than malicious efforts to cheat an MNC, stresses Ekkehard Rathgeber of Bertelsmann Direct Group Asia. "Ninety percent of [Chinese] JV partners are very serious with their time," he says. Still, problems arise simply because the two partners have "very different targets, different ideas, and different mindsets," he says. As an example of the gap, Rathgeber explains that while many MNCs focus their operational goals tightly on profits, the Chinese partner may place a higher priority on other goals, such as impressing government officials by adopting advanced technology. Problems can also arise when the MNC introduces the Chinese partner company to operating procedures used globally. One common rough spot: the domestic partner may balk at the salaries offered to foreign managers in China. Working through such issues can be extremely time-consuming, Rathgeber warns.

> *"The key to success for partnerships is the alignment of your strategic interests, your ability to maintain the alignment over a significant period of time, and making sure your partner can contribute to those strategic interests."*
>
> **Dr. Gary Dirks,**
> President and CEO,
> British Petroleum China

Strategy #5: Set the Correct "Marriage" Terms

Setting the best terms of the partnership is, of course, extremely important in alleviating problems once the joint venture starts operating. During negotiations, both sides typically struggle to obtain the largest percentage of ownership possible, and to protect their rights while limiting their obligations. Our international managers offered several bits of advice on surviving this process in China.

Microsoft China's Jun Tang, who oversees two JVs and one WFOE, advises establishing the JV as an entirely new entity. "If you do want to set up a JV, it is better to start from scratch," he says. Starting from zero allows both partners to adopt a new mindset, rather than continuing operations according to established methods. For example, in staffing, both partners can choose key personnel to send to the new company. This avoids a mindset of "outsiders" and "insiders"; everyone is an outsider in the new venture. "With a new entity, you can create a new culture, a new business model, a new atmosphere," Tang says. "To change an existing organization is very difficult. That is why we see a lot of JVs fail." Tang insists on establishing a new company even if nearly all members of the partner companies are hired into it.

TIP Assess a potential JV partner by making on-site visits, requesting detailed financial and operating records, and gathering input from industry insiders.

One rule of thumb which attorney Norman Givant of Freshfields Bruckhaus Deringer shares with international clients in China: steer clear of 50–50 joint ventures. "That just builds gridlock into the structure," he says. Unless regulations require 50% Chinese ownership, Givant encourages MNCs to demand a majority share.

Givant also advises considering alternatives to straight joint venture models, as more options are opening for MNCs as regulations liberalize. Givant expects MNCs to undergo more mergers and acquisitions in the future as foreign companies take equity interest or procure stakes in listed Chinese companies, or buy companies outright. He also predicts that foreign companies will become more active in China's financial markets as regulations are liberalized. "You will see a growing sophistication both in terms of acquisition and participation in financial markets," he says.

Meanwhile, two of our international managers mentioned the benefits of establishing as a joint stock company (or "company limited by shares") in which the Chinese partner company is given a minority interest in the company. This allows the MNC to retain management control. Both Unilever and Alcatel have used such a method. Regulations were changed in 1994 to allow MNCs to register as joint stock companies, although relatively few have been approved.

Managing the Partner-to-partner Relationship

Our interviewees stressed that forming the partnership is the beginning, not the end, of the negotiation process for MNCs operating in China via a joint venture. The hard work really comes when the two sides begin working together.

In understanding the importance of good relations to the success of a JV, Seiichi Kawasaki's metaphor of a JV being "like a marriage" is particularly useful. Like a marriage, a lasting, efficient, and prosperous joint venture depends on the willingness and ability of the two sides to set the same goals and to cooperate in meeting them.

The China hands we interviewed offered a wealth of information on making business partnerships work in China. They listed four critical success factors:

- Mutual trust
- Good communications
- Effective decision-making
- Shared ethics and standards

TIP **It is critical that you and your JV partner agree on goals and priorities. The problem of "same bed, different dreams" has led many JV partners to divorce.**

Critical Success Factor #1: Mutual Trust

International managers agreed that lack of trust is the root of many problems arising in foreign–domestic JVs in China. Given the differences in culture, language, and business orientation, an element of suspicion or resentment easily develops between the partners.

Philips China's David Chang understands this well. His position entails overseeing the company's 17 JVs and 17 WFOEs in China. Managing a successful JV is a tricky, delicate business, he says. "Around the world, forming JVs is an art. This is not unique in China." But he stresses that JVs—even government-arranged partnerships—can bring value to MNCs in China. The secret to success, he says, lies in winning the trust and support of your partner. He says that joint ventures often break down when the two sides distrust each other, each fearing that the other side is looking out only for itself.

To avoid a breakdown in relations, Chang urges international managers to try and see the partnership through the eyes of their local partner. He says that many domestic companies believe foreign enterprises come to China mainly for quick returns.

Another CEO goes further, explaining that some local managers think that "All you foreigners, you come here to steal." Many local managers also perceive an imbalance in the level of

TIP When forming a JV, it is best to create the organization from scratch to avoid bringing old mindsets to the new entity. Steer clear of 50–50 partnerships. Consider JV alternatives such as a merger or acquisition.

investment made by the two partners. Some Chinese managers believe that foreign investors can recover their investment as soon as the partnership is formed. This is because MNCs often invest in a joint venture "in kind," by providing technology and equipment. Another source of friction: Chinese partners often provide land and buildings, which appreciate over time, but MNCs tend to provide technology and equipment—items that devalue over time. Third, resentment can arise simply because the Chinese enterprise lacks leverage in negotiations because it needs the foreign technology. Such thinking, Chang says, can lead local partners to "take a negative or hostile view toward their partner."

How can an MNC alleviate such negative suspicions in its Chinese partner? Chang first urges MNCs to stress their long-term commitment to China and their dedication to seeing both partners benefit from the partnership. Second, MNCs should ease the perception of imbalance in the JV by clarifying the value of their own contribution, and by acknowledging and emphasizing the value contributed by the Chinese partner. "Try to create opportunities in which the Chinese company can prove its contribution," says Chang. "You build trust and create value. Finally, they will become a source of help rather than being hostile."

At Airbus China, Guy McLeod agrees that trust is a make-or-break quality in any joint venture. Partnerships often fail, he says, when the foreign partner takes a short-term, profit-oriented view. McLeod works hard to assure JV partners that Airbus's goals are beneficial to the Chinese side. "We want to ensure that the standards for pilot and engineer training in China are the highest. Our training center [in China] is not different from the ones we have in Miami or Toulouse. That was our goal," he says. Such a mission, of course, wins the support and trust of the Chinese JV partner.

Critical Success Factor #2: Good Communications (Direct Talk vs. "Face" Saving)

One of the biggest trouble spots for international managers working with Chinese business partners is learning to communicate effectively without causing a loss of "face." The central problem is that Westerners strive for clear, unambiguous communication, while Chinese often rely on an imprecise, indirect manner.

One common form of cultural disconnect in joint ventures, identified by our interviewees, is the tendency for the Chinese partner to avoid telling the international side about problems and difficulties. The reason for this is cultural: Chinese managers tend to be trained in a business culture in which it is better to avoid mentioning problems to a superior if possible. Troubling the boss can be considered rude and would likely be seen as an admission that the manager was to some degree responsible for the problem.

TIP Build a sense of trust within a JV by stressing your long-term commitment to China, and by acknowledging the value which each side brings to the partnership.

In general, the Chinese preference for vague communication provides two benefits: avoiding conflict by preserving harmony, and preserving "face." BearingPoint Greater China president Bryan Huang explains the culture clash. "Almost all Americans or Europeans get very confused when they first visit Japan or China. Western culture places a high value on being very specific. But in Japan and China, things are more ambiguous, on purpose. This makes communication very difficult."

The first reason for being indirect concerns the Chinese concept of "face" (*mian zi*), which roughly translates into "one's public image or sense of self-esteem." Because "face" is considered extremely important in Chinese culture, causing someone to "lose face" is a serious offense.

International executives point out that the idea of "face" exists in Western cultures, but to a lesser degree. Says Philip Murtaugh of General Motors China: "People in the U.S. have 'face,' too—people like to be appreciated, like their contribution to be recognized." But he explains that the degree of impact if a person loses "face" is more significant in China. "In the U.S., it is unusual to belittle somebody in a group, and certainly it's not a pleasant experience. But in China, it is *never* done. So if it happens, it becomes a bigger issue." For example, if a manager embarrasses a business partner in the U.S., such as by joking to a client about the partner firm's inability to meet deadlines, the incident might trigger a follow-up discussion or complaint. But if such a scenario took place in China, business relations between the two partners could be gravely or irreparably damaged.

The danger for a foreign manager in China is that he or she can inadvertently cause loss of "face," simply by speaking too bluntly. "One word can hurt someone's feelings forever," says Jun Tang, of Microsoft China. "American culture is very direct. But people [in China] are so sensitive. Sensitivity is part of their 5,000-year-old culture." Forgetting to invite a manager from the JV partner company to a business lunch, for example, could cause serious resentment. "If you let somebody lose 'face,' it will be very difficult to rebuild a trusting relationship," Tang says. "And if you lose their trust, you lose everything. Trust is the most important value in the Chinese community."

The flip-side of the need to save your own "face," is the precautions Chinese take to preserve "face" for others. Chinese professionals tend to be extremely cautious about expressing opinions, because doing so could embarrass a supervisor. For a Chinese staff member, the simple act of voicing a direct opinion could be seen as disrespectful. Paolo Gasparrini of L'Oréal China explains that this thinking is rooted in the Chinese education system. "My mother taught me that when the teacher asks a question, you raise your hand and answer it. Here, it's different. They are taught, 'Don't make waves.' So when we asked our managers to react to something, to give their opinion, they didn't want to. For them, every time they expressed an opinion, they were disrespecting authority. However, things have changed a lot over the years."

Freshfields Bruckhaus Deringer's Norman Givant gives foreign clients this advice when dealing with Chinese business partners or staff members: "You have to be sensitive to cultural mores of the country you are working in. Some managers take a bark-and-bite approach to management, but that method doesn't go down very well here." Givant advises foreign managers to portray an image of being firm but personable. "People who work with you have to understand that you mean what you say, but you have to say it with a smile," he says.

A final point: Interviewees stress that the preference for indirect communication in order to protect "face" is diminishing among young-generation Chinese. In fact, Korn/Ferry's Helen Tantau says that some local professionals now prefer Western-style direct communication. She says the stereotype of Western managers is: honest, open, and—when it comes to things Chinese—humble. Such a profile is attractive to more internationalized domestic employees, she says.

Critical Success Factor #3: Effective Decision-making (Individual Action vs. Consensus)

Another source of frustration for our interviewees in working with JV partners is the tendency for Chinese executives to avoid personal accountability for business decisions. Many Chinese professionals come from an extremely hierarchical business culture in which younger and lower-ranked personnel are expected to passively take orders from superiors. Making decisions—or even making suggestions toward a decision—can be considered rude or improper. Ekkehard Rathgeber of Bertelsmann Direct Group Asia explains how this mindset evolves: "Normally, the way [Chinese] are trained is that one supervisor tells them what to

CASE STUDY

ALTERNATE VIEW AT SONY, CHINA

At Sony China, Seiichi Kawasaki offers a different take on adapting his communication techniques to China. In contrast to Western managers, he has had to shift his management style to be more direct in China than is the norm in Japan. "Japanese people are very vague. We guess each other's meaning. But the Chinese are much more direct and clear," he says. Kawasaki finds Chinese businesspeople "closer to the world standard" in terms of communication, especially younger-generation executives. After five years in China, Kawasaki has come to appreciate the Chinese style. "This open communication is much more effective," he says.

Kawasaki warns Japanese managers coming to China not to assume that the workplace culture is the same as in Japan, "Many Japanese wrongly assume that a similar approach can be made when working with Chinese. But Chinese are much more straightforward, while Japanese try to respect the consensus. Our approach is very different."

"

You have to be sensitive to cultural mores of the country you are working in. Some managers take a bark-and-bite approach to management, but that method doesn't go down very well here. ... People who work with you have to understand that you mean what you say, but you have to say it with a smile."

Norman Givant, Shanghai Office Managing Partner, China Practice Group, Freshfields Bruckhaus Deringer

do. But the minute that person isn't there, the process collapses." In other words, in a traditional Chinese company, only the boss or supervisor makes decisions for a particular department or sub-department, and no one else can make decisions within his or her realm of responsibility. The result: reluctance among local staff to take responsibility or to work independently, and a preference for making decisions based on past precedent.

Standard Chartered China CEO Stanley Wong, a Hong Kong native, agrees that the reluctance to stick one's neck out is a cultural characteristic in China. If asked to take a public stand, many Chinese professionals will hesitate out of a real fear of making a bad decision, and then being punished harshly for it.

Given this culture of fear, if Chinese managers or employees do need to make decisions without input from their superior, many take a frustratingly long time in doing so, said our interviewees. Many approach problem-solving by consulting with a host of friends and family members, then carefully considering how various possible decisions would affect the larger network of persons involved. Dr. Ernst Behrens of Siemens China explains that, because of China's political and economic past, staff members over the age of 40 are used to an environment of collective rather than individual decision-making. "A Chinese employee will consult friends or relatives on a problem he faces at work, but will not discuss it with his direct superior for the fear of losing face," says Behrens. "By the time he tells you, the roof is on fire." Such delayed communication often leaves Western superiors frustrated, but Behrens warns against reacting angrily. "You will have his resignation letter on your desk the next day." This is likely an outcome that neither side wanted. To avoid such an escalation, Behrens says international managers must understand the Chinese mindset on decision-making and informing superiors.

The tendency toward avoidance and lack of accountability is particularly strong among the generation of over-45-year-olds. Helen Tantau of Korn/Ferry explains: "There is a tendency for those who lived through the Cultural Revolution, or who have worked in the SOE system, to avoid accountability. The thinking is: 'I don't make decisions; the guy above me will make the decision.' Those who are multinational born and bred don't have this mindset."

TIP **When communicating with your Chinese partner, remember to preserve their "face." Sometimes indirect communication is more effective.**

Hilton Shanghai's Volkmar Ruebel says the tendency to avoid decision-making can be changed. The solution is to empower employees with the ability to solve problems independently, step by step. "This country is built on the idea of: 'Don't do anything on your own'," he stresses. "If you look back 15 years, thinking was detrimental to your health." When he began in his position in 1994, Ruebel says the hotel staff operated by "hiding behind rules and regulations," meaning that no one took responsibility or made decisions. After setting to work to "deregulate" the hotel, Ruebel says he has instilled a culture of "don't only *think* it, *do* it" at Hilton Shanghai. "We changed from a military management—'Do as you're told or…,' or a management of fear—to a management of 'Let's move forward.'"

At GM China, Philip Murtaugh has promoted a "team-based culture" in which individual personnel must contribute to solving problems as a group. He says this method helps in two ways: it encourages contribution from team members without putting individuals on the spot, and it flattens the hierarchical structure so that team members don't worry that their suggestions would cause a supervisor to lose "face." Murtaugh uses teams to "force decision-making at an appropriate level." For example, he says the group structure has helped GM China to break out of an environment of dysfunctional meetings. When he first took the helm, only Chinese supervisors spoke during meetings with Chinese managers and staff. "For two whole years, when we had meetings only one person spoke from the Chinese party. Others had no words other than, 'That is a good idea'," Murtaugh says. Slowly, he began asking other personnel to contribute ideas in small groups. "It's a gradual process, but people have started to voice their own opinions." With time, he says, employees began appreciating the change. "We create an environment where, throughout the company, people have a lot of empowerment and influence over their jobs. People like to work here because they can make decisions."

The efforts of Standard Chartered's Stanley Wong also show that the mindset of fear can be changed, but slowly. Wong has

TIP Encourage Chinese colleagues to voice their opinions. Create an environment in which honest mistakes are accepted.

worked hard to stress a corporate culture that recognizes and rewards decision-making—through simple public praise or more official recognition such as bonuses. He stresses to staff and colleagues that occasional honest mistakes are inevitable and will not be punished. In some cases, he offers rewards to people who took initiative even if the results turn out imperfectly. "Recognition is also about senior management being able to support some well-meant business failures and well-intentioned mistakes. If it is a well-meant mistake, I think the effort itself should also be recognized."

Critical Success Factor #4: Shared Ethics and Standards

One of the areas posing the highest risk of friction in a JV or cooperation between MNCs and Chinese firms is in reconciling differing concepts of ethics and standards. For most international companies, the MNCs must find ways to ensure that the local partner adopts corporate practices and procedures.

Christopher Shaw, president of Eli Lilly China, explains his method of introducing global standard practices for working in China. Every Eli Lilly employee in China receives a copy of the company's "red book" outlining corporate policies that provide clear guidelines on how to operate with customers, suppliers, and others. This is complemented with in-depth training, which is repeated every year, and further reinforced through company brochures and newsletters. "China has lots of different practices. There are a lot of differences in the way [Chinese companies] operate," says Shaw. "You have to make sure the message is very clear and that it reaches all the way through. I spend a good amount of time on it."

In some cases, introducing corporate policies and procedures in China can bring the MNC in opposition to local business practices. JV partners may argue that following international practices will only give local competitors an edge. 3M's Kenneth Yu has faced such pressure. "In the early days, people said when you do business in a developing economy, you do it differently—you have to take care of the interests of more people. We do make sure everyone gets their fair share, but when it comes to business ethics: there is no compromise, from Day 1." Yu has had to fight internal battles in order to introduce the importance of maintaining corporate standards. When he began working in China off and on in the late 1980s, he worked with some "very new young sales reps" who had joined straight from university or from SOEs. They pressed Yu to change his policies to fit the China market, warning that if they didn't adopt market practices, they would lose customers. "And we did lose business in the early days," he says. "We'd rather lose a customer than taint our squeaky-clean reputation."

"

This country is built on the idea of: 'Don't do anything on your own.' If you look back 15 years, thinking was detrimental to your health."

Volkmar Ruebel, General Manager, Hilton Shanghai

Yu has met with similar obstacles in initiating 3M's environmental protection policies in China. "Environmental law here, although it is getting tighter, isn't like in the U.S.," Yu says. Thus, the corporation's environmental protection policies sometimes exceed the requirements in China. But Yu insists to employees and business partners that 3M operates under the same procedures in China as elsewhere worldwide. This has also caused a backlash among business associates, who charged 3M with wasting money, he says. "At the beginning, we raised eyebrows," Yu says. He adds that maintaining environmental standards later benefited the company's ventures in China. "Over time, it has given 3M a lot of good publicity, and we eventually got benefits from the host government in the area."

The bottom line, Yu says, is that while MNCs often must respect the local business culture in China, "some corporate culture has to take precedent over local culture." Last, he also points to 3M's performance in China as proof that "it is okay to adhere to your own corporate standards."

Conclusion

Managing a joint venture or business partnership is like managing a marriage. The first decision for MNCs in China is to decide whether to marry (form a joint venture) or stay single (operate

TIP While you must adapt to Chinese business practices, corporate culture, values, and ethical standards must not be compromised.

as a wholly foreign-owned enterprise). Regulations now allow international companies to invest as WFOEs in more sectors. Thus, the first step is to be clear on current regulations. While most interviewees recommend forming a WFOE if legally possible, all acknowledged that JVs can offer significant benefits, especially in providing expertise in negotiating with government, detailed market knowledge, and established operations. For MNCs that choose to form a JV or business partnership, the following box summarizes the key advice of our interviewees.

SUMMARY OF TIPS

WORKING WITH BUSINESS PARTNERS

TO JV, OR NOT TO JV?

1. Know the Regulations

The first task for any newcomer is to fully investigate how the regulations pertain to your sector, your company, and the region of China you seek to enter. What was true six months ago may no longer be valid today.

2. The Case Against JVs

Avoid JVs unless you are required to form one or are certain of the benefits. WFOEs are generally simpler, faster, and more efficient to operate.

3. The Case For JVs

Use JVs when the local partner offers connections with authorities and market knowledge that a WFOE would be unable to achieve on its own.

PARTNER SELECTION, PARTNERSHIP TERMS

1. Choose a Weak, Silent Partner

When regulations force you to form a JV in which the partnership adds limited value to the business, choose a weak partner that you can easily control.

2. Choose an Active, Value-added Partner

Companies that choose to form a JV today can look for Chinese partners that can contribute toward the company goals by bringing insight into the local business environment, established operations, a strong client base, and skill at negotiating with government.

3. Know Your Partner

Assess a potential JV partner by making on-site visits, requesting detailed financial and operating records, and gathering input from industry insiders.

4. Align Your Goals

It is critical that you and your partner agree on goals and priorities. The problem of "same bed, different dreams" has led many JV partners to divorce.

5. Set the Correct "Marriage" Terms

When forming a JV, it is best to create the organization from scratch to avoid bringing old mindsets to the new entity. Steer clear of 50–50 partnerships. Consider JV alternatives such as a merger or acquisition.

MANAGING THE PARTNER-TO-PARTNER RELATIONSHIP

1. Mutual Trust

Build a sense of trust within the JV by stressing your long-term commitment to China, and by acknowledging the value which each side brings to the partnership.

2. Good Communications

When communicating with your Chinese partner, remember to preserve their "face." Sometimes indirect communication is more effective.

3. Effective Decision-making

Encourage Chinese colleagues to voice their opinions. Create an environment in which honest mistakes are accepted.

4. Shared Ethics and Standards

While you must adapt to Chinese business practices, don't compromise your corporate culture, values, and ethical standards.

Chapter 4
Communicating With Headquarters

"Our CEO and the whole corporate leadership have had a laser light focused on China during the last 24 months. It's one of the few countries nowadays whose economy doesn't show signs of slowing down."

Charles Browne, President, Du Pont China

“

Our headquarters realize that China is a very big market. Because of this, the expectation tends to be built very high. But China is going to be a very long-term play. China is about potential, potential, and potential.”

Stanley Wong, Chief Executive, China, Standard Chartered

Introduction

No matter how fast or how powerful global communications technology becomes, international managers of MNCs in China still face serious problems communicating with their headquarters back home. In fact, the 20 top executives we interviewed described facing a perpetual struggle to keep their supervisors in the U.S., Europe, or Asia fully informed of—and supportive of—operations in China.

Simply put, pitching China to the team back home can be challenging. Steve Schneider of GE China explains it this way: “You do two types of selling: selling your company to China, and selling China to your company. Both are tough sales. There is still a fair amount of mystique to overcome when selling China to your company.” Paolo Gasparrini of L’Oréal China describes the communication gap more succinctly: “People who live [in Shanghai] may have a different vision from those in Paris.”

And when communications falter, misunderstandings occur and business suffers. One popular misperception faced by international managers is the unrealistic growth goals for China ventures from the executives back home. “Our headquarters realize that China is a very big market. Because of this, the expectation tends to be built very high,” says Stanley Wong, CEO China for Standard Chartered. “But China is going to be a very long-term play. China is about potential, potential, and potential.” Wong says it can be difficult to explain the obstacles to growth that he encounters, because such hurdles simply don’t exist at the bank’s headquarters in London.

The opposite problem also occurs: home-office executives unnecessarily, and unwisely, lose faith in the China operations. One of our top executive interviewees points out that if the corporate head office leaders never visit China, they may fail to recognize that the country is ultimately “a great place to invest.”

The main message relayed by our interviewees is that the amount of support China-based managers receive from corporate headquarters is proportional to how well those at headquarters understand China’s business environment. Therefore, good communication with the home-office executives is essential to the success of China operations. A case in point is Sony. Sony China's Seiichi Kawasaki witnessed a dramatic change in the support he receives from headquarters. "Five years ago, when I would explain the possibility of development in China, some people [at HQ] were hesitant. But now, because China's exposure in Japan is very much increased, more people understand what is happening here. So they are very much easier to convince," he says.

In fact, Kawasaki has a "much easier" time winning support from supervisors in Tokyo than he did when stationed elsewhere in Asia. He says the decision-making for Sony's China business is now quite effective, mainly because attention at the top levels of the company is focused on China.

This chapter focuses on the advice of our 28 top China executives and consultants on establishing effective communication with headquarters.

Communications Challenges

China-based executives face three main obstacles to communications with their supervisors back home (see Figure 4.1):

- Geographical distance (including time difference)
- Informational distance (lack of knowledge about China back home)
- Cultural distance (misperceptions about China)

If these obstacles are not cleared, our China hands explained, they can damage or even destroy an MNC's China operations.

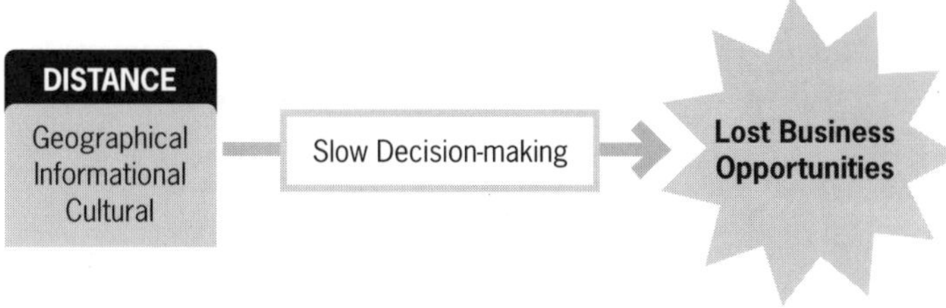

FIGURE 4.1 *China Office-to-HQ Communications Challenges*

Geographical Distance

"

Problems that seem urgent to an international manager in China can seem unimportant to the upper management in Pittsburg or Paris."

The authors,
China CEO

The simple phenomenon of being located on the other side of the globe from the top decision-makers in your corporation presents several unavoidable challenges. Du Pont China's President Charles Browne says he and his team sometimes disagree with headquarters simply because "we are here and we know much better what is happening in this country." He says that risks or opportunities that seem urgent in China can seem distant and relatively unimportant to the upper management in Pittsburg or Paris. Particularly challenging is when China-based executives find themselves competing for resources or funding against managers located nearer to the headquarters. Out of sight can mean out of mind, says Browne. "The problem is that if you are away from home, you are out of the system."

Even the simple act of scheduling time to phone one's supervisors poses logistical problems. The time difference means that Shanghai-based managers must wait until 2 PM to contact a supervisor in Brussels or until 1 AM to reach a director in Los Angeles. Many China-based managers spend their days in the office, and their nights at home on the phone to their supervisors.

The second problem our China hands discovered is that even when interest in Asia is high, understanding may be low. Kenneth Yu of 3M China says that knowledge of the region has increased over the last two decades. In 1984, when Yu's predecessor first recommended to the home office that 3M establish a representative office in Shanghai, the response was: "Where is Shanghai?" While Yu says that such a response would not happen today, the current "China fancy" in the West has not translated into a deep understanding of market conditions, business culture, or economic development. "For executives, particularly those in Fortune 500 companies, China [operations] are still only a fraction of the total corporation. In a typical Fortune 500 company, the home-office executives' understanding of China tends to be limited," Yu says. "Yes, China gets a lot of attention, a lot of hype. But ask what [executives] know about China, and they'll probably say there are a lot of opportunities—that's about it, in most cases."

Siemens China's Dr. Ernst Behrens describes a similar situation back home. "In general, in Europe, the understanding of China is disappointingly bad," he says. "People understand by now that China is a country that has opened up substantially and is extremely successful economically. But they still tend to believe that it is much like the old Soviet Union, with an outdated political system and little freedom for the individual people." He says most first-time visiting friends or colleagues from Europe are surprised to see the Chinese enjoying the kinds of personal freedoms that are common in Europe, such as people dyeing their hair blonde. "Most are positively shocked to see the actual life of the Chinese people and the way China is managing its economy and developing its industry today," he says.

Misperceptions of life in China can lead to misunderstandings about business opportunities, says Microsoft China's Jun Tang. "Some [Westerners] think of China as being still in the bicycle [era]," he says. He tells of recently playing a joke on an American colleague visiting Shanghai for the first time. When the visitor asked if there were many cars in Shanghai, Tang told him to expect a city with 10 to 20 vehicles. Upon arrival, the visitor was shocked to see the city's roaring freeways, subway system, and mag-lev train. Such misunderstandings can also affect business decisions, Tang says. For this reason, he frequently corrects perceptions from headquarters concerning business plans in China.

Happily, several interviewees reported that the information gap is shrinking as interest in China has grown in the West. Eli Lilly China's Christopher Shaw has seen a new curiosity about China in North America. "People think [China] is interesting and they want to come visit," he says. While most visitors come with preconceived, and incorrect, "images from the past," these impressions are quickly corrected upon arrival. "They come here and their minds change," Shaw says. "I encourage as many people to come here from the head office as possible, because by doing that, they can see what is happening; they can see the quality of people; they can see the eagerness to grow and develop."

"

Some [Westerners] think of China as being still in the bicycle [era]."

Jun Tang,
President, Microsoft China

"

The current 'China fancy' in the West has not translated into a deep understanding of market conditions, business culture, or economic development."

The authors,
China CEO

Informational and Cultural Distance

Misperceptions about the number of cars one might expect to find on the roads in Shanghai or about other factual data are fairly easily corrected. Far tougher to correct, our China hands said, are misunderstandings based on cultural differences—how and why business practices in China differ from those back home.

Airbus China's Guy McLeod says a regular part of his job entails explaining to headquarters "why things are a little bit different here." For example, McLeod frequently reminds those at headquarters that business decisions in China may not be final even when they seem to be final. He describes the difference in negotiating styles: "In Europe or the States, 'yes' means 'yes,' so we can work together toward a common goal. Here, 'yes' doesn't always mean 'yes,' and 'no' doesn't always mean 'no.'" In other words, a verbal—or even a written—commitment from a Chinese business partner does not necessarily mean the deal is sealed. Traditionally, Chinese business culture placed less importance on honoring the details of an agreement and more emphasis on building a strong long-term relationship. For example, a Western buyer might be expected to accept a smaller order than was agreed upon if the Chinese supplier has had unexpected difficulties producing the full amount. Accepting the reduced amount—and showing flexibility—proves commitment to the relationship.

Another lesson on China that McLeod teaches to top executives back home is: don't give up. Just when it seems that a particular business venture cannot possibly get off the ground, an unexpected solution may emerge. Brinkmanship is another common quality in Chinese business negotiations. Says McLeod: "One piece of advice I give people about China: everything is difficult, but everything is possible."

Also difficult for superiors in the West to grasp is the political side of business dealings in China. In particular, an MNC's launch and expansion in China can require approvals from many different government entities. The officials involved will be assessing the project based on how well it matches political, not business, goals. "The important thing for the executives in London to understand is how this notion of national interest manifests itself in the way the industry is developing," says Dr. Gary Dirks of BP China. Dirks says it is critical for executives in the head office to understand the role that different government entities play in business decisions—from the city and provincial levels, to the central government level.

Rapid change in the Chinese business environment can present another dangerous stumbling block for China-based managers communicating with headquarters. So says Gordon Orr, a director in the Shanghai offices of McKinsey & Company. "For MNCs, the pace in China is one of the more difficult things to handle—in terms of the size of market opportunities, the way the regulations change," says Orr. "The pace of change means that there is a big challenge often for the head of the China Business Unit to keep the global leadership of the MNC sufficiently informed about why they are making the choices they are making, why the situation is different now from a year ago." Orr says this issue is one of the key challenges McKinsey & Company assists international clients with in China.

> *"In Europe or the States, 'yes' means 'yes,' so we can work together toward a common goal. Here, 'yes' doesn't always mean 'yes,' and 'no' doesn't always mean 'no.' ... One piece of advice I give people about China: everything is difficult, but everything is possible."*
>
> **Guy McLeod**, President, Airbus China

Distance = Slow Decision-making = Lost Opportunities

Given the fluctuating state of the Chinese business environment, quick and nimble adaptation is often essential to success. But fast reactions are nearly impossible when decisions must be made back in the corporate headquarters.

At BearingPoint, Dr. Bryan Huang says the most serious problem for his clients in dealing with headquarters is that decision-making slows dramatically. "In our current environment—the market-oriented economy—you have to react fast," he says. "But the time needed for communications [with headquarters] can be very long."

Huang illustrates the frustration many international managers feel with a joke. A local manager in Shanghai sees that it is raining and contacts his headquarters for permission to purchase an umbrella. After several weeks of discussion at the home-country office, he receives a reply stating: "Why do you need an umbrella? The best training method is to experience the rain."

After MNCs reach a certain size and maturity level, a transfer of power typically takes place in which the China-based management is allowed to make more decisions without consulting headquarters. With more independence, communication with corporate head offices becomes more streamlined, channels of communication flatten, and the local operation achieves the status of strategic partner.

> "*In our current environment—the market-oriented economy—you have to react fast. But the time needed for communications [with headquarters] can be very long.*"
>
> **Dr. Bryan Huang**, Senior Vice President and President Greater China, BearingPoint

Growth Phases in China Operations

Specific advice for establishing and maintaining China–HQ relations depends largely on the stage of development for the MNC's China operations. The types of challenges named by our interviewees, and the best solutions to these problems, varied widely depending on the scale, scope, and maturity of the local business ventures.

Our China hands described three phases in the typical development of an MNC's overseas operations (see Figure 4.2), giving advice on maintaining good relations with the corporate headquarters for each phase.

FIGURE 4.2 *Three Stages of China Operations Development*

Phase 1: Infancy (Launching in China)

In the beginning stage of establishing China operations for an MNC, a single executive is often sent to Shanghai or Beijing alone as a pioneer. Six of our 20 top executive interviewees entered China as such trailblazers. In this phase, communication with headquarters is most often a simple matter of the lone country manager checking in regularly with his superiors at head office.

Our interviewees at British Petroleum, Siemens, L'Oréal, Hilton, and Microsoft passed through such an initial "lone ranger" period in China. L'Oréal's Paolo Gasparrini arrived in Shanghai in 1996 with one assistant and a suitcase of cosmetics samples. By 2005, the company had become one of China's largest cosmetics enterprises. In the six years he spent running Microsoft China, Jun Tang built the company from a one-man show into a company employing 400 workers in Shanghai alone. During his 11 years spent overseeing British Petroleum in China, Dr. Gary Dirks has led BP to become among the largest foreign investors in the country. "The BP that exists today is nothing like it was in 1995 when I arrived here. After many mergers and acquisitions, we are a hugely different company," says Dirks. During the growth period, Dirks' own role has shifted from "hands-on" to "more strategic."

At the start-up stage, the burden of relaying information to and from the corporate headquarters most often relies solely on the pioneering China manager. Dominique de Boisseson of Alcatel remembers the exhaustion that came with serving as the sole communications channel between the company's China operations and his superiors worldwide. "When I first arrived in China [in 1997], I needed to spend days in the company and nights on the phone. It was very tiring," he says. "My boss was in Paris, but the product line headquarters were dispersed around the world. I spent my life on the phone. It was a difficult time."

Relying on a single person for all China–HQ communications is simple and clear-cut, but also risky for the company (and exhausting for the top China executive). Luckily, this stage typically doesn't last long. Most companies quickly move into a period of fast growth—the "youth" phase.

Phase 2: Youth (Fast Growth)

During the "growth spurt" period of establishment, MNCs in China expand operations by adding employees, increasing production, entering new markets, and adding new products. At this stage, communicating with corporate headquarters involves more people, adding new layers and potentially creating new problems.

One typical model for structuring communication with headquarters is seen at Carrefour China. When Jean-Luc Chereau took over China operations in 1999, the company had 14 stores. By 2003, that number had more than doubled and the company was planning to continue growing by 10 to 15 stores per year. After four years in the position, Chereau was overseeing a team of seven division managers in China. These managers report to him, while Chereau reports to two levels of superiors: to an Asian regional supervisor in Hong Kong, and to the headquarters in Paris. "It is very simple; there are not so many levels of hierarchy," says Chereau. He enjoys easy access to both supervisors because they understand China and appreciate its strategic importance to the company.

A different corporate structure was developed by Philips during its fast-growth phase in China. When the company returned to China in 1985, Philips set up a series of independent individual product divisions, each of which operated as a separate joint venture company. Philips China's David Chang explains the thinking back in headquarters: since market conditions vary widely from product to product, each product should be developed and marketed under a separate company. "Philips has a very clear policy: we try to delegate, as much as possible, the responsibility to local organizations," he says. Rather than establishing China-to-headquarters communication, the company operates as many separate entities reporting to separate headquarters overseeing specific products.

Today, Philips operates more than 34 legal entities in China, directly employing more than 20,000 people. The downside is that after nearly 20 years of growth, Philips China was suffering from a rather chaotic corporate structure. "Philips has been very much scattered in China," says Chang. Managing operations of such scale and scope requires "a more cohesive approach." One of his first tasks after taking the helm in 2002 was to create an overall organizational structure with "cross-divisional coordination." Chang has been tasked with standardizing HR policy and accounting procedures, centralizing financial control, and setting overall corporate strategy in China. One of the biggest challenges he has faced has been to help coordinate Philips' bid to supply a package of products and services for the 2008 Olympics, a project requiring close coordination between separate divisions in China. As Chang puts it: "Now Philips finally needs to have a One Philips approach."

Another company facing a similar challenge in managing fast growth among a series of divergent operations located across China is Du Pont. One of the key responsibilities for head of China operations Charles Browne is to coordinate and manage a network of individual businesses throughout the country. When the company re-entered China in 1984, Du Pont opened representative offices in Beijing and Shanghai. As the company began establishing operations throughout China, Du Pont began lobbying the Chinese government to allow it to establish a holding company. Browne says the company's goal was to "manage operations in a cohesive way" and to "unite all the operations with a common culture, common values."

Du Pont was granted approval to form the first holding company in China in 1988. Browne says this structure provides an efficient method of managing China operations. "It is more efficient. You can leverage all of your business support and services." Today, Du Pont China Holding Co. acts as the overall owner and the "link" between the company's 21 operations scattered around China. "My responsibility as a country manager is to see that we are doing the business correctly, we are growing from the corporate point of view, we are expanding as fast as we can, and we are not missing any opportunities," says Browne. From his vantage point overseeing all the China operations, Browne can then adequately relay information on China directly back to corporate headquarters. A similar holding company structure is used at BP China and Sony China.

Phase 3: Adulthood (Maturity and Autonomy)

After MNCs reach a certain size and level of maturity in China, the China-based management typically is allowed the autonomy to make many decisions without consulting company headquarters. When more decisions are made independently, communication with corporate head offices becomes more streamlined and channels of communication flatten and simplify.

At this stage, the local operations achieve the status of strategic partners with the corporate head offices. This concept is explained more fully in the next and final section of this chapter.

Ideal China-to-headquarters Communications

Throughout the growth of an MNC's operations in China, communication with and support from headquarters are essential to success, our interviewees stressed. Dr. Elmar Stachels, Bayer Greater China CEO, describes ideal two-way communications in this way: "You cannot expect [headquarters] to make the right decisions if you don't supply them with comprehensive information. It is our responsibility to give them a comprehensive picture." At the same time, he says, the China-based management must "try to take the global perspective into account." The upshot is that both sides must "talk to each other and respect each other."

Even with such positive intentions in mind, China-to-HQ communication will sometimes falter. When asked how to safeguard against communication breakdown, our featured China hands described four main critical success factors for effective China-to-headquarters communications:

- Head-office commitment to China
- Corporate clout for the China head

- Bring China to the headquarters (arrange VIP visits, education on China)
- Shift power to China (autonomy for the China operations)

See Figure 4.3.

FIGURE 4.3
HQ–China Office Guanxi

CSF #1: Head-office Commitment to China

The first element necessary for successful China operations–headquarters relations is a strong commitment to China from the top echelons of the corporation. Most of the 20 international managers we interviewed reported having achieved strong high-level support.

The support given to Du Pont China is typical. Company president Charles Browne describes it this way: "Our CEO and the whole corporate leadership have had a laser light focused on China during the last 24 months. It is one of the few countries nowadays whose economy doesn't show signs of slowing down."

A similar mindset is driving decision-making at Microsoft. "China is the priority at Microsoft," says Jun Tang, the company's China president. "Everybody understands that this is a country

TIP Try to establish support for China operations among the top management at corporate headquarters. Having two or three top decision-makers take an interest in your operations will make things much easier for you.

we cannot lose." Support from the top has allowed Tang to set an ambitious growth pace. "I want China to be the fastest-growing subsidiary of Microsoft for the next three to five years," he says. "It is now one of the fastest-growing—every year, the growth rate is 30–50%—but it should be the fastest-growing subsidiary. I want China to be number 1."

Dr. Ernst Behrens of Siemens China reports enjoying similarly solid support from the highest corporate level. "We are fortunate because the CEO of Siemens, Dr. Heinrich von Pierer, in 1999 told the company: 'We have to go to China. It is vital for our future successful existence.'"

At BP China, Dr. Gary Dirks agrees that support from the top is essential to effective China–HQ relations. "There has to be a deep interest at the center of the company in wanting to do something in China," Dirks says. "If there are two or three top guys who are really interested in your project, that eases things up. If I can speak to them and they listen, that can save a lot of time."

CSF #2: Corporate Clout for the China Head

International managers stress that another critical success factor for smooth relations with headquarters is that the manager leading China operations have the ability and be given the authority to make certain types of decisions on his or her own, and that his or her opinions and recommendations are respected.

McKinsey & Company director in Shanghai, Gordon Orr, tells his clients that the most critical quality in a head of China operations is "someone with credibility back at corporate headquarters." He recommends that companies send to China a person with a well-established record back at the main office. "In many ways, having a depth of understanding of the corporation is more important than having a depth of understanding of China," Orr says. While the head of China operations can find many local staff members to educate him or her on China business practices, the most important quality he or she should bring to China is the ability to work effectively with the main corporate office. By contrast, Orr says, a China-based manager who is "an unknown quantity" at the corporate center often faces serious challenges in winning top-level support. "I'd recommend sending someone who is a heavyweight in the organization," says Orr.

BearingPoint gives similar strategic advice to its multinational clients in China. Dr. Bryan Huang says that one of the most important keys to success in China is to "give the China unit more authority to determine product strategy, marketing strategy, even HR strategy." Ideally, once operations have developed and matured, the China-based management is often given control of daily operations. Only decisions with far-reaching implications, such as financial allocation or a shift in branding policy, must be determined at the corporate headquarters level.

L'Oréal China's Paolo Gasparrini says he could not succeed if his superiors in Paris didn't give him the autonomy to act on his own. "You need someone with credibility [heading China]," he says. After 15 years spent as a L'Oréal country manager abroad, Gasparrini has earned respect and trust from the corporate head office. "If I say something, people tend to listen to me."

Gasparrini says that although he and his supervisors in Paris share "the same objectives," it is up to him to determine how a plan is implemented. "If you are here just to do what [headquarters] tells you, they don't need you," he says, adding that he often alters and adapts corporate plans to match the Chinese business environment. "It is my responsibility sometimes to fight and have confrontations—especially when something cannot be adapted to China," he says. Although he tries to "make everyone happy," he sometimes needs to ruffle feathers. "You cannot say 'yes' all the time. Sometimes you have to discuss and sometimes you have to say 'no.' It is my job; I am paid for this," he says. "I have to be listened to. You cannot escape from the fact that the [China leader] is important."

A hard-to-beat track record of 41 years spent working overseas also provided Hilton Shanghai's Volkmar Ruebel with the necessary clout to take on his position. "I had a reputation before I came," he says. Today, he says, he has been given "a high level of autonomy" in running his operations. "My direct boss has a reasonably good understanding about what happens here [in China], but he relies very much on our interpretation, our guidance on how to approach things," Ruebel says. The hotel business relies primarily on understanding the market well. Therefore, directives must come from a manager on the ground who is tapped into the day-to-day operations. "Our industry is very close to people. If you don't understand people, you cannot operate a hotel," Ruebel says. "If someone in Beijing or Chongqing doesn't understand the market in that city, he can't do business [there] and needs to get up to speed."

Ruebel says the input he receives from the company's London headquarters is generally supportive. "They are listening to us, rather than dictating how much we have to make. They say, 'What is the best way to go about this?' I am very happy with them," he says.

Another example of the China leadership position held by a corporate heavyweight can be seen at BP China. Dr. Gary Dirks came to China after nine years with BP, including two years spent overseas. "I have more autonomy only because of my rank in the company," says Dirks. "Of course, this is a reflection of the importance of China, and also of the complexity of what goes on here."

"Good support and understanding from the headquarters" has also been a critical element in the success of Siemens' China operations, says Dr. Ernst Behrens. He stresses that he communicates directly to the head offices in Germany, rather than going through a regional office. Most importantly, those at the headquarters trust and respect his decisions, understanding that his input from the ground in China is vital. "We have to give [headquarters] necessary input to help them understand the risks and opportunities here," says Behrens. "If somebody in Germany thinks he understands the whole world, let him go ahead."

At 3M, each of the corporation's 67 country-based subsidiaries worldwide is led by a managing director who runs his operations essentially as an independent company. Kenneth Yu, managing director for China, says 3M differs from other MNCs by giving more autonomy to country managers. While peer companies often give their China-based top executives an "administrator role," Yu says 3M gives its managing directors the role of prime

"

You cannot say 'yes' all the time. Sometimes you have to discuss, and sometimes you have to say 'no.' It is my job; I am paid for this. I have to be listened to. You cannot escape from the fact that the [China leader] is important."

Paolo Gasparrini, President and Managing Director, L'Oréal China minister, rather than king or queen. "And what does the prime minister do?" asks Yu. "He delivers results."

While Yu reports to the vice president of Asia-Pacific, he stresses that, on issues concerning China operations, "I am expected to make most of the decisions." For instance, he handles all hiring and operational decisions on his own. Only "major decisions," such as making a new investment, building a new plant, or producing a new product, are made jointly by the 3M subsidiary and the home office. As Yu puts it, "3M subsidiaries have a lot of autonomy."

When good communications are established between China operations and corporate headquarters, the two sides cooperate to promote China operations while ensuring that China fits into the corporation's global strategy. As Alan Brown of Unilever China explains, this can mean striking a delicate balance. He describes his own relations with corporate headquarters in this way: "We have a high degree of autonomy, but also a high degree of engagement because China is a must-win battle." Ideally, good relations with the home office provide China operations with the right mix of freedom and support. "[Corporate-level leaders] need to agree more or less with what we want to do," says Brown. "It is extremely important that the people on the ground [in China] have strategic capability, not just operational capability. Consistency is everything. If you zigzag, you are in real trouble."

TIP **Appoint a China top executive who is well-respected and well-connected at headquarters. Improve efficiency by giving autonomy to the China operations wherever possible.**

CSF #3: Bring China to the Headquarters

One of the key methods used by our interviewees to build support for China operations at their home offices was to bring information on China to those at the headquarters, either by arranging for education delegations to visit the headquarters or by encouraging the company's VIPs to visit China.

Several of the multinationals we have profiled regularly send China experts to their headquarters. One method, used by 3M, is to send rising stars from their Chinese staff to the U.S. for work stints in the main office. Such a program gave current China managing director Kenneth Yu two years of training at corporate offices in St. Paul, Minnesota, while also allowing Yu to "transfer knowledge about China to the home-office executives." Yu says such programs "certainly help to shorten the learning curve in the headquarters."

Another way to boost support from the head offices is to bring top-echelon executives to China. Many of our interviewees arrange regular visits from senior executives. Microsoft's Jun Tang says Bill Gates visits China "once every couple years," while the group CEO visits yearly. Meanwhile, the Airbus group president comes to China once a year, while Airbus China hosts two to four visitors yearly from the corporate board level.

L'Oréal China's Paolo Gasparrini says bringing corporate VIPs to China not only bridges the information divide, but also raises the status of his operations within the global corporation. "In our case, we are lucky because the president himself makes an effort to know and understand China," says Gasparrini, adding that the global president has spent a week in China every year for six years running. "For a worldwide CEO, this is important. He follows our business. It is very important that the number 1 of the company is directly interested in China. It helps us a lot within the international structure." Paying such regular visits also benefits L'Oréal China in another way; Gasparrini says the L'Oréal president now has established relationships with a wide range of Chinese officials, business partners, and the local team. "He knows many people [in China] at the first level, but also at the second and third levels," says Gasparrini.

Among the MNCs featured in this book, Sony China takes the award for most frequent visits from corporate headquarters. "There are constant visitors from headquarters coming to China. The number is large—almost every day," says Sony China's Seiichi Kawasaki. In fact, his offices are so often visited that Kawasaki jokes about sometimes wishing Tokyo were a little further from Shanghai.

One warning voiced by Airbus China president Guy McLeod regarding corporate visitors is that VIP guests can acquire a slanted impression of China after several days of being whisked around Shanghai or Beijing. "If [executives] come here for two or three days, they may think China is so wonderful, so easy," says McLeod. "Of course it is easy when they stay in the best hotels and you arrange their car and translators."

BP has developed a solution to this problem. The company not only flies VIPs from headquarters to China each year, but also sends them to classes on local business culture. "There are people from London [BP headquarters] coming all the time. They love it," says Dr. Gary Dirks, of BP China. The course—"China Through Chinese Eyes"—is conducted at Beijing's Tsinghua University and features Chinese professors, journalists, and businesspeople sharing their "vision of China." Dirks says the course offers a valuable introduction. "So often, you hear Chinese stories told by Westerners. If you listen to the Chinese tell their story, it is very different," he says.

TIP **Bring people from headquarters to China regularly. This will further their understanding of business conditions and your operations.**

CSF#4: Shift Power to China

The ultimate goal for many of our profiled top China executives in creating effective relations with headquarters was to see China operations gain autonomy within the global corporation. Many of the interviewees sought to transfer more decision-making powers to China, allowing for faster, more efficient management of operations. At many of the featured companies, such a transfer of power was in keeping with the importance of China to the company's worldwide operations.

In the case of British Petroleum, the company achieved this power transfer by installing a corporate group vice president as the president and CEO of country operations. Worldwide, only four regional presidents of BP also hold the rank of group vice president, the title held by China top executive for the company, Dr. Gary Dirks. He describes the corporate structure in China as a "matrix organization" in which he serves simultaneously as the chief executive, handling day-to-day operational issues, and the group VP, handling strategic issues.

Installing a top-ranked executive as the head of China operations allows BP to make more decisions without HQ input, and when decisions do need input from the corporate leaders, discussions are generally efficient. Business units elsewhere report to a

TIP It is essential that corporations give those on the ground in China strategic capability, not only operational capability. Corporate headquarters must recognize the fast growth and rising importance of their China operations.

vice president, then a "stream chief executive," then the group CEO. In the case of BP China, one of these layers is removed.

Another company that has made a power shift into China is 3M. There, China managing director Kenneth Yu also holds the title of regional director for Greater China which means that he oversees operations in China, Hong Kong, and Taiwan. Giving Yu dual responsibilities helps to consolidate decision-making and oversight for all three places. "At 3M, counterparts in all three [Greater China] subsidiaries work very closely together in a team," says Yu. This structure allows him to coordinate operations in the region and to communicate efficiently with headquarters.

An even bolder transfer of power has taken place at Alcatel China. In 1998, the company opened a small research and development (R&D) center in China. The division now employs 2,000 researchers. In 2000, the company moved its Asia-Pacific headquarters to Shanghai, and elevated the president of the region to also serving as a member of the Corporate Executive Committee. For chairman and CEO of China operations Dominique de Boisseson, it meant that all regional vice presidents for the corporate division were located in one building in Shanghai. "Now, when we need to make a decision, all the people involved in the decision-making are right there," he says. "Only some very important decisions go to the chairman." The result, de Boisseson says, is very efficient communication. "I believe we save 30% of the time we used to spend on decision-making. This means we have 30% more time to spend on the business."

Other profiled MNCs have also opened R&D centers in China, following a growing trend among international companies to establish research in China for China. The number of foreign-invested R&D centers increased from 200 to 600 between 2002 and late 2004.

General Electric opened a Global Research Center near Shanghai in 2003, one of the corporation's three such centers worldwide. Meanwhile, Bayer moved its regional headquarters functions to Hong Kong and Shanghai. The change allows Bayer to be more effective, says the company's China CEO Dr. Elmar Stachels. "There are a lot of difficulties getting fast information about China," he says. "It is very important for headquarters representatives to be close to the market. They have to know exactly what is going on in China. If they were located in Germany, it would be much more difficult, even impossible, to be effective."

One logical end-point for this power transfer is for MNCs to locate their Asian regional headquarters within China. Shanghai, for example, witnessed an influx of regional headquarters establishing in the city during 2004 and 2005. As of late 2005, the city was home to 104 regional HQs for multinationals, many moving to the city from Singapore, Hong Kong, or elsewhere in Asia.[1]

Such moves help to propel the China operations of an MNC toward achieving the correct balance between autonomy (ensuring efficient, competitive operations speeds) and interdependence (ensuring that China develops in synch with the company's global strategy). Our interviewees generally agreed that, in today's China, creating an ideal communications model with headquarters often hinges on recognizing the importance of China operations to the global corporate strategy. McKinsey & Company's Gordon Orr says the firm's client work in China is changing based on this shift. "For the MNCs, the initial era was market development: what should we be doing in China, finding the route to market, treating China as an isolated entity. But these days, you really don't do China strategies; you do global operations strategy, global operations platform, global market strategies—and China is a core element in that. The number of global team projects we are involved in [in China] is three to four times higher than it was three years ago." Thus, establishing good China-to-HQ communications relies first on recognizing the fast growth and maturation of many MNCs' China operations, and the rising importance of China operations to many global companies.

Conclusion

A critical challenge for the heads of China operations is communicating with their headquarters in the home country. Not only

1 Shanghai Foreign Economic Relation & Trade Commission.

are China managers geographically distant from their supervisors (out of sight, out of mind), but those at corporate headquarters may have little understanding of China's business environment and little appreciation of the challenges and the pace of activity. These gaps can lead to slow decision-making and lost business opportunities. For these reasons, the goal of many of the top executives we interviewed is to increase autonomy for the China operations, thus improving efficiency of operations.

Many of the China operations of the 20 MNCs we have profiled have passed through (or are passing through) development stages similar to the development of a human being: infancy, adolescence, and adulthood. The final stage is reached when the local China operations achieve the status of strategic partner to the headquarters.

SUMMARY OF TIPS

COMMUNICATING WITH HEADQUARTERS

1. Head-office Commitment to China

Try to establish support for China operations among the top management at corporate headquarters. Having two or three top decision-makers take an interest in your operations will make things much easier for you.

2. Corporate Clout for the China Head

Appoint a China top executive who is well-respected and well-connected at headquarters. Improve efficiency by giving autonomy to the China operations wherever possible.

3. Bring China to the Headquarters

Bring people from headquarters to China regularly. This will further their understanding of business conditions and your operations.

4. Shift Power to China

It is essential that corporations give those on the ground in China strategic capability, not only operational capability. Corporate headquarters must recognize the fast growth and rising importance of their China operations.

Chapter 5
Facing Competitors

"China is full of contradictions. Here we are in a socialist country, but it's one of the most competitive societies on earth."

Simon Keeley, Head of the Hewitt Asia Leadership Center (HALC), Hewitt Associates China

INSIDE CHAPTER 5

Introduction

Fierce competition from unexpected sources. Decidedly unlevel playing fields. A still-developing legal system offering uncertain protections for business operations. These are the factors that our interviewees listed as turning the China market into a murky, confusing, and frustrating terrain for MNCs.

Listening to international managers describe their struggles against the varied opponents they face when competing in the China market conjures up images from a new Game Boy release—in which our MNC executive (the digital hero) faces a constant onslaught of attacks from a host of increasingly strange and deadly combatants. After analyzing the responses of our 28 China hands, we found that most identified three categories of strong, but very different, competitors jostling against them for the China market: global rivals, local competitors, and intellectual property rights (IPR) infringers.

Chapter 5 covers international managers' advice on coping with the main groups of legitimate competitors: global rivals and domestic competitors. (*Note:* Chapter 6 covers our interviewees' advice on battling IPR infringers.)

Global Rivals (Fellow MNCs)

The first opponents many MNCs face in China now are the global corporations in their industry that have already arrived. Thousands of companies have rushed into China since the nation opened its doors widely to foreign investors in the mid-1980s. Foreign direct investment into China climbed through the 1980s and 1990s until, in 2003, the country overtook the United States as the most popular destination for FDI. In 2004, China attracted FDI of US$153.5 billion (by contract value), including US$60.63 billion in utilized capital. In cumulative terms, as of the end of 2004, China had attracted FDI of US$1.097 trillion (contract value) and US$562 billion (utilized) since economic opening began. In addition, nearly 51,000 foreign-funded companies had been set up in China in the previous 20 years, and more than 400 of the Fortune 500 had operations in China.[1]

The upshot is that most of the world's largest companies are already in China, and a wave of smaller, more specialized companies across a wide spectrum of fields has arrived in the years following WTO accession. Today, many foreign-invested enterprises are now both well-experienced and well-entrenched in the Middle Kingdom.

> *All the big guys are [in China], right down the list. For the international players, this is a dog fight."*
>
> **Dr. Gary Dirks**, President and CEO, British Petroleum China

Thus, for many global corporations, winning in China means battling the same major international rivals faced elsewhere in the world. The experience of British Petroleum is typical. "All the big guys are here, right down the list," says Dr. Gary Dirks of BP China. "For the international players, this is a dog fight."

Kenneth Yu of 3M China portrays the battlefield this way: "You face the normal competition in China, but you get more competition because you're not the only smart person: everyone wants to come here." The result, Yu says, is "a lot of international competition." Seiichi Kawasaki of Sony China describes the competitive arena he faces in China: "I can say this is the most competitive market in the world. There are a lot of international companies here—Japanese companies, American and European companies—plus local companies. They all try to compete in China." At L'Oréal China, Paolo Gasparrini finds a similarly volatile environment in the cosmetics industry. "We have all the international competitors here that we have everywhere in the world, such as in the U.S., France, Germany. Plus, local competitors are becoming stronger and stronger because they are learning and growing."

In China, MNCs tend to compete against fellow MNCs in a number of capacities—not only vying for customers, but also jostling against each other to win government approvals, recruit and retain key personnel, form partnerships and alliances with local companies, or to secure land, facilities, equipment, and supplies.

Over the past two decades, BearingPoint has seen a maturation of the competition between multinationals in China, as

1 Ministry of Commerce, China, statistics for 2004.

"*I can say this is the most competitive market in the world. There are a lot of international companies here—Japanese companies, American and European companies—plus local companies. They all try to compete in China.*"

Seiichi Kawasaki, Director and President, Sony China

Bryan Huang explains: in the first years of economic reform, many MNCs hurried into China with seed money but little understanding of how to operate. In the early 1990s, global firms moved their manufacturing to China to save costs. In the late 1990s, international companies entered with the goal of selling to the burgeoning domestic market for both industrial and consumer goods. Today, the thinking has shifted again, Huang says. "Now we are at another turning point of foreign companies' investment in China—[MNCs] are considering China as an integral part in their global strategy." In other words, more multinationals are treating China as a key component in their overall corporate goals, taking into account a full range of strategic opportunities, from manufacturing to R&D to domestic sales.

The Boston Consulting Group has noted a similar shift in the mindset of its MNC clients. When Greater China managing director John Wong arrived in 1995, much of his work focused on entry strategies for multinational firms setting up in China. Today, more of his international clients have already established in China, and are now looking to expand in terms of geography or business scope. "A lot of our business shifted from looking from the outside in, to building businesses in China where the company already has a base," Wong says.

For MNCs in China, all of this means that competition from fellow international firms is now fierce in many industries and will become fiercer as foreign companies gain experience, build networks, and localize. Then, too, China's accession to WTO in 2001 offered a three-year grace period for many regulatory changes. Thus the deadline of December 2004 brought significant market opening in many sectors (especially retail and distribution). Most WTO-accession regulations must be in place by 2007.

But there is another fast-growing group of competitors, which, in many ways, is proving even more difficult to compete against than MNCs. That is because these newly developing competitors are often unknown quantities—young, aggressive, and unpredictable. They are China's domestic firms.

Emerging Domestic Opponents

Many MNCs in China now are hit from two sides. On the one hand, their global competitors are in many cases well-entrenched in China and are quickly learning to succeed here. On the other hand, domestic companies are changing fast to adapt to the new market-oriented economy. Gone are the days when international firms enjoyed a wide quality gap ahead of local competitors; in all but the most specialized technical sectors, domestic firms are making headway.

The result, for many international companies in China, is a "two-way squeeze." Dr. Elmar Stachels of Bayer China says, "Here, we have the combination of local companies that are globalizing more and more, and global players that are localizing in China." He describes the change in recent years as follows: "In many areas, Chinese companies are improving in quality and climbing up. This is a fact." The result is a market that is "very attractive to customers" but very difficult for MNCs.

One of the surprises in writing this book was the realization that, for many MNCs, the most challenging competition they face in China comes not from international players but from emerging local companies. The reason is that fellow multinationals tend to be familiar rivals that compete according to established and respected rules. After all, many leaders of global companies share a similar grounding in basic Western-oriented business theory and strategies, often studying similar courses in their MBA or other graduate programs (Porter's Five Forces, the BCG Matrix, PEST and SWOT analysis). But domestic competitors are a totally unknown force, often following unfamiliar, confusing, or even illogical business strategies. Thus, an analogy is that international managers are finding that fellow MNCs use standard battle procedures (even in China), but Chinese companies engage in guerrilla warfare.

Du Pont China's Charles Browne describes a two-tiered competitive arena in China: "We know our international competitors very well—we do business with them in the U.S. and Europe. They know us, we know them." But Chinese companies tend to be difficult for foreign managers to assess. Browne says that

"Here, we have the combination of local companies that are globalizing more and more, and global players that are localizing in China."

Dr. Elmar Stachels, CEO, Bayer China

even those domestic firms that Du Pont seeks to cooperate with, rather than compete against, are hard to analyze. "With Chinese companies, it takes longer for us to form a relationship with them, build trust, understand their ways of doing business," he says.

Coca-Cola has also found local companies challenging to compete against. In China, the cola giant faces off against international rivals Pepsi in carbonated drinks, and Danone and Nestlé in bottled water. But in the packaged tea and juice drink market, Coke China competes against two large-scale Taiwanese producers and one major Chinese maker. And in the bottled water sector, the company also squares off against a "formidable" Chinese maker, says Coca-Cola China president Paul Etchells. The biggest difficulty in facing domestic producers, Etchells says, is unpredictability. The two strongest Chinese beverage companies are especially difficult to analyze, he says, because they tend to be inconsistent—marketing aggressively for a time, then backing off suddenly. Creating an effective strategy is extremely difficult when fighting an on-again, off-again rival.

Home-court Advantage: Low Price, High Quality

The most serious challenge described repeatedly by our MNC managers across the full range of industries profiled in this book is that local competitors in China are now wielding a double-edged sword created by rapidly improving in quality while maintaining low price levels. When Dr. Ernst Behrens began as president and CEO of Siemens China in 1997, the company faced two clear categories of competition: global rivals in the high-priced segment, and local competitors in the low-priced sector. Today, however, low-end local electronics and telecom product manufacturers are improving product quality and are appealing to the mass market. "We have to adjust our products into that [low-priced] range—there is the real volume," says Behrens. "The local companies are moving up to the upper level. Look at Huawei, Haier, Lenovo. They are now very strong competitors; they are becoming multinational. We are facing a real challenge."

Traditionally, Chinese manufacturers have produced low-end products sold at low prices relative to international markets. After the full opening of China to foreign investment and foreign products in the mid-1980s, a large gap developed in many sectors where foreign brands attracted the top consumer income brackets while domestic companies retained the rest of the market. Today, however, many MNCs are finding that local competitors are fast approaching international standards of product quality, but maintaining a significant price gap with foreign-branded goods.

BearingPoint's Bryan Huang says that many of his international clients in China initially followed a strategy of high-end positioning. "The Japanese companies [in particular] feel that they cannot compete on price, so they move to the high-end market," he says. "They are launching new products in China at the same time as in Japan." Ultimately, however, Huang believes that remaining strictly high-end is "not a long-term sustainable strategy for multinationals." He agrees that domestic companies are quickly improving in quality and are repositioning upscale. Huang points out that many Chinese companies are now "very rich in cash," allowing them to acquire the technology to upgrade products. In fact, the lead time for local companies to adapt a product to international-class specifications is often "only a few months."

The result is that Chinese companies narrow the quality gap but leave a large price gap. Consumers find products that are close to international brand-name quality at prices far below international brand-name rates—a tough combination for MNCs to compete against. In fact, in some sectors, this combination has effectively locked out foreign companies from the China market. Consider the white goods industry, now dominated in China by Chinese maker Haier. International companies can no longer find a foothold in a landscape crowded by high-value, low-cost domestic makers. In 2001, eight international makers held roughly 15% of China's white goods market, each one holding a fractional market share. Meanwhile, Haier alone owned 28%.[2]

Sony China's Seiichi Kawasaki is intimately familiar with the

---

2 China Europe International Business School case study.

trend among local competitors to move upscale while keeping prices down. Traditionally, Kawasaki says, many domestic IT product manufacturers have followed a pattern of producing as many products as possible, saturating the market, then slashing prices in order to move inventory. This method has wreaked havoc in China's IT products and electronics industries, rendering many sectors unprofitable. One example: Kawasaki says it is now nearly impossible for foreign firms to produce a color TV that can sell at a profit in the China market.

To avoid price wars with Chinese makers, Sony has followed a policy of maintaining price but continually increasing product value by introducing new features. But this strategy has been less successful in China recently, Kawasaki says, because "another type of competitor is coming." He explains the change: "What Sony does is to introduce new concepts into its products, but this creates other problems. The features of the product are very easy [for Chinese competitors] to learn. They can make a cheap imitation." As a result, domestic IT product makers quickly launch similar products, typically at steep price discounts.

Today, Sony maintains an edge in China by speeding product development even faster and by aggressive marketing—one area in which local companies still tend to be weak. "We have to add more value through the marketing. It is constant fighting, constant changing."

Many of the international managers interviewed for this book described a similar "squeeze" in their industries as the gap between international and Chinese products narrows both in terms of quality and price. Alan Brown of Unilever China saw a dramatic shift in the consumer goods industry soon after he took up his post in 2001. "Prices have moved down for foreign products and up for local products—so they are coming closer to each other. There has been an extremely painful period of readjustment."

According to McKinsey & Company, there is often a pattern in newly opened developing markets in which domestic companies in various sectors enjoy boosted sales after an influx of upscale MNCs. Gordon Orr, a director in the company's Shanghai office, describes a pattern that international companies often fall victim to when entering emerging markets. Soon after a protected market opens, the top international companies in that field enter simultaneously, "each hoping to capture 20% of the market." Most see results that are more modest. "Then comes frustration," says Orr.

> "*Prices have moved down for foreign products and up for local products—so they are coming closer to each other. There has been an extremely painful period of readjustment.*"
>
> **Alan Brown**, Chairman, Unilever China

Fast Learners

Most of our 20 top executive interviewees expressed a significant degree of concern over how fast and how far domestic companies are advancing technologically. Consider the fixed communication infrastructure market. Dominique de Boisseson of Alcatel China Investments explains the scenario in his industry: Alcatel's main competitors in China are now Chinese. The company's largest opponent, Shenzhen-based Huawei Technologies, employs 30,000 personnel in China and achieved contracted sales of US$5.6 billion in 2004. Not only is Huawei a large company even by international standards, but it is developing very rapidly. For example, as a method of upgrading quickly, in 1999 Huawei cooperated with IBM on an internal reengineering project that included sending several IBM engineers to work with Huawei in China. "These are the new Chinese companies—with advanced products and global competitiveness," says de Boisseson.

Even in highly specialized industries such as pharmaceuticals, Chinese companies are making headway. Christopher Shaw of Eli Lilly China tells of dramatic changes in his industry. Traditionally, Lilly's main competitors in China have been international firms with brand-name products. Meanwhile, local makers have focused on lower-end generic drugs in the smaller hospitals where economy is the biggest driver. "[Chinese companies] are competitors, but they primarily operate on price and we operate on value," says Shaw. Eli Lilly's strategy has been to position as a top-quality product, supported by medical marketing, consumer education, and patient support. But while a strategic divide still exists in China's pharmaceutical industry, it is narrowing. "The leading domestic firms are becoming more market-driven," says Shaw. "They are learning fast; they are hiring people from

> *"These are the new Chinese companies—with advanced products and global competitiveness."*
>
> **Dominique de Boisseson**, Chairman and CEO, Alcatel

the multinational companies." He points out that several domestic pharmaceutical firms now operate on a national scale, distributing throughout China.

The pharmaceutical industry is currently in a "transition stage," Shaw says, in which "China is developing remarkably." In this industry, MNCs are motivated to weather the current difficulties because the overall field seems certain to grow aggressively for the next several years. China moved from being the world's 10th-largest pharmaceutical market in 1997 to eighth-largest in 2003. By 2010, industry analysts say, China could be the fourth-largest, driven by the size of the population and the trend toward increased longevity.

And this is only the beginning of the development of local pharmaceutical companies, Shaw says. At present, international pharmaceutical manufacturers have complained that when they seek to register a new product, there is inadequate protection for their pioneering research data.[3] Local applicants can gain access to the data, then use it to submit their own application. MNCs are also pressing the government to extend patent terms in order to provide a protection period for products in which the patent life is "unreasonably short" due to a long development cycle or delays in regulatory approval. This will protect international pharmaceutical companies from introducing new products to China only to lose their patent in too short a time to recover costs.

Within a decade, interviewees in the field expected to find the pharmaceutical market in China operating more similarly to that of the West—with two distinct tracks: R&D of new products, and generic production of older pharmaceuticals that are no longer protected by patent. At such a stage, the industry will operate more harmoniously, with the two industry sectors working "with each other, less in direct competition," Shaw says.

---

3 2005 White Paper on American Business in China, American Chamber of Commerce in China, American Chamber of Commerce in Shanghai, (2005).

Services Squeezed, Too

Manufacturers are not the only MNCs feeling pressure from local Chinese competitors. The trend toward stiff competition from domestic companies is also being felt among international managers in the services sector. This counters the widely held belief that Chinese companies are mostly one-trick ponies: skilled at replicating manufacturing processes but unable to upgrade "software"—factors such as customer service and marketing. Today, international firms operating service companies are also finding local competitors improving and competing head-on.

Several service-sector expatriate managers we interviewed reported the same problems with copycats faced in manufacturing: local firms have learned to replicate their services and sell them at a steep discount. When the publishing giant Bertelsmann Direct Asia launched an online book club in 1997, company president Ekkehard Rathgeber says it quickly became a victim of its own initial success. "It had a very big impact on the market, so that many people tried to copy it," he says. "They are pretty good in copying things." Within 18 months, several competing book clubs were operating online. These offered consumers fewer features but far lower prices. "Always, they immediately go for price competition," says Rathgeber. One upside for Bertelsma nn: Rathgeber says the online book-selling market offers such narrow margins that Bertelsmann's largest international competitors have stayed out of China. "Foreign companies think it's not worth it," he says.

The hotel industry offers one of the clearest examples of the evolution of Chinese companies in the services sector. Shanghai, for example, is now home to 20 five-star hotels, making it a major hospitality center in the region. But the city also has 27 four-star and 118 three-star hotels, which are mainly ambitious locally owned companies.

Shanghai Hilton's Volkmar Ruebel has seen massive changes in his business during his 11 years in China. In the early 1990s, he says, virtually all domestic hotels operated on a very low budget, offering low-grade facilities and minimal service for a low rate. During the 1990s, business at these hotels picked up as travel increased among Chinese businesspeople and tourists. These hotels suddenly saw their occupancy rates soar and their profits surge. Many used the cash in-flow to upgrade their facilities, then bumped up their nightly rates from RMB100–300 (US$12-37) to RMB400–500 (US$39-54). As a result, China's two- and three-star hotels became a "pretty strong force," Ruebel says, turning a good profit by offering clean, modern facilities for Chinese travelers. This has led to a hotel building boom that is ongoing. By 2003, Shanghai had some 48,000 hotel rooms; by 2010, Ruebel expects the city to have over 60,000 rooms.

Commitment to Professionalism

Despite representing vastly different industries, our interviewees repeatedly mentioned one clear trend among Chinese firms: a marked shift toward greater professionalism driven by the emerging market-based economy. Dr. Ernst Behrens of Siemens China explains the change: "It is no longer the government determining who does what. Fifteen years ago, [the Chinese government] said, 'You make bicycles; you make washing machines.' Today, companies develop by themselves. This is the great change. Competition now exists."

While many traditional domestic businesses have shut down during the past 15 years of reform, those that have survived largely have done so by becoming more streamlined and market savvy. One indication that Chinese companies are gaining competitiveness: more are willing to pay professional consultants for their services. Each of the four consulting companies we interviewed—McKinsey & Company, BCG, BearingPoint, and Hewitt Associates—reported that their China operations now serve mainly Chinese clientele. (Even the senior executive recruitment firm Korn/Ferry, which serves mainly MNCs in China, has taken on a growing number of Chinese companies since 2001.)

Our eight consultant interviewees were generally surprised at the strong interest among domestic firms in using their services. Consider Hewitt Associates, which entered China planning to focus only on MNC clients. In mid-2000, the company management voted to expand and attempt serving Chinese clients—a move that seemed "audacious" at the time, remembers Hewitt executive Simon Keeley. Hewitt hoped to receive 20% of revenues from local clients within the first year; in fact, the company was receiving nearly 70% of its earnings from Chinese firms 12 months later.

Several years on, Keeley still calls the interest among local firms "explosive," adding that Hewitt could receive 100% of its human capital consulting business from Chinese companies, but chooses to maintain a mix of multinational and local clients. "The real growth area in consulting today is with Chinese clients," he says. Much of his HR work for Chinese clients consists of "designing from the bottom up" in terms of clarifying roles and responsibilities, setting salaries, and managing employee performance. "They have so much to do," Keeley says. "Multinationals already have their [HR] systems, which they import to their China operations, but many Chinese companies don't have a structure to start with."

Keeley describes four types of Chinese client companies: first are SOEs that are "really serious about getting competitive and becoming global," such as CNOOC (China National Offshore Oil Corp.). Second are SOEs that are "being pushed into becoming more competitive, many kicking and screaming." Third are large and successful private companies, such as Huawei, many of which are exploding in growth and emerging as "very serious competitors with global ambitions." Last are private family-owned companies, often established in rural areas such as Zhejiang or Jiangsu province. Keeley says many of these family businesses founded by former farmers or factory workers have grown into multimillion-dollar operations but so far lack the resources to internationalize. He advises not "underestimating" the potential of these fast-growing companies.

It was China's WTO accession in 2001, Keeley says, that triggered many Chinese firms to seek international consulting services. "A lot of companies were getting nervous about what WTO [accession] means. So they are rapidly trying to professionalize like their multinational competitors," he says. Helen Tantau of Korn/Ferry Shanghai agrees that the joining of WTO pushed many Chinese companies to begin competing aggressively both domestically and internationally. Korn/Ferry has found that domestic firms make ambitious clients, especially in recruiting executives away from multinational firms. Tantau tells of one Shanghai-based food products company that recently lured one-third of its professional staff from MNCs.

Tantau stresses that those Chinese firms that have aggressively pursued internationalism and competitiveness have tended to win big—meaning that some are now beating MNCs at their own game. "Within China, many successful Chinese companies are much more successful than their international counterparts," she says. In industries such as computers and consumer electronics, she stresses, several domestic players are now "huge" and are fully committed to maintaining their advantage. "They are spending money and they are doing all the right things," she says.

McKinsey & Company China works both with SOEs and a growing number of private domestic companies, mainly in industries facing "substantial competitive pressure," says company director in Shanghai Gordon Orr. He is focusing on two industries in particular: consumer electronics and insurance. In the past few years, Orr has seen a rapid evolution in the types of issues Chinese clients seek help in addressing. Initially, many sought assistance with either streamlining their organization or setting strategy. But lately, the company is tackling a third set of issues: fine-tuning operations to improve overall competitiveness. Orr is now assisting Chinese firms with streamlining supply chain management, upgrading assembly at the factory, analyzing route to market, or sharpening branding skills—similar issues to those McKinsey addresses for clients in developed markets worldwide. "It is amazing to see that the issues you need to address in the China market have become very similar to what you see everywhere else," says Orr.

The Boston Consulting Group has also seen a "dramatic change in the ability and attitude of Chinese companies toward using consultants," says company managing director for Greater China John Wong. Domestic firms now "recognize what consultants are," Wong says, and are paying for top-quality services. Today, half of BCG's clients in China are domestic firms. The change Wong notes is that the gap in needs between his Chinese and international client companies is narrowing. "We make a distinction between MNCs and Chinese companies, but five years from now, that distinction will be less and less," says Wong. "Chinese companies are trying as fast as they can to develop many of the capabilities they see in MNCs. So, the distinctions are going to blur."

> *"Chinese companies are trying as fast as they can to be like MNCs. So, the distinctions are going to blur."*
>
> **John Wong**, Managing Director Greater China, The Boston Consulting Group

At BearingPoint China, 85% of clients are local companies. Bryan Huang, company president of Greater China, says management consulting began to be recognized by domestic firms in the late 1990s, but "really took off" in 2002. Today, he says, "There is a big transition in the market to more and more recognition of consulting services."

Most of BearingPoint's Chinese client companies are state-run companies looking to modernize and internationalize operations. "[SOEs] badly need management consulting and implementation consulting," Huang says. "Most just left the planned economy a little more than 10 years ago. They are facing a lot of challenges in the market economy." For example, some of Huang's manufacturing clients are used to measuring how much product they produce, rather than how much they sell. "From this, you can see that their mindset is still in the planned economy," he says.

Despite the socialist roots, Huang says many SOEs are modernizing rapidly. The Chinese managers he works with tend to be very aggressive about transforming their companies. In fact, many top executives at client firms spend their days working and their evenings and weekends taking EMBA courses. "They have great enthusiasm for learning more about management," he says. Another indication of the commitment to change: when hired by Chinese companies, BearingPoint consultants often work directly with the very top level of management. "We always work with the chairman or CEO, even for an ERP [enterprise resource planning] project. Instead of just asking 'How is it going?' from time to time, they are involved in very deep discussions," Huang says. He adds that many Chinese companies are now paying consulting fees in the same range as Western or Japanese clients.

Coming Soon: Chinese MNCs

The next step in the evolution of the market economy, China hands agree, will be the emergence of Chinese multinationals. Domestic companies, including Huawei (telecom), Haier (white goods), and Lenovo (computers), are already producing and selling branded products internationally. The consensus among our interviewees is that this is just the beginning; many more Chinese brand names will appear on the global market in the next decade. BCG's John Wong calls such a development "inevitable."

Steve Schneider of GE China is one top China executive who is preparing for this shift. In GE's "short-cycle" businesses (consumer products, plastics), its China competitors are already mainly domestic companies. In the company's "long-cycle" businesses (aircraft engines, transportation systems), its competitors in China are now mainly European and American companies, but Schneider says this will soon change. "Twenty years from now, there won't be this distinction—it will all be global competitors [in China]," he says, explaining that all sectors of the China market will soon be dominated by world-class companies, both international and domestic firms.

Even in high-entry-barrier industries such as oil and gas, Chinese MNCs are expected to emerge as international players. "I don't see any reason why we won't see Chinese multinationals in our industry," says Dr. Gary Dirks of BP China. While Dirks warns that the biggest challenge for Chinese firms in the petroleum industry is that they are coming "late to the game" and thus facing difficulty finding new reserves of oil and gas, he adds that those that are successful will benefit from being able to tap into China's vast market from the inside.

Even within the services sector, which has been one of the slowest fields to develop in China, interviewees expect that world-class Chinese companies will soon appear. In the hotel business, for example, as Volkmar Ruebel of the Hilton Shanghai points out, a precedent has already been set in other Asian countries. "If you look at the Japanese or the Hong Kong hotels operating internationally, or at Shangri-la Group of Malaysia which operates all over Asia and Europe, why wouldn't there be a Chinese group in the future?" he asks. Ruebel adds that the population of traveling Chinese businesspeople and of Chinese working overseas has created necessary volume. "Look at the Chinese market overseas. If we could move a Chinese hotel into Thailand or Germany, why not?"

Our interviewees stressed that the Lenovo purchase of IBM's PC division in 2005 is just the beginning of what the world can expect of Chinese companies in the near future. Worldly, professional, and highly ambitious, Chinese companies are winning the competition battle in China and are now starting to look abroad. As Dr. Ernst Behrens of Siemens China explains, "The Chinese have a vision of what they want to be—they want to be a technologically leading country in the world, and they are going in that way." Another interviewee put it more bluntly, saying: "It would be very naive to say that Western companies will still be king in 20 years."

TIP **For MNCs targeting the China market, there are some battles not worth fighting. Avoid competing against domestic cost-based products.**

Strategies for Battling Chinese Competitors

Given the atmosphere of increasing competition from domestic firms, our 28 expert China hands gave their best advice for surviving in today's China market:

- Pick winnable battles
- Innovate ...
- ... But beware of over-innovation
- Don't fight, merge

Strategy #1: Pick Winnable Battles

Our interviewees stressed that some sectors are now dominated by Chinese firms offering market-accepted quality at prices far

TIP The best survival strategy is to keep moving: continually upgrade to stay ahead of competitors.

below those of MNCs. These sectors are now nearly impossible for international firms to penetrate if targeting a mass market. Simply put, there are some battles not worth attempting. Says Korn/ Ferry Shanghai's Helen Tantau, "For foreign companies that want to compete in the consumer electronic sector—washing machines, air-conditioners, refrigerators—they find it very hard to compete as it is a volume game that is very difficult to win."

Strategy #2: Innovate ...

Many Chinese firms are becoming expert at developing products and services on a par with those introduced by global companies. Thus, international firms say the best survival strategy often is to keep moving: continually upgrading to stay ahead of the local firms.

"Local competitors study companies like ours, our products and how we market them. They study and try to learn what we do, and they are very good at determining what works," says Charles Browne of Du Pont China. He adds that this adaptability, coupled with deep understanding of the local market, gives Chinese companies the best of both worlds. "After all, local companies know the culture much better than we do. So they can be very fierce and strong competitors." Du Pont's solution, Browne says, has been to steadily introduce new products and features. "Constant innovation is a must. We still succeed because we have been in business for a long time and we can develop new products and technology faster than they do. But it doesn't take long for local companies to catch up, so we cannot stay static. We have to keep moving and improving our products and services and our understanding of our customers' needs."

Strategy #3: ...But Beware of Over-innovation

Consultants agreed that one dangerous tendency among foreign companies targeting the China market is to introduce higher-end products that are not only priced out of range but that include features that domestic consumers do not need. In particular, BearingPoint Greater China's Bryan Huang warns clients in the IT field against misdirected over-engineering. For example, he points to international companies that recently introduced mobile phone handsets built to last 10 years and phone batteries with 20-year warranties. "Who will use a mobile phone for more than two years?" he asks. "There is a lot of waste in those products." Huang explains that when these products were recently marketed in China by global makers, local manufacturers responded by developing versions with similar features—except the enhanced life-span—but sold at far lower retail prices.

TIP Avoid over-engineered products. Offer quality and functionality that matches demand, but don't lose sight of cost.

Other sectors susceptible to over-engineering, says Huang, are TVs and home appliances. In these sectors, local companies are now adept at reverse-engineering foreign-made products, preserving the most-preferred functions and reducing price. Says Huang: "You get the quality and functionality, but not the cost."

TIP If you can't beat 'em, join 'em (or buy 'em).

Strategy #4: Don't Fight, Merge

If you can't beat 'em, join 'em. One method of meeting the challenge of increased competition from Chinese companies is to join forces rather than continuing to fight. One popular strategy among our 20 featured MNCs in China is merging with or acquiring local firms. Consultants expect this strategy to be used increasingly going forward. For many firms, mergers and acquisitions (M&As) offer the benefits of a JV partnership without the risks and threats.

Conclusion

As one of our interviewees explained, China is a "dog fight." Another described China as the "most competitive" market in the world. MNCs find all of their familiar global rivals in China, and some may have been there for up to 20 years. Meanwhile, domestic competitors are leaping ahead in quality, sophistication, and speed. Many international companies are now squeezed by local players adept at replicating their best product features while slashing selling prices. The necessary survival skills for China now are innovation, speed, flexibility, marketing, and careful tracking of consumer preferences.

SUMMARY OF TIPS

FACING COMPETITORS

1. Pick Winnable Battles

For MNCs targeting the China market, there are some battles not worth fighting. Avoid competing against domestic cost-based products.

2. Innovate

The best survival strategy is to keep moving, continually upgrade to stay ahead of competitors.

3. But Beware of Over-innovation

Avoid over-engineered products. Offer quality and functionality that matches demand, but don't lose sight of cost.

4. Don't Fight, Merge

If you can't beat 'em, join 'em (or buy 'em).

Chapter 6
Battling Intellectual Property Rights Infringers

"The more successful you are [in China], the more IPR issues you will suffer from."

David Chang, CEO, Philips China

Introduction

It takes only a day or two for most visitors to China to find evidence of the extent of intellectual property infringement taking place in the nation. On their first stroll away from their international hotel, travelers will find markets peddling phony Gucci bags, North Face jackets, and Nike shoes, or street-side vendors with carts full of pirated new-release Hollywood (and Bollywood and European) movies. The pirates are hard to beat in terms of selection; some films are on offer in China via street peddlers before they are officially released in their home market. (The pirates obtain pre-released copies, or make their own handheld films during a movie preview.) The counterfeiters are also masters at delivering convenience and low price. In Shanghai, for example, it is common for vendors to slip from pub to pub, inviting patrons to shop for an appealing film or TV series from their barstool—all for less than US$1 per DVD.

China's pirating of film, music, and software is well known, but the nation's IPR violations extend far beyond DVDs, reaching into such alarming sectors as pharmaceuticals, pesticides, and automobiles. China has been consistently rated as one of the world's most serious violators of intellectual property rights for the past 25 years. Beginning in 1989, the U.S. government has consistently ranked the nation as one of its worst offending trade partners in its annual assessment by the office of the U.S. Trade Representative. Since then, China has either been listed as a Priority Foreign Country or been included on the more-serious Priority Watch List—a status that requires monitoring under the U.S. Trade Law. In May 2005, China was again "upgraded" to the Priority Watch List, together with India and Brazil, due to "serious concerns" about compliance with the WTO Agreement and other international agreements. Both U.S. and European government sources estimate that 15% to 20% of all consumer goods in China are fake products.[1]

European governments and companies are also highly concerned. The amount of counterfeit products intercepted at the

1 U.S. Department of Commerce website; European Commission, *EU-China Business Summit Report* (2004).

EU border by the Customs patrols of member states is increasing rapidly. In 2002, fake products to the value of 85 million euros were seized; in 2003, 50 million euros-worth were seized in the first six months alone. Among these fake goods, 60% originated in China. In fact, since 2001, more MNCs worldwide are noting the growth in exports of phony products from China—a factor of the increasing sophistication and globalization of piracy operations.

> *"Each of the 20 multinational companies profiled in this book, with the exception of Airbus, has suffered directly from at least some degree of IPR infringement in China."*
>
> **The authors,** *China CEO*

Exactly how widespread is counterfeiting and other IPR violations in China? One oft-quoted estimate within business circles is that one-fifth of China's economy is dependent upon counterfeiting. Pinpointing this figure is difficult, because few companies are willing or able to provide hard data to government or industry associations on the losses they incur. Jack Chang, chairman of the Quality Brand Protection Committee (QBPC) of the Beijing-based, 1,200-member China Association of Enterprises with Foreign Investment says that because of this reluctance and lack of a reliable formula, it is difficult to calculate the monetary loss, job loss, and tax loss caused by counterfeiting in China.

Each of the 20 multinational companies profiled in this book, with the exception of Airbus, has suffered directly from at least some degree of IPR infringement in China. But while Airbus China's Guy McLeod declares, "You can be sure all Airbus aircraft are made by our company; they are not made in Hunan [province] or somewhere else," another interviewee explained that the aircraft industry as a whole has not entirely escaped from reports of piracy. One China expert told us of an incident that took place in the mid-1980s. When placing an order for airplanes and aircraft engines, China had ordered more engines than plane bodies. "Why did they buy so many engines?" he asks. "What they were trying to do was to reverse-engineer the plane itself. Unfortunately, instead of using aluminum, they used steel, so the animal never got off the ground." During the past 20 years of economic development in China, the rule of thumb seems to be: anything that can be copied has been, and anything that cannot be copied, has been attempted.

Among our interviewees, those most troubled by counterfeiting, not surprisingly, are manufacturers of high-priced, easy-to-copy items such as software and luxury goods. However, our profiled companies have experienced pirated copycat goods in a wide spectrum of categories, from soda pop to laptops, cosmetics to cars. As Philips China's David Chang explains, "The more successful you are [in China], the more IPR issues you will suffer from."

One important point to stress: for all of our interviewees, IPR infringement represents a hindrance, but not a dire threat,

IPR Basics

What exactly are intellectual property rights? The term became more widely used after January 1995 when the World Trade Organization adopted the Trade-Related Aspects of Intellectual Property Rights (a.k.a. the TRIPS Agreement). This agreement was negotiated in the 1986–94 Uruguay Round of WTO negotiations in response to an increased need to protect ideas and knowledge in international trade, according to the WTO website.

The TRIPS Agreement details five types of intellectual property rights protection that WTO member countries must offer:

1. How basic principles of the trading system and other international intellectual property agreements should be applied.
2. How to give adequate protection to intellectual property rights.
3. How countries should enforce those rights adequately in their own territories.
4. How to settle disputes on intellectual property between members of the WTO.
5. Special transitional arrangements during the period when the new system is being introduced.

The agreement covers the following broad types of intellectual property: copyright, trademarks, geographical indications, industrial designs, patents, layout designs of integrated circuits, and trade secrets.

Copyright and related rights give the authors of literary and artistic works (books and other writings, musical compositions, paintings, sculpture, computer programs, to their success in China. Even Microsoft, which estimates that 90% of its branded product sold in China is counterfeit, is still growing aggressively in China and is optimistic about its long-term prospects (see below). In a 2004 survey by the QBPC of its 100-plus China-based companies, only five reported that the losses they were incurring in China due to IPR infringement were larger than their revenues. Most surveyed MNCs reported losing 5% to 15% of potential revenue to pirates—a danger, but not a disaster. None of our interviewees said that the problem of

and films) protection for a minimum period of 50 years after the death of the author. Copyrights also protect actors, singers, musicians, and other performers, plus the producers of sound recordings and broadcasting organizations. The main social purpose of protection of copyright and related rights is to encourage and reward creative work.

Industrial property rights include the protection of distinctive signs—in particular, trademarks (which distinguish the goods or services of one undertaking from those of other undertakings) and geographical indications (which identify a good as originating in a place where a given characteristic of the good is essentially attributable to its geographical origin).

To establish protection, patents, industrial designs, integrated circuit designs, geographical indications, and trademarks must be officially registered. The registration includes a description of what is being protected—the invention, design, brand name, or logo—and this description is public information. Copyright and trade secrets are protected automatically according to specified conditions. They need not be registered.

Other conditions may also differ—for example, the length of time that each type of protection remains in force.

Concerning enforcement, as the WTO website states: "[H]aving intellectual property laws is not enough[;] they have to be enforced." The TRIPS Agreement states that WTO member governments must ensure that IPR can be enforced under their laws, and that the penalties for infringement are tough enough to deter violations.

lack of adequate IP protection was large enough to deter them from aggressive investment into China. The *2005 Business Climate Survey* conducted by the American Chambers of Commerce based in Beijing and Shanghai found that, while 80% of the 450 companies surveyed said China's IPR enforcement is "ineffective" or "totally ineffective," those companies polled were also distinctly positive about the overall business outlook. Fully 86% of companies polled saw revenue increase from 2004 to 2005; while in 2005, 87% saw their level of business activity in China increase and 79% named China as their company's "top foreign direct investment destination." Thus, while IPR concerns are serious in some industries, they should be considered within the context of an otherwise extremely attractive market.

This chapter starts with a brief explanation of China's long history of IPR infringement; it then turns to our interviewees for front-line accounts and advice on fighting China's pirates.

China's Long History of IPR Infringement

Consider this quote: *"The Chinese are very ingenious at imitation. They have imitated to perfection whatsoever they have seen brought out of Europe. In the province of Canton, they have counterfeited several things so exactly that they sell them inland [as] goods brought out from Europe."* [2]

These words aptly express the mix of awe and frustration many of our interviewees voiced in describing counterfeiting and other IPR infringements in China. But there is one large difference between the speaker quoted above, Domingo Navarrete, and the 28 international managers and consultants we interviewed: it was after a visit to China in 1659 that Navarrete made this statement.

Our point is: the production of fake goods has a very long

[2] Jonathan D. Spence, *The Chan's Great Continent* (New York: Norton and Company, Inc., 1998).

tradition in China. It is also a widespread practice and, in many ways, has been a rather well-respected practice. The concept of a single person or single company holding exclusive intellectual property rights to a work of art has not been well developed in Chinese culture and society. Consider the fact that traditional Chinese art is largely based on the ability of apprentices to replicate exactly a master's work.

Second, in a broad sense, Chinese culture is based largely on the concept of supporting the collective group, rather than respecting individuals. During the Communist era, in particular, individual rights and individual property were strictly limited or even non-existent. Thus, even now, the concept of IPR remains misunderstood or not well supported, in many cases.

Third, the concept of rule of law is still rather new in China. Traditionally, Chinese societies have been monitored by government policy rather than by a body of law. "This is a country in which, traditionally, personal relationships and issues of power frequently dominated the outcome of disputes," says Norman Givant, Shanghai office managing partner for the China Practice Group at Freshfields Bruckhaus Deringer law offices. In other words, there is no "tradition of the sanctity of law" in China. As an example, another interviewee points out that contracts in China are "frequently breached without much thought." Understanding the problem begins with the realization that the concept of a formal legal system is still relatively new and only shallowly rooted in China. The mindset is best summed up by the saying, "In China, people obey people, not laws." In other words, China has for centuries operated under the rule of *guanxi* (rule of relationships) rather than Western-style rule of law.

> *"During the past 20 years of economic development in China, the rule of thumb seems to be: anything that can be copied has been, and anything that cannot be copied, has been attempted."*
>
> **The authors**, *China CEO*

Rule of Law Takes Root

During the upheaval of the 1940s to 1970s, China had no legal system, per se; instead, all legal power was held by government policy. "In the period of 1949 to 1979, the Chinese Communist Party wasn't terribly interested in the law and courts," says Givant. "What they were interested in was the exercise of government policy and power."

"

In the period of 1949 to 1979, the Chinese Communist Party wasn't terribly interested in the law and courts. What they were interested in was the exercise of government policy and power."

Norman Givant, Shanghai Office Managing Partner, China Practice Group, Freshfields Bruckhaus Deringer

This began changing in the 1980s under Deng Xiaoping, when the government began correcting the arbitrary regulatory decisions made during the Cultural Revolution and began creating a legal system that would attract investment. In recent years, China's lawmaking body, the National People's Congress (NPC), has passed a flurry of laws designed to attract investment and comply with WTO accession requirements. "They are putting the legal system in place," says Givant. In fact, he says, the NPC has been "in overdrive" in its rush to establish a full legal structure.

Legal experts and business executives agree that today, the problem with inadequate rule of law lies not with China's business-related laws, which are now—after years of reform in order to attract investment and to comply with the WTO—generally at or above international standards. Instead, the trouble lies mainly with enforcement.

Givant sums up the situation in this way: "You have a growing body of law to guide commercial behavior, but the real question is: do people view these laws as binding on them? And are there effective mechanisms in place for enforcing rights?" He points to Shanghai traffic as an example of the mindset of many Chinese citizens toward the law. At his neighborhood traffic light, whenever a traffic cop oversees morning traffic, drivers are extremely careful to follow every rule to avoid paying fines. But when the traffic cop is absent, the corner devolves into chaos—drivers make U-turns, motorcyclists ride on the wrong side of the street, and pedestrians struggle to jay-walk over traffic meridians.

IPR Enforcement

In the case of IPR, the gap between stiff laws and lax enforcement is particularly large. QBPC chairman Jack Chang stresses that China has created a broad range of IPR laws and regulations as well as an intellectual property tribunal at civil courts to hear IPR cases. "China has been responsive to the needs of its trading partners," he says. However, most of the counterfeiters run their operation "underground." In such cases, the brand owners generally cannot identify the counterfeiting party, let alone find and freeze their fixed assets—steps generally taken before initiating civil lawsuits.

One problem with the implementation of IP protection in China is that the country's court systems are notoriously undeveloped and prone to corruption. (For more on China's court system, see Chapter 8.) "Getting judgments in your favor is already problematic; enforcing them is doubly so," says legal expert Norman Givant. For one thing, central government decisions don't fully "carry downward" to provincial and municipal levels. Then, too, local officials and local law enforcers are geographically, as well as socially and culturally, "close" to the infringers and may sympathize with them over a foreign and distant legal IP holder. "If you look at local governments," says Givant, "the authorities have every vested interest in squelching intellectual property rights."

"

The problem is that officials have to execute the court decisions. The [enforcement officers and IPR infringers] still have their network; they rely on one another."

David Chang, CEO, Philips China

Our interviewees explained that, while lawmakers and the central government have bought into the need for protecting IPR, many local-level law enforcers have not yet done so. "The government could close down [fake] VCD makers. If every foreigner knows where to buy them, why don't the police know where they are?" asks Ekkehard Rathgeber of Bertelsmann Direct Asia. The problem is that IPR infringers are often well connected and therefore protected. "Corruption is part of the problem. A lot of people benefit from the [pirating] business," Rathgeber says.

Philips China's David Chang agrees that the laws exist, and the courts often rule to protect IPR, but the process tends to break down in the execution of legal decisions. Says Chang, "The [enforcement officers and IPR infringers] still have their network; they rely on one another." (For more on enforcement challenges, see the section below.)

Reports from the IP Battle Front

Airbus China's Guy McLeod shares a story that gives insight to the mindset of China's counterfeiters. "One of my close friends works for Coca-Cola. He told me that they once discovered a chap making fake Coca-Cola [in China]. They asked him how he could produce fake Coke. The man answered, 'Of course it is fake. The guys at Coca-Cola won't give me the recipe. If they keep it secret, how can I make real Coke?'" The main message from our interviewees is that respect for IPR is still new and undeveloped in China.

Coca-Cola China confirms that the company faces a continuing problem with producers of fake products. "Our brands are very famous worldwide brands, so there is obviously a strong motivation for counterfeiters," says Paul Etchells of Coca-Cola China Beverages. The problem is not large enough, however, to seriously damage business—he estimates that fake Coke products amount to less than 10% of his production volume, and adds that the local governments have proven helpful in cracking down when pirates are found. The biggest challenge Etchells faces is that it is so easy for pirates to start, and to restart. "We take action whenever we are aware of it. But shortly afterward, it all starts up again," he says. "These manufacturing operations are very small, and are located in all sorts of obscure places in this huge country." He has come to consider counterfeiting as "a cost of doing business" in China.

High-risk Industries: Software, Music, and Movies

Software is clearly one of the industries most affected by piracy. The U.S.-based Business Software Alliance estimates that 90% of all software used in China in 2005 was counterfeited. Not surprisingly, Microsoft suffers the most among our 20 profiled companies. The good news for Microsoft is that China's computer-using population has boomed to 80 million, the vast majority of whom are using Microsoft software. The bad news for the software giant is that, since only an estimated 10% of copies sold are legal, booming popularity does not mean booming business. Jun Tang of Microsoft China concedes that the "IPR problem is the biggest obstacle to our growth."

While a small fraction of fake MS Office software or other Microsoft products are sold to buyers who think they are buying authentic software, virtually all sales are made to consumers who know they are buying a low-cost fake. "In most cases, in the street, everybody knows it is an illegal copy," says Tang.

Tang has little hope of dramatic improvement in the short term. While Microsoft has hired personnel to track and stop IPR infringers, he says the real solution will come only after the need for IPR protection is felt among Chinese firms. He says the process is already under way. "Local software companies are facing the same IPR problems and high-level government officials know this," says Tang. "Microsoft is one victim, but the larger victim is [China's own] local software industry."

Another industry victimized by pirating is entertainment—movies and music on CD and DVD. Music CDs are one product on offer by Bertelsmann Direct Group Asia, making the company a prime target for piracy. Company president Ekkehard Rathgeber says his main competitor in the CD and DVD business in China is "illegal sales." It is the vast price differential that sends many customers to vendors for fake copies. Bertelsmann's legitimate copies sell for RMB80 to RMB100 (US$10 to $12); fakes sell for one-tenth that cost or less. Street prices for movies on DVD actually came down from 2003 to 2005, from RMB10 to RMB7 in many cases.

Worst of all for Bertelsmann, since the fake copies are digitally produced, the quality of bootleg DVDs can be virtually the same as legitimate ones. "The price difference is too huge; you have to be a saint not to buy [pirated copies]," says Rathgeber. Another advantage pirates have over legitimate sellers is accessibility; the government has long restricted imported music and films, allowing in only 10 international movies a year before WTO accession, and 20 per year since. In contrast, illegal vendors sell whatever titles they choose, selling them in subway stations, pedestrian underpasses, and at elementary school gates. "You see DVDs and VCDs anywhere, everywhere. You can buy them by the hundreds and thousands," says Rathgeber. Although perhaps one-third of fake music and movie CDs sold are of such poor quality that they cannot be listened to or watched, the low price makes the risk worthwhile.

With software, music, and films, there is a widespread mindset among Chinese consumers—and even among the authorities—that the licensed sellers are setting profit margins too high, says Rathgeber. He points out that if a DVD costs RMB1 to produce but sells for RMB80, RMB79 of the selling price is sent to an MNC outside China. In such a scenario, he says, law enforcement

"

We take action whenever we are aware of [IP infringement]. But shortly afterward, it all starts up again. These manufacturing operations are very small, and are located in all sorts of obscure places in this huge country."

Paul Etchells,
President, Coca-Cola Beverages China

> *You see DVDs and VCDs anywhere, everywhere. You can buy them by the hundreds and thousands."*
>
> **Ekkehard Rathgeber**, President, Bertelsmann Direct Group Asia

officers are "probably not very motivated" to protect wealthy and powerful foreign IPR holders.

As a result, many of the MNCs selling intellectual property-protected works in China are making little money. For example, Bertelsmann has had relatively little success selling its licensed CDs of U.S. jazz saxophonist Kenny G in China despite the jazz musician's widespread popularity. "Kenny G's music is heard everywhere [in China]—[in] all the shops, hotels," says Rathgeber. While Bertelsmann has sold roughly 50,000 copies of his works, as of 2003 the company believes millions of illegal copies have been sold.

Can a software or music company survive in China? Like Microsoft, Bertelsmann's strategy is to wait for the local market to mature. Says Rathgeber, "We cannot prevent people from copying. Our market is the growing legal market." The company is banking on demand growing eventually for high-quality legal products and for the extra convenience of purchasing online and requesting door-to-door delivery.

"Infringement is very much a critical issue," says Seiichi Kawasaki of Sony China. Because the company faces infringement in its software, games, and music products, it has set up specific departments in Beijing and Hong Kong to oversee IPR protection in China, in collaboration with the local government authorities.

Kawasaki will not estimate what percentage of Sony products sold in China are fakes, but says all company products are vulnerable, even low-end items such as batteries. Not only does piracy cut into Sony's profits and damage its name, but some fake products pose a health risk to consumers, he says.

Fighting Dangerous Counterfeiting: Chemicals and Pharmaceuticals

Another industry where piracy poses the problem not just of lost profits, but also of potential environmental or even health risks, is agro-chemicals. Production of fake Du Pont products, especially agricultural chemicals, has not only allowed pirates to "make a lot of money in a short time," according to company president for China Charles Browne, but has endangered the company's reputation with customers who don't realize they have purchased counterfeits. "We have to defend our trademark and reputation at all costs," he says. "Farmers are irritated with us because the products [pirated agricultural chemicals] they bought were defective." Most troubling, says Browne, is the health risk posed to consumers who don't realize they are buying produce grown with fake, unauthorized, unsafe pesticides, fungicides, or herbicides.

One of the most serious IPR problems China faces now is in counterfeiting of pharmaceutical products. The European Union Chamber of Commerce in China (EUCCC) estimates that 10% to 15% of all medicines sold in China are counterfeits. Such a volume of phony medicines has disastrous implications for public health. Our pharmaceutical industry interviewees said the Chinese government acknowledges the seriousness of the issue and has been cooperative in addressing it.

In addition to the health hazards posed by counterfeiting, multinational pharmaceutical companies are also concerned that unlicensed production of patented medicines cuts into sales from the companies that developed them. The result: corporate support for R&D into new medicines is squelched. Dr. Elmar Stachels of Bayer China voices the frustration common within his industry: "Everybody engaged in [pharmaceuticals] would like to see a return on their investment, otherwise there will be no research and development. The inventing of a substance takes many years. And when you have the substance, the manufacturing is only a small part of the cost. If somebody just copies the ingredients, they can save all the money spent on R&D and then offer lower prices. The price pressure really falls on those research-based companies."

In the field of pharmaceuticals, Eli Lilly China's Christopher Shaw stresses that progress is being made, not only in the passing of new patent laws but in the enforcement of them. "The new policies are very positive," he says, explaining that Eli Lilly can now receive 20-year patents on pharmaceutical products in China, a period that is "comparable to any country in the West." New laws also grant six years of data exclusivity—a time-span comparable to that of some European countries. Also, China's "patent linkage rule" stipulates that regulators should not approve a new drug unless it has been proved that there is no patent existing.

Shaw says, "While these are significant developments and the Chinese government is to be congratulated, there are still areas for development." In particular, he names the relatively long time required to gain market approval—a process that can take as much as three years longer in China than in other countries, effectively reducing the product's life span. Shortening the approval processes is "the next stage" for China's maturation in pharmaceutical regulation.

The Most Frequently Encountered IPR Challenges

While situations vary from industry to industry, the MNC top executives we interviewed identified several central challenges, which nearly all had encountered in protecting their intellectual property rights in China:

- Lack of governmental support
- Small fines, big rewards
- Sophisticated pirates
- Internationalized infringement

Challenge #1: Lack of Governmental Support

International managers in China explained that in seeking support for their IP protection, they often find a subtle but widespread attitude of tolerance for IP infringements. This *laissez-faire* attitude is especially widespread at the local government level—a phenomenon our consultant interviewees say is typical for developing countries.

After all, a primary goal for the Chinese government is to see the country develop and prosper as quickly as possible. Therefore, especially a decade ago, "reverse engineering" of high-value foreign-made products seemed a logical method for upgrading manufacturing. "The idea was: Buy one, copy it, and go from there," says one interviewee. "And that mentality still prevails in many instances. If China can copy something, then they save themselves a great deal of foreign exchange by producing it here."

Ekkehard Rathgeber explains the thinking of many Chinese officials, especially in the rural areas: "My people are poor; people in western China are making RMB200 (US$24) per month. Now a bunch of foreigners want me to protect their Gucci handbags? I couldn't care less."

China's serious unemployment problem also plays into the underlying tolerance of IPR infringement. While the official target unemployment rate is around 4.7%, this figure underreports the problem. First, it does not include unemployed or under-employed agricultural workers, a group that still accounts for more than half of China's population. Second, the rate includes only those urban residents who are officially registered as unemployed—ignoring migrant workers who come to China's cities from the countryside and laid-off workers who receive only a basic stipend. Taking these factors into account, many Chinese analysts put the unemployment rate at 8% to 10%. With this lack of jobs in mind, many officials and law enforcers consider the local economy to be better off with piracy than without it.

Norman Givant agrees that encouraging IPR protections can be a hard sell. "There are many vested interests protecting and preserving the counterfeiters, for many reasons—employing redundant workers, generating profits and tax revenues, and even developing export markets."

He gives an example: "You have a factory in a province in the heartland of China that is making antiquated products that have no market; it also has the heavy burden of a redundant workforce. All of a sudden, it finds that it can start ripping off branded products and selling them. It now has a product it can market domestically or export to countries that are not interested in IPR but are interested in price. It is providing workers who would otherwise go on the dole with a job, and is now supplying the local government with taxes." All these factors are skewed against the protection of IPR.

"

My people are poor; people in western China are making RMB200 (US$24) per month. Now a bunch of foreigners want me to protect their Gucci handbags? I couldn't care less."

Ekkehard Rathgeber, President, Bertelsmann Direct Group Asia (explaining the mindset of many rural officials)

In some small, remote Chinese cities, Philip Murtaugh of General Motors China comments, the majority of the population may depend on counterfeiting as their livelihood. In such a scenario, an IPR crack-down would be disastrous for townspeople and the government. "It is impossible to shut down the only livelihood of the whole city; the city loses 95% of its tax revenue," Murtaugh says. "If you were running the government, you wouldn't do that."

Our interviewees generally agreed that the worst gaps in IP enforcement today take place at the local government level. QBPC chairman Jack Chang says officials at some county and city entities are "not yet determined to fight," because there is too much to lose in many rural villages. Until the economic scenario changes and there are more incentives to switch to legitimate work, IPR infringements will likely remain a significant concern for MNCs and Chinese domestic industries in China for some years.

However, despite the general agreement among interviewees that IP enforcement is lacking in China, many said the attitude of the authorities is improving, especially those in the central government. Most of our interviewees who had fought specific IP violations had found government officials to be helpful. British Petroleum China's Dr. Gary Dirks says that when the company faced cases of counterfeited lubricants, the government was responsive. "When we have been able to provide the authorities with evidence about what is going on, by and large, they have been very good at cleaning things up," he says.

Bayer China also has experienced cooperation from the government. Company CEO Dr. Elmar Stachels says, "The interest [of the Chinese government] in supporting us with regards to IPR protection is increasing. [For example], the government acted very cooperatively in a large project concerning a heart disease medicine. We found some counterfeiting, and we went to court. The court ruled in our favor and the fake medicine was destroyed."

Challenge #2: Small Fines, Big Rewards

One of the biggest problems is China's history of light punishment for IPR infringement. Most fines levied amount to between

RMB10,000 and RMB100,000 (US$1,200 – US$12,000)—an amount far lower than the potential profits for many counterfeiting operations. The Administration for Industry & Commerce (AIC) may fine infringers up to three times the value of the illegal operation, but no minimum fee has been set. Also, if the value of the illegal operations cannot be determined, the AIC uses its discretion to set the fine. In such cases, there is no minimum fine and the maximum is set at RMB100,000. One consultant interviewee explained that China's IPR regulations generally state only the maximum amount that a court or administrative authority can impose on infringers, leaving actual fines to the discretion of court personnel. "Our observation is that the actual fines or penalties given out so far are not very high," he says.

And even if fines are increased, tougher regulations will not solve all problems for companies defending their IPR. One interviewee tells of a recent raid in which the counterfeiters escaped punishment by arguing that they were not planning to sell the products, but were only collecting and then destroying them.

Challenge #3: Sophisticated Pirates

After 15 years of booming business, counterfeiting and other IPR infringements in China are now sophisticated sectors. While China's central government has become more focused on fighting IPR over the past decade, infringers have become far more difficult to stop. As their wealth has grown, so has the technology used in production, distribution, and even surveillance. Today, pirating is often a complex, large-scale business, with R&D and product design taking place in an urban center while actual production happens in a scattering of remote Chinese villages where law enforcement is relatively weak. Counterfeiters often spread their operations across several provinces so that when one production center is detected, others can continue production. Some counterfeiters also operate legitimate businesses as a cover, making it even easier to shift pirating operations whenever the law enforcement officers close in.

Paolo Gasparrini of L'Oréal China describes the situation concisely: "The problem is that you close down one [counterfeiter], and another one opens somewhere else." Attorney Norman Givant puts it this way: "You cut off one counterfeiter and two spring up in his place. Sometimes, they are the same persons with different names. And sometimes, they may close their factory, give the equipment to their brothers-in-law, and open a new facility in the village down the road."

"

You cut off one counterfeiter and two spring up in his place. Sometimes, they are the same persons with different names. And sometimes, they may close their factory, give the equipment to their brothers-in-law, and open a new facility in the village down the road."

Norman Givant, Office Managing Partner, China Practice Group, Freshfields Bruckhaus Deringer

Challenge #4: Internationalized Infringement

One alarming recent change is the growing percentage of China-made fake products being exported to major international markets. The Quality Brand Protection Committee (QBPC) reports that counterfeiters now often operate at international trade fairs, directly competing with legitimate competitors by soliciting sales from international trading companies.

In a growing percentage of cases, pirating operations are controlled by operators outside China, QBPC chairman Jack Chang says, such as from the Middle East and South Asia. "We know that a lot of counterfeiting products are exported from China. During raids [in rural China], we found packages marked 'Made in France' or 'Made in Italy.'" Today, Chinese manufacturers are being approached by international counterfeiting groups. They bring samples to China and look for local manufacturers.

In the *2005 Business Climate Survey* (from the American Chambers of Commerce based in Shanghai and Beijing), 9% of responding companies claimed that IPR infringement in China is causing "material damage to global operations." The two chambers (in the *2005 White Paper on American Business in China*) urge the Chinese, EU, and U.S. governments to increase Customs interception activities and to improve three-way cooperation in cross-border criminal investigations.

The globalization of IPR infringement does not bode well for combating—or even containing—the problem, Chang says. He points out that many factors are helping to expand, not reduce, the piracy business: liberalized trading rights, increased manufacturing in China, and growing expertise among counterfeiters in selling their products internationally. "The high potential profits will attract more people into this underground economic system," says Chang.

Although Chinese police and Customs are now focusing on these emerging challenges in protecting IPR, Chang says infringers are also adapting themselves quickly to the new legal environment. Thus, Chang expects the IP battle to continue in China until at least the turn of the decade.

One current focus of the QBPC is to promote international cooperation in fighting piracy. Chang argues that the international community should recognize that counterfeiting is a global problem and "start working together, rather than pointing fingers at each other." While counterfeiters now cooperate across borders, law enforcement entities often face restrictions in working with their international counterparts. "We have not yet seen enforcement agencies cooperate systematically and effectively across borders," says Chang. As a first step, he applauds efforts by both the WTO and INTERPOL to establish channels for information-sharing among law enforcement entities throughout Asia.

Strategies for Battling IPR Pirates

Because 19 of our 20 top executive interviewees had directly experienced IPR infringement of their company products in China, most had strategies in place for addressing the problem. Some companies had established sophisticated IP protection systems. In addition, the business consultants we profiled regularly give advice on handling infringement. This section synthesizes the six main strategies of our interviewees for battling infringement.

Strategy #1: Work Positively With Government

One of the messages from our 28 China experts is that the central government is generally more sympathetic and more efficient at addressing the IPR concerns of MNCs than are local government entities. Says L'Oréal China's Paolo Gasparrini: "At the central government level, they understand [about IPR]. The key is to get the cooperation of the government at all levels."

If any company should know intimately about fighting counterfeiting, it is Microsoft, since 90% of the product sold in China bearing its name is fake. One way to win support at the local level, advises Microsoft China's Jun Tang, is to ask local government entities to lead by example, signing (and enforcing) agreements not to purchase counterfeit product. Microsoft has signed an agreement with the Shanghai Municipal People's Government to legalize every single piece of software in every computer throughout its offices. This policy of "zero compromise on illegal copies" has established a model for Microsoft to introduce to other government agencies, arguing that if the Shanghai government has adopted such a policy, they should too.

Once government entities have accepted such agreements, Tang believes individual companies—and even individual consumers—in China will also sign on. "We are very confident. It takes time, but we will see these things improve," he says. Tang adds that such battles are not limited to China. "Even in Western countries, you don't have 100% IPR protection. Individual or small organizations will still use illegal software."

Jack Chang gives specific advice to member companies of the QBPC on working successfully with government entities on IPR. First, he says the committee learned a very important lesson soon after it launched: based on first-hand experience, he strongly advises MNCs not to adopt a confrontational attitude concerning IPR violations. Such an attitude alienates the Chinese government, putting them on the defensive. "We have learned to be patient," he says. "We decided to make it our mission to work cooperatively with the Chinese government. We realized that confrontation will not get us anywhere."

Chang says the QBPC benefited quickly after adopting a sympathetic stance. "Because we changed our mindset from frustration to cooperation, we gradually saw the government's mindset change as well," he says. "When we were sort of pushing, the Chinese government became defensive. But when we became cooperative and patient, they listened to us. Gradually, they became cooperative as well. Now they have even become proactive, approaching QBPC members to see if they can help our members with difficult cases." Chang advises companies to relay a similar message to government, stressing that "we're in this fight together."

One of the most effective methods the QBPC has used to foster goodwill and cooperation with law enforcement agencies is to organize awards for honourable IPR achievement—such as cases in which police refuse bribe offers or in which police cooperate effectively with Customs or other entities to solve a crime.

The QBPC launched the awards in 2002, recognizing the 10 best cases of honest and effective law enforcement action against IPR violations. To add clout to the awards, winning law enforcement officials were brought to Beijing and presented with the award by the minister or vice minister of commerce—a move that gave the awards critical weight with recipients. By 2005, the awards competition had attracted 27 cases competing for 10 awards.

In an effort to win the support of local governments, the QBPC recognizes their IP protection efforts and includes them in the awards. Chang says enthusiasm has grown for the awards program in China's less developed inner provinces (such as Sichuan and Shaanxi), since these regions are now aggressively seeking foreign investment.

Finally, the QBPC also selects four government agencies to receive "outstanding achievement" awards, thus building support among Customs, inspection, and quarantine entities, and other enforcement agencies involved with IPR. "The purpose of these awards is to build good role models. When you recognize and reward people's sense of honor, it makes a difference," says Chang. Showing the ultimate governmental approval for the QBPC's work—and a 180-degree change from the hostile relations with government in the past—China's vice premier Wu Yi referred to the QBPC as "my capable right-hand assistant" at a meeting with international business executives in 2004.

> "
>
> ***When we became cooperative and patient, [the government] listened to us. Gradually, they became cooperative as well. Now they have even become proactive, approaching QBPC members to see if we can help with difficult cases."***
>
> **Jack Chang**, Chairman, Quality Brand Protection Committee, China Association of Enterprises with Foreign Investment

Strategy #2: Join Forces

One of the most effective methods for fighting piracy is also one of the most difficult to conduct: lobbying for change by banding

TIP When approaching the Chinese government for support in protecting IPR, avoid taking a confrontational stance; seek to help the government in its work to fight infringement.

together with other companies in the same industry. Working with competitors on this common problem, and sharing information on solutions, is a hard sell in China's super-competitive arena, but our interviewees who have tried this route, swear by it.

Paolo Gasparrini of L'Oréal China admits the company faces counterfeiting. Famous-brand cosmetics such as those owned by L'Oréal are a preferred target for counterfeiters. Gasparrini says L'Oréal has benefited from teaming up with fellow cosmetic or skin-care product companies to fight the practice. "We are very active together with other companies [on this] because it is a big problem, especially in some areas," he says.

An example of a more narrowly focused industry group is the Research & Development-based Pharmaceutical Association in China (RDPAC), consisting of 40-some member companies. The RDPAC focuses strictly on pharmaceutical industry concerns, including IPR.

Another function of industry associations is to assist and encourage government and law enforcement personnel. For instance, QBPC jointly runs an annual training program with police officers specializing in economic crime. Jack Chang says the program now operates smoothly despite getting off to a rough start. "When the QBPC first started organizing programs with the police, nobody knew us," says Chang. "Initially, 50% of the officers left the meeting during the QBPC member presentation, saying: 'We have been police officers for 20 years—why should we listen to them?' But once the police started listening to us, they realized that we know what we are talking about and we were able to work together."

One goal for the QBPC at present is to enhance criminal enforcement of IP laws; China has traditionally relied on administrative enforcement for IPR, which tends to result in lighter consequences for infringers. As a step toward this outcome, a judicial interpretation issued in December 2004 lowers the bar on the types of counterfeiting that can be considered as "criminal" offences.

Creating awareness among Chinese consumers is another tactic used by the QBPC and other industry associations. "If only 5% or 10% of consumers change their mindset, it will make a big change," says Chang. But achieving such a switch in consumer thinking is extremely difficult. In a 2000 study of 2,500 Chinese consumers on IPR awareness, the results were "pretty discouraging," according to Chang. "They said they didn't care about counterfeiting as long as the quality was acceptable, and that buying counterfeit goods only damages the foreign brand owners, who are not their concern."

TIP **Join forces with other businesses and associations in the IPR battle to share best practices and present a common front to the government.**

Chang points out that Chinese consumers are not the only buyers of counterfeit goods in China. Many tourists, including Western businesspeople working for MNCs, visit local markets for counterfeit souvenirs. "We are sorry to see that the employees of multinational brand owners who come to China for business meetings look for and buy counterfeit goods," says Chang. In that situation, it is difficult to convince Chinese consumers that they should respect IPR laws. He is pushing for the creation of

Quality Brand Protection Committee

The Quality Brand Protection Committee of the China Association of Enterprises with Foreign Investment was officially launched in China on March 2, 2000. As of 2005, it had attracted 120 multinational companies concerned with the impact of counterfeiting. QBPC members represent more than US$40 billion in investment in China.

The committee's mission is "to work cooperatively with the Chinese central and local governments, local industry, and other organizations to make positive contributions to intellectual property efforts in the People's Republic of China." Its main goals are to represent its membership in lobbying for improvements to IPR protections in China and to serve as a bridge between China and the international community in this effort.

The QBPC achieves these goals by working with government to improve legislation and strengthen enforcement of IP protections and to deepen public awareness of the importance of IPR. The committee also assists members in improving their in-house IP protection systems. The activities of the QBPC are supported by nine industry working groups and by sub-committees focusing on: Best Practices/Enforcement, Communications, Customs, Government Cooperation, Legal Issues, Membership Services, and Patents.

TIP **Dedicate resources and personnel to protecting IPR in-house. Build awareness and support for IP protection throughout the company.**

public service announcements, ideally promoted by celebrities, to deliver the message that buying pirated goods means supporting child labor and criminals. On the other hand, refusing to buy fake goods will kill the pirating industry.

Strategy #3: Dedicate In-house Resources

Among the MNCs profiled in this book, different companies had adopted vastly different in-house IP protection strategies based on the significance of the problem to their operations. British Petroleum China operates an IPR "security group" to seek out and report on infringers. Says BP China's Dr. Gary Dirks, "Our people are trained to be very vigilant about counterfeit products. We are pretty aggressive about going after counterfeiters." L'Oréal China has hired a full-time monitor of IP infringements. Meanwhile, Unilever China has dedicated a 12-person team to work with government agencies on IPR. Although the company's China chairman, Alan Brown, says the expansion of retailing via supermarkets and hypermarkets has cut down on IP violations, problems continue to exist. He declares: "[Fighting counterfeiting] is a constant battle. The bigger the brand, the more copyright issues you face."

For most MNCs, QBPC's Jack Chang recommends establishing a coordinated global brand protection system, with personnel sharing information from key infringement centers. In a survey of 100 QBPC members, only 30 companies had established global anti-counterfeiting measures and had set aside specific resources, while 40 companies reported dedicating resources for fighting counterfeiting in the Asia-Pacific region. Chang urges member companies to increase the financial and human resources dedicated to this fight.

Strategy #4: Focus on Prevention

Another QBPC recommendation is that companies in China shift their IPR strategy from "fire-fighting" to "fire prevention." Jack Chang points out that catching and deterring individual IPR infringers is very difficult. Instead, companies can benefit from focusing on preventing future infringement.

First, he urges companies to conduct an "IP audit." Many companies lack an exact knowledge of the areas in which they are vulnerable to attack from counterfeiters.

Second, Chang stresses that it is critical for international companies in China to obtain full buy-in on fighting infringement from senior management. That means dedicating time to talking directly to government authorities on the issue.

The top executive should also convey a sense of urgency on the issue to the entire company so that employees are encouraged to act as the eyes and ears of the organization, reporting IPR infringements whenever they are discovered. Another tactic is to encourage the entire supply chain—including upstream and downstream suppliers—to become involved in detecting IPR infringements. Many of our interviewees stressed that companies must develop a clear code of ethics regarding IPR—offering ethics training for all employees and suppliers—and must enforce punishment when the rules of ethically protecting IP are broken.

Catching counterfeiters involves gathering evidence, then working with the police to conduct raids. Particularly worrisome, says Chang, is a new trend: pirates are penetrating the downstream supply chain of legitimate manufacturers and buying raw materials and packaging components. He urges companies to assess their entire supply-chain system to close any loopholes that are allowing infringers to make inroads.

As another way to bolster prevention, Chang is lobbying the government to instruct the electric power bureau not to supply 380-voltage industrial power to civilian residences. During raids, he has found that most of the production facilities used by counterfeiters require 380-voltage power to operate. Cutting off this power supply would leave 80% of the underground counterfeiting plants unable to run their machines.

Strategy #5: Use Contractual Safeguards

For white-collar professionals, China's job market is an employee's market. Turnover rates of 20% annually for professional staff, especially at the management or specialist level, are now

TIP Top executives should personally convey the importance of IP protection to employees and to the government. Conduct company-wide IP audits to detect vulnerable areas.

common in many industries, our HR consultant interviewees said. Many firms struggle to recruit and retain professional staff, and poaching is rampant between competing firms.

HR shortages relate directly to IPR concerns, because when employees leave, they take with them the knowledge they gained in their previous company, including intellectual property information. Certainly, knowledge of a competitor's business operations—especially IP secrets—is a powerful draw for poachers from competing companies. Another potential threat: employees quit, then use inside knowledge of their former employer's IP systems to launch their own competing enterprise.

While it is extremely difficult for an MNC to prevent former employees from selling company secrets after they have left the company, managers can take some preventative actions. In order to attract investors, municipal governments in Beijing and Shanghai have adopted labor regulations giving trademark holders the option of including in employment contracts either a three-year non-compete clause or a six-month prior notice to resign clause. Jack Chang is unsure how effective these regulations will prove, but stresses that the rules "at least indicate that Shanghai and Beijing want to provide more benefit to investors. They offer more legal methods for protecting IP rights."

Similar safeguards also can be written into employment contracts with JV partners and suppliers, especially when the partnerships involve access to corporate technology or other specialized know-how.

Strategy #6: Protect Sensitive Technology

Another method recommended by our interviewees for protecting your corporate technology in China is: keep it out of China. Unfortunately for China, in some cases the consultants we have profiled recommend this method to their clients. The *2005 White Paper on American Business in China*, published by the American Chambers of Commerce based in Shanghai and Beijing, shows that chamber member companies are using this method to protect IP. In a survey of member companies of the two chambers, 73%

of U.S. high-tech companies polled said that poor IPR protection "influences" their R&D investment into China. In other words, companies are thinking twice, and in some cases withholding research investment, due to concerns over IP protection.

At Freshfields Bruckhaus Deringer law offices, Norman Givant advises his clients to be cautious when bringing technology to China. "For technology that is critical to the long-term survival of the company, it's better not to bring it here," he says. "If it's copied, it's not only the business in China that will be adversely affected—its corporate existence may be challenged."

For technology that must be brought to China, it is critically important that companies ensure that all patents, trademarks, and copyrights imported into China are registered and recognized there. Holding a patent registered in your home country or elsewhere does not ensure protection within China.

Once the key technology is in China, managers should ensure that it is not easily accessible to unauthorized employees. They should also divide the dissemination of sensitive information so that no single person has access to the complete technology. Interviewees also stress the importance of conducting a thorough background check on all personnel who will be given access to critical corporate information.

TIP **Be extremely selective in giving employees or business partners access to core technologies. Be clear on the regulatory tools available to employers in protecting against employee misuse of critical IP information.**

Conclusion

IPR infringement is a huge industry in China with a very long history. While China has recently improved its IP protection laws, especially since joining the WTO in 2001, enforcement remains weak. Nearly all MNCs in China experience piracy of their products. (Among our profile companies, only Airbus was exempt.) Of particular concern is piracy of such products as pharmaceuticals and chemicals, in which public safety is at risk. Enforcement suffers partly because the rule of law remains shallowly rooted in China, and because piracy is a key source of economic activity in many parts of the nation. Challenges faced by MNCs include: lack of government support (especially at the

TIP **Create safety mechanisms to limit employee or partner access to core technologies. In some cases, companies may not want to bring critical technology to China.**

China's IPR Future: Bleak or Bright?

Given the breadth, depth, and sophistication of China's underground IPR infringement industry, what hope should MNCs have for improvement in the future? Our interviewees looked to other developing Asian countries in answering this question.

Kenneth Yu of 3M Greater China says: "The problem I see today in China in terms of protection of copyright is very similar to what I saw in Taiwan in the 1980s. You could buy a Rolex look-alike in Taiwan in the 1980s for US$20. This is no different from China or other developing economies. When the economy is developing quickly, people tend to take shortcuts. But as the economy develops further, the host government will do a better job of regulating."

Dr. Ernst Behrens of Siemens China agrees. "I always compare this situation with Japan and Taiwan 25 years ago. I think [IPR infringement] will diminish over time because there are more and more local companies which have the same interest in IPR protection that we have."

Most of our interviewees voiced the belief that, once a significant volume of Chinese companies develop IP products needing protecting, law enforcement will improve. Legal expert Norman Givant of Freshfields Bruckhaus Deringer aptly declares, "Only when the Chinese authorities see that the domestic industry is affected by counterfeiting, and only when domestic industries start clamoring for more stringent IP protection, will the government be persuaded to see that it is actually in China's long-term interest to have a strict system of IP protection."

Ekkehard Rathgeber of Bertelsmann Direct Group Asia shares the same opinion: "When will the problem be solved? When you have local companies suffering from the same thing—local music industry, movies, software. If the government wants these domestic industries to develop, they need to take action."

There are signs that such a change is under way in China. Data from the State Trademark Bureau shows that between 2000 and 2004, 90% of the 91,000 IPR enforcement actions undertaken in China involved protecting the rights of domestic firms. As local firms fight for protection of their IP rights, enforcement should improve and the overall environment for IP protection should benefit greatly.

local level); rewards outweigh the risks for many infringers; and growing sophistication and internationalization of many piracy operations. China's IPR infringement industries will likely die down with economic development (as has been the case in other developing countries). The true key to improving enforcement will likely come when more Chinese businesses begin fighting to protect their own intellectual property rights.

SUMMARY OF TIPS

BATTLING CHINA'S IPR INFRINGERS

EXTERNAL MEASURES

1. Work With the Government

When approaching the Chinese government for support in protecting IPR, avoid taking a confrontational stance; seek to help the government in its work to fight infringement.

2. Join Forces With Others

Join forces with other businesses and associations in the IPR battle to share best practices and present a common front to the government.

INTERNAL MEASURES

1. Dedicate Resources

Dedicate resources and personnel to protecting IPR in-house. Build awareness and support for IP protection throughout the company.

2. Focus on Prevention

Top executives should personally convey the importance of IP protection to employees and to the government. Conduct company-wide IP audits to detect vulnerable areas.

3. Use Contractual Safeguards

Be extremely selective in giving employees or business partners access to core technologies. Be clear on the regulatory tools available to employers in protecting against employee misuse of critical IP information.

4. Protect Sensitive Technologies

Create safety mechanisms to limit employee or partner access to core technologies. In some cases, companies may not want to bring critical technology to China.

Chapter 7
Winning Over Chinese Consumers

"It is impossible to sell second-rate technology in China. Chinese want the best. China is often the first place we introduce a new technology. Chinese are very demanding customers."

Dominique de Boisseson, Chairman and CEO, Alcatel China

INSIDE CHAPTER 7

Introduction

The place: the city of Wuhan, Hubei province, central China. The scene: a crowd of incredulous onlookers and news-hungry reporters gather around a sparkling-white Mercedes SLK230 convertible sedan. Given the okay from the car's businessman owner, two young men with sledge-hammers approach the car. As the TV cameras roll, the men swing at the car, shattering the windshield, twisting the steering wheel. Within minutes, the US$85,000 sports car is dented and battered.

The reason: car owner Wang Sheng is angry at Mercedez-Benz for selling him what he considers a sub-par automobile. Wang told reporters he began experiencing problems with his car within days of purchasing it. After five attempts to have it repaired, and several attempts to return it to Mercedes, Wang took drastic measures. The story made the evening news in China and newswire headlines internationally.

In response, Mercedes claimed that Wang's car troubles were the result of his using improper fuel, not of quality problems. After the public car-pounding, the company reportedly threatened to sue Wang but later reconsidered. Even if there were no faults with the car, Mercedes-Benz does seem to have made one mistake: that of misjudging Wang and vastly underestimating the lengths to which a Chinese consumer would go if dissatisfied.

Meet the new Chinese consumer: demanding, outspoken, full of attitude.

Although few Chinese customers would go to the extremes of Wang Sheng, international managers familiar with the Mercedes case tend not to be shocked. Among the top executives interviewed for this book, most described Chinese consumers as extremely tough customers. Particularly in the urban areas, a growing percentage of the population possess the maddening combination of being demanding, worldly, impatient, price conscious and, worst of all, fickle.

This chapter discusses first the challenges foreign managers of MNCs face in winning over customers in today's China. We begin by detailing the expansion of the consumer population in terms of population size, spending power, and expectations. We then discuss challenges to reaching consumers, and conclude with the advice of our interviewees on best practices for reaching China's evolving and demanding consumers.

"

A lot of people come to China assuming that Chinese customers' expectations are low. What I've found out is that consumer expectations are much higher in China than in other countries, such as Japan. My impression is that Chinese consumers are among the most sophisticated in the world."

Philip Murtaugh, General Manager and CEO, General Motors China

The Lure of 1.3 Billion Customers

Securing a slice of the Chinese market is crucial to the global business strategies of many MNCs for the simple reason that the growth potential of the nation vastly outshines that of virtually any other market worldwide. The world's most populous nation now offers a consumer base that is not only vast but also wealthy, worldly, and willing to spend. All of this is good news for MNCs bringing their goods and services to an increasingly open China. Average annual per capita income nationwide increased from US$267 in 1994[1] to over US$1,000 in 2003 and should reach nearly US$8,000 for Shanghai residents by 2007 (as stated in our Foreword). Per capita annual consumer expenditure also increased dramatically in the past decade. Spending on housing has soared—as people have moved away from subsidized housing to renting or purchasing their own apartment. Nationwide, average annual housing spending rose from US$12 per capita in 1994 to US$50 in 2004. During the same years, spending on transportation and communications jumped from US$17 to US$90, while spending on education and leisure rose from US$16 to US$56 per year.[2]

In China's urban centers, consumer spending is soaring much faster than the national average, as more families are buying their own apartment and increasing spending on pricier lifestyle items such as telecommunications and vacations. In terms of durable goods, some 95% of Chinese urban households now own the big-ticket household items of a color TV, refrigerator, and washing machine. This figure drops to 30% in rural areas.[3] The rate

1 Economist Intelligence Unit statistics, 2004.

2 *China Statistical Yearbook, 2004.*

3 Economist Intelligence Unit statistics, 2004.

of Chinese urbanites owning a home-use PC is now 30%, while 90% own a cell phone.[4] Looked at another way, between 1999 and 2002, the number of color TVs per 100 urban population in China increased from 11 to 25, PCs increased from 1.9 to 6.8, internet users rose from 0.7 to 5.3, mobile phone subscribers rose from 3.4 to 16, and automobiles rose from 0.1 to 0.3.[5]

Increasing consumer spending is widely considered to be at the beginning of a long-expected upswing driven by China's economic expansion of 9% annually. Consider that the deposit interest rate dropped from 11% in 1994 to 2.1% in 2004, fueled by government efforts to encourage consumer spending. One example is the central government's decision to launch two "golden week" holidays; since 1999, Chinese citizens have enjoyed a seven-day break from work each May and October, during which they are encouraged to travel, shop, and dine out.

In addition, China's one-child policy has meant that children make up a powerful set of consumer decision-makers well funded by parents and grandparents. On the other hand, improved nutrition and healthcare have resulted in an increasing population of retirees. (The over-64 age group accounted for 7.6% of the total population in 2004.) Meanwhile, the salaries of working professionals are rising rapidly in many sectors, creating vast opportunities for businesses.

Not only are China's consumers growing wealthier, but they are growing more accessible to MNCs. During the initial economic opening in the late 1970s, foreign investment was restricted mainly to manufacturers producing in China to sell abroad. This model shifted during the mid-1990s, picking up speed following WTO accession, to allow more production in China for the Chinese domestic market. As domestic markets opened and import tariffs fell, MNCs switched from using China as the world's factory to viewing the nation as the world's shopping mall. Evidence of this trend is found in the *2005 Business Climate Survey*, which polled member companies in the American Chambers of Commerce based in Beijing and Shanghai. The

---

4 *China Statistical Yearbook, 2004.*

5 China Internet Network Information Center; *China Statistical Yearbook, 2004*; McKinsey analysis.

survey found that 62% of the 450 China-based U.S. companies surveyed said their number 1 goal for their China operations was to "produce goods or services in China for the China market." Only 14% named as their top priority producing goods or services in China for the U.S. market.

The upshot: China's combination of vast market size and rapidly developing consumerism has made the nation a major focal point—if not *the primary* focal point—of global strategy for many international companies now operating in China, and is clearly so for the 20 MNCs profiled in this book.

> ***"The world's most populous nation now offers a consumer base that is not only vast but also wealthy, worldly, and willing to spend."***
>
> **The authors,** *China CEO*

General Motors is one such company. "China is a top priority for us," says Philip Murtaugh of GM China. Although the country brings GM a relatively small part of its global sales revenue, the market offers tremendous potential for expansion at a rapid rate. Most importantly, the company's robust growth in China—where car sales for GM went from 0 to 258,000 annually in its first four years of operations—stands out among GM's other important markets worldwide. "We are contributing positive profits to the company, while those [operations] in Europe and Latin America are going through serious problems. So, GM China is growing very rapidly and the contribution from it is going to be very important. How to manage a large group is my next concern, as the company is expanding quickly."

Companies in the services industries are also preparing for an emerging Chinese consumer market. Hilton Shanghai's Volkmar Ruebel says Hilton is gearing up for increased business from Chinese nationals both in and out of China. "China is becoming a huge market for us, not only in terms of the hotels operated in this country, but also in terms of Chinese travelers going overseas. Within the next 10 years, you will see Chinese become the largest group of travelers in the world."

The growth and maturation of the China market is also impacting business-to-business suppliers. A case in point is GE, which sells parts to manufacturers across a spectrum of nine major industries. "Right now, and for the next 20 years, China is probably going to be one of our largest customer bases," says GE China's Steve Schneider. Specifically, over the next 15 years, China will likely become GE's largest buyer of power generation equipment

"*Right now, and for the next 20 years, China is probably going to be one of our largest customer bases. China is a very important part of our strategy.*"

Steve Schneider, Chairman and CEO, General Electric China

worldwide (in terms of gigawatts), the largest buyer of aircraft, and the largest buyer of consumer and commercial finance services. "China is a very important part of our strategy," says Schneider. GE expanded from operating four business sectors in China when Schneider took the head position in 2001 to operating nine major industrial sectors by 2003. During those years, the company grew from 26 to 36 entities nationwide. Schneider expects growth to pick up even further through 2005 because economies of scale for GE's China operations are increasing. "Now, the amount of growth in dollars and people and companies is going to increase. And that will create some challenges."

While the fast growth and maturation of the Chinese market is well known to MNCs, access to the market—legally and logistically—is often somewhat unclear. That brings us to the next two sections of this chapter.

Regulatory Challenges

The first step for an MNC seeking to reach Chinese customers and clients is ensuring the legal right to do so. This simple statement introduces an obstacle that is far more complex than it seems. China's regulatory environment, although generally improving in terms of business practices and market access, is in a period of transition. While the nation has been steadily opening its markets to foreign investment since the late 1970s, and although a flurry of legal changes have been enacted following accession to the WTO in 2001, the terms of specific laws often remain unclear to foreign investors. Our international executive interviewees describe grappling with new laws that are vague and incomplete, or that are interpreted inconsistently by different local governments. As a result, international managers sometimes find themselves struggling through legal gray zones.

For most sectors, access to the domestic Chinese market has improved recently; in some cases, dramatically so. Our interviewees tell us that this has created vast opportunities, as well as new challenges. Consider the radical changes experienced by international players in the carbonated beverage sector. Up until 2002, the international beverage bottlers in China faced a highly restrictive operating environment. In the case of soda giants Coca-Cola and Pepsi, the Chinese government required case-by-case approval for each new bottling plant that either producer sought to open, and set an unofficial policy of most often approving either Coke or Pepsi to bottle in a given city, but not both. Second, producers faced production quotas; when either one saw its sales reach maximum limits in the peak summer season, the company had to apply to extend the production quota rather than immediately expanding production to meet demand. Third, in order to help develop the domestic beverage industry, Chinese law stipulated that foreign beverage makers produce a certain percentage of their production volume as Chinese brand-name products, which forced international producers to spend a portion of their company resources on developing, producing, and marketing domestically branded drink products.

All of these requirements were dropped in 2002, affording sudden freedom for the two soda giants. The result since 2003 has been a race between the two to reach untapped Chinese cities and to enter cities formerly held by the rival company. In the two years after regulations were eased, both companies embarked on aggressive advertising campaigns and rushed to introduce new products; Coke launched canned Nestea (in a joint venture with Nestlé) in 2003, Icy Mint Sprite in 2004, and Vanilla Coke in 2005, while Lemon Pepsi was released in 2004.

In other sectors, two of the most important and furthest-reaching regulatory changes under WTO came in 2004 with the passage of the Measures for the Administration of Foreign Investment in the Commercial Sector and the 2004 revisions to the Foreign Trade Law. Together, these two regulations open the retail, wholesale, and import–export business to wholly foreign-owned enterprises. In addition, while previous regulations restricted foreign-invested manufacturers to selling in China only products they manufacture in China, the new regulations allow such manufacturers to import and sell finished products in China. Last, the new rules have allowed WFOE retailers or wholesalers to establish anywhere in China since December 2004, ending geographic restrictions. These regulations are just one example of the highly significant changes brought on by WTO accession, creating vast new opportunities for MNCs targeting this market.

The atmosphere of rapid regulatory change may be slowing somewhat: the bulk of the commitments China made on entering WTO were to come into effect within three years of accession, meaning by December 2004. The good news for MNCs is that China has largely fulfilled its requirements to amend regulations on schedule. The *2005 White Paper on American Business in China,* published jointly by the American Chambers of Commerce based in Beijing and Shanghai, states: "China has generally complied with its WTO commitments since its accession in 2001." The document commends China for reducing customs duties on agricultural and industrial products and opening previously closed markets, stating: "This has led to an 80 percent leap in U.S. exports to China [from 2001 to 2005] … and the favorable investment climate has spurred record numbers of U.S. companies to set up in China." However, the document also raises concerns over missed deadlines and other delays in meeting commitments to opening specific sectors—in particular, the distribution and direct selling industries—to foreign investment.

The chambers also stress that while many of China's business-related laws have been passed or expanded, law enforcement sometimes lags behind. This is especially true in the inadequate enforcement of intellectual property rights laws. (For more on IPR infringement, see Chapter 6; or on government support of business interests, see Chapter 8.)

Logistical Difficulties

After clearing all regulatory challenges and restrictions to setting up and operating in China, MNCs often face a number of logistical difficulties in the mechanics of reaching their customers—particularly in the distribution of goods. This section covers the advice and experiences of our interviewees in overcoming difficulties in getting products and services to end-users.

"Distribution" posed the single-most prevalent logistical problem for the 20 China-based international managers featured in this book. As the interviewees explained, markets are now opening faster than MNCs can devise ways to reach them. One such company feeling the pressure to expand distribution quickly is Coca-Cola China, perhaps the most ambitious distributor among the 20 companies in this book. Says company president Paul Etchells, "There are huge untapped opportunities, but the size of the country is an impediment to realizing the potential that is out there. That is the single largest challenge."

Interviewees stressed that China's infrastructure is rapidly improving, even beyond the major cities and into what international managers call second- and third-tier cities. Alan Brown of Unilever China praises the nation's infrastructure development. "The progress in infrastructure is almost unbelievable—the airports, railroads, and incredible roads. Compared to any other big country such as India or Indonesia, it is really awesome. The progress is without parallel."

But accessing decent-quality roadways is only one of the difficulties that must be overcome in arranging distribution. Bertelsmann Direct Group Asia's Ekkehard Rathgeber sums up other challenges this way: "Since China is a huge marketplace and there are many provinces, it is an extremely diversified distribution network. It is difficult to make sure product gets distributed in a proper way." Rathgeber explains that it is generally very difficult to control distribution, as there are "challenges that have a constant impact on your distribution channels."

International managers agreed that some distribution challenges have recently eased. For example, manufacturers interviewed said they used to face more serious local protectionism when seeking to bring their products into a new province or municipality. In such cases, although the company had the legal right to distribute there, local governments managed to find ways to block or delay transportation.

Today, such problems are diminishing, especially in the more developed areas. One American manufacturer explains that the central government is "working very hard" to get rid of regional protectionism. "Today, it's not as important an issue as it was seven years ago," he says. Instead, foreign companies are now more likely to experience more standard obstacles such as a local government preference for competing companies already established in an area. "If another company has already made a large investment in a certain city through a joint venture, you will be at a disadvantage if you want to promote your products there," says one German manufacturer.

Distribution Challenges

More problematic than local protectionism to many foreign managers is the challenge of efficiently managing the transportation of goods across China. At L'Oréal China, Paolo Gasparrini names distribution as "one of the main challenges" to the company's aggressive growth plans. He stresses that while the China operations of L'Oréal draw on the parent group's international expertise to succeed in other business aspects—such as product development and marketing—achieving reliable and efficient transportation is one area in which MNCs lose out to local competitors. "The distribution side depends very strongly on local knowledge and is closely linked to the Chinese context," Gasparrini says.

Foreign companies' weaknesses in distribution stem largely from the fact that the field was heavily protected against foreign investment until recently. It was only in 2003 that foreign firms gained the right to form majority-invested JVs in distribution, and that limitations on the location and size of foreign-invested distribution operations were lifted. As of December 2004, WFOEs in the retail, wholesale, and franchising sectors gained distribution rights, although the government was slow to issue clear guidelines on applying for such rights and relatively few companies applied in 2005.

At least for now, most MNCs are using Chinese distribution networks to transport goods—a system that is often confusing and cumbersome. As Unilever China's Alan Brown explains, China's existing channels for transportation of goods through wholesalers to distributors to retailers are based on a complex system that has developed over decades, even centuries. "There is a long-standing, historic, deeply embedded network of wholesale markets in China which goes back to the Silk Road," says Brown. "A good understanding of the main flows of this network is essential and that really can only be [set up] by local people. You have to have local employees or local partners who understand this."

> "
>
> ***The rate at which modern [retail] trade is developing in China is without parallel. It has never happened before, not even in Europe."***
>
> **Alan Brown**, Chairman, Unilever China

Brown explains that distribution in China is organized into distinct "tiers" that products pass through as they move from wholesalers to retailers—a system that can be confusing and even inaccessible for foreign companies. "There is a very particular way of managing the flow of your goods as they cascade down the wholesale markets," he says. In simplified terms, Tier One wholesalers sell to Tier Two wholesalers, Tier Two wholesalers sell to Tier Three vendors, and Tier Three vendors sell to retailers. "The best people to understand the levels are those on the ground, managing the cascade of product," says Brown. "The fact is: local operators just know better than international operators. Regional companies know how to operate this. This is a bit of a black box for international operators."

Another common concern among interviewees: MNCs distributing through wholesalers often experience lengthy delays in collecting payment after their products are sold. The top executive for China at one German company told us: "Wholesalers and retailers are often very reluctant to pay; the motivation for them to pay is very low. You tend to finance your wholesalers quite a lot, but you don't get the money back. Payment is rather a big problem in China."

The bottom line is that, for companies in the consumer products sector, sales and distribution are "the most serious challenge" faced in China, says Alan Brown. But he adds that distribution and sales are improving for MNCs in China because the retailing sector is undergoing a "seismic shift" in changing from traditional sales channels—wet markets, street vendors, and mom-and-pop shops—to modern retailing. He explains: "The rate at which modern [retail] trade is developing in China is without parallel. It has never happened before, not even in Europe." He cites an AC Nielsen report showing that 50% of consumer sales in China's larger cities

CASE STUDY

WINNING AT DISTRIBUTION: COCA-COLA (CHINA) BEVERAGES

One MNC renowned for successful strategies in overcoming China's daunting distribution problems is Coca-Cola. Coke re-entered China in 1979 (following a 30-year hiatus), making it one of the first Western firms to enter following the Cultural Revolution. Pepsi entered in 1981. By 2005, both had invested more than US$1 billion in China. (Coca-Cola made this investment indirectly, via its JV bottlers.) However, Coke had expanded far faster, operating 32 bottling plants and employing 20,600 employees to Pepsi's 14 bottling plants and 10,000 employees. In 2005, Coke held 53% of the carbonated soft drinks market in China, while Pepsi had gained 22%. Both beverage giants closely guard sales and profit information, but unconfirmed reports state that Coke China has been profitable since 1995, while Pepsi was still in the red as of 2003.[6]

After two-and-a-half decades of head-to-head competition in China, Coke's distribution strategy is widely believed to be a significant factor in its substantial lead over Pepsi. In our interview with Coca-Cola China's Paul Etchells, he explained the delicate balance the company has achieved between expanding distribution while containing costs. The first step in the company's distribution strategy is opening bottling plants near its major consumer markets. In building its empire of bottling operations nationwide, Coke chose not to invest directly, but to use three partner bottlers—Hong Kong-based Swire Beverages and Kerry Beverages, and China's COFCO. This leaves the investment and operational costs to the partners, but still allows Coke to retain a level of influence because each of the three partners has strong and deep ties to Coca-Cola. Swire, for example, partners with Coke elsewhere internationally.

Another factor in Coca-Cola China's successful distribution strategy is its use of "managed distribution partners." Rather than directly hiring distribution personnel, Coca-Cola contracts individual "partners." Before signing them on, Coke seeks exclusivity agreements to ensure that the partners do not handle competitors' products. Again, this policy allows Coke to manage retail distribution without the expense of hiring full-time employees. It seems clear that, after 25 years of leading China's soft-drinks market, Coca-Cola can expect its bottlers and distributors to accept special terms before working together.

6 Economist Intelligence Unit, 2003; company sources.

are now made at "modern" retail outlets such as supermarkets, hypermarkets, chain stores, and department stores. He believes the transformation toward modern shops is taking place in Shanghai and other major cities at the fastest pace worldwide, a change that is "absolutely phenomenal" given the size of China, he adds. Retail sales in China for 2003 stood at nearly US$500 billion, and are expected to grow to US$723 billion by 2008. [7]

Tough Customers

Getting products and services to the Chinese consumer is only half the battle for foreign managers; getting them to purchase them is the other half. It is no longer true that the first task is the more difficult of the two. The overriding shift described by the 28 international managers and consultants interviewed is that while logistical difficulties are easing (given China's infrastructure development and market access opening), the challenges of meeting consumer tastes tend to be worsening.

This section details the primary challenges faced by foreign managers in luring and retaining customers among Chinese consumers and buyers:

- Sky-high demands
- Pricing constraints
- Mismatched products
- One China, many markets
- Low brand loyalty
- Lack of reliable consumer market information

Challenge #1: Sky-high Demands

While none of the international managers interviewed for this book had faced a PR crisis involving the destruction of their

---

7 Economist Intelligence Unit forecast, 2005.

product on national TV (such as Mercedes-Benz did in Wuhan), all agreed that international companies often underestimate the sky-high expectations of today's Chinese consumers. As Steve Schneider of GE China puts it, "A lot of [Western] people have the wrong impression that Chinese customers would accept outdated, poor-quality products." On the contrary, Schneider describes Chinese consumers as extremely demanding, especially of foreign-made products. In fact, he says, MNCs often face unreasonable expectations from consumers of their internationally branded products.

Schneider points to Chinese consumer attitudes toward foreign-brand automobiles as an example of impossible expectations. "In the U.S., Japan, or Germany, customers understand that every car company produces some cars with problems," Schneider says. But in China, due to the lack of consumer experience, buyers tend to expect 100% perfection in foreign-made products. "In China, the customer might be the first person in the entire history of the family who has ever bought a car. Consumers don't know that cars are extremely complex products and sometimes develop problems. [However, the customer] is paying a huge amount of money for a [foreign-made] car, and if he cannot get a perfect car, he gets very upset." Although GE is not in the car business, the company has met with the same unrealistic expectations from Chinese customers. In fact, Schneider says, GE's greatest challenge in China is "meeting the customer's expectations."

Sony China's Seiichi Kawasaki also describes facing consumers with high quality expectations in China. Kawasaki points to TV sets as an example of the high expectations of Chinese customers. "The expectation of the picture quality of the color TV is very high in China. It may not even be so high in Japan," says Kawasaki. "And for product design, [Chinese consumers] expect much more. The Chinese consumer has high expectations for our products. We have to listen to them carefully."

For consumer product manufacturers such as those in the electronics field, China is becoming a first-run market for launching new features. "It is impossible to sell second-rate technology in China. They want the best," says Dominique de Boisseson of

Alcatel China. "China is often the first place we introduce a new technology. The Chinese are very demanding customers." As an example, he points to short messaging services (SMS), which have boomed in China. In 2005, Chinese cell phone users were sending close to 1 billion short messages via mobile per day. De Boisseson stresses that China was the first country in which Internet portals began making money on SMS.

Today, China is a booming but very discriminating market for mobile phones. "Young people are well-educated and they want the latest products. In China, we find a very developed market—we have customers who want the latest style, the latest technology, the latest applications, the most advanced services," says de Boisseson.

The consultants we interviewed have made it one of their focus areas now to help clients adapt to the changing needs and demands of Chinese consumers. At BearingPoint, Bryan Huang tells his clients that the tendency for Chinese customers to have high expectations of foreign goods is not only the case for high-end goods. "When you offer a product to Chinese consumers, even if it is a low-end product, the customers are always demanding. This is a part of the Chinese character," says Huang.

Part of the advice that McKinsey & Company gives its clients is that Chinese consumers are "well informed," says company director in Shanghai Gordon Orr. "There is a lot of consumer information out there." The trick, says Orr, is for multinational firms to understand where potential customers are getting their information and how to influence it. He stresses that today's Chinese consumers tend to collect information from many sources, weighing the input before making a purchase—as do consumers in developed markets. For this reason, influencing purchasing decisions is now as difficult in China's urban centers as in major Western cities. "Building a brand takes much more than just placing ads on CCTV [television station]," Orr says.

Demanding and discriminating customers are a fact of life not only for MNCs retailing directly to consumers but also to those selling to business-to-business buyers. Du Pont China is one such multinational selling to domestic manufacturers across a spectrum of industries including automobiles, textiles, and

"

The expectation of the picture quality of the color TV is very high in China. It may not even be so high in Japan. And for product design, [Chinese consumers] expect much more. The Chinese consumer is very demanding. We have to listen to them carefully."

Seiichi Kawasaki,
Director and President,
Sony China

"

Chinese customers have very high expectations. They are very demanding on quality. ... They are also superb negotiators on price."

Charles Browne, President, Du Pont China

plastics. The company's Charles Browne describes his clients in this way: "Chinese customers have very high expectations. They are very demanding on quality."

The good news, for MNCs, is that the growing sophistication of consumers in China is creating new markets for their products. Many say that internationalism and growing product awareness are allowing them to introduce products that Chinese consumers would not have been interested in 10 or even five years ago. Bayer has experienced such a shift. "Our [China] customers are asking for international quality more and more," says Bayer China's Elmar Stachels. "The more they are globalizing, the more they are climbing up, the more chances we have for our quality products. This is the trend in China."

The bad news for foreign managers of MNCs is that the high demands of Chinese consumers and buyers are often matched with relatively limited spending power.

Challenge #2: Pricing Constraints

Du Pont China's Charles Browne followed his comment on Chinese customers having very high expectations and high demands on quality with another observation: "They are also superb negotiators on price." Consumers with both tough standards and limited budgets create an extremely tough market for many companies. Even worse, given the fast-growing competition among MNCs in China, the result in many sectors has been narrowing profit margins.

Many of the international managers we interviewed are under pressure in China to offer top-quality products and services, but to keep prices lower than elsewhere worldwide. Interviewees named consumer products such as flat-screen TVs, DVD players, and digital cameras as having razor-thin profit margins in China.

It is not only higher-end items that face pressure to reduce prices, however. As Sony China's Seiichi Kawasaki explained in Chapter 5, it is nearly impossible now for international makers to produce a profit-earning color TV in China for the domestic market. MNCs simply cannot produce a product that meets local demands for quality but stays within pricing constraints.

Even in low-tech consumer products, the squeeze is being felt. Coca-Cola China's Paul Etchells explains that "a large number of people [in China] can't afford our products." He says Coke faces a similar issue in India, Africa, and Eastern Europe, and in each place the solution is the same: maintain quality and standards, reduce price, and survive via high volume sales. As we mentioned in the Foreword, China was Coke's fifth-largest market in terms of volume consumed in 2005, and could become third-largest by 2008 (after the United States and Mexico).

> "
> ***Sometimes products are over-engineered [for the China market]. People won't pay for things they don't need."***
>
> **Kenneth Yu**, Managing Director, 3M China

Challenge #3: Mismatched Products

One of the most common mistakes foreign-based MNCs make in China is bringing in product that is simply not suitable for the target market. One interviewee has seen multinationals commit such serious "mismatches" as importing processed cheese spread to a non-cheese-eating market, sports drinks into non-sporting communities, and high-priced imported beers into markets with strong (and cheap) local labels. He says such errors are quickly discovered when products fail in the market. "If you do make a mistake in China, you realize it quickly. The feedback is very, very fast."

Kenneth Yu of 3M China explains from experience that some East–West mismatches are difficult to detect until it is too late. Yu says that 3M suffered in "the early days" in China because the company sought simply to bring in top-quality products without gauging buyer needs first. The thinking back then, he says, was that Chinese buyers would adapt to the higher-quality products being introduced—a mindset Yu calls "wrong." Introducing high-grade products, even a relatively inexpensive item such as sandpaper, will fail if consumers don't feel a need to pay more for it. "Sometimes products are over-engineered," says Yu. "People won't pay for things they don't need." Yu stresses that he doesn't recommend bringing cheaper products to China, but that companies must "meet local customers' requirements."

Challenge #4: One China, Many Markets

Another common challenge in reaching Chinese customers is the wide variation in demographics, preferences, and even cultural norms throughout the nation. As a result, MNCs must sell to many different markets within the country. David Chang of Philips China sums up the message from many international managers: "China isn't a homogenous country. The challenge for Philips is: in such a non-homogenous situation, how do you find the right strategy?" He explains that the China market includes the full spectrum of customer groups. "You can see the whole value-chain in China: underdeveloped, developing, developed; or from labor-intensive to capital-intensive, to brain-intensive. In China, they all exist simultaneously." This variation means that MNCs must cater their products to a wide range of customer needs simultaneously. Says Chang: "For a global company to fully tap into the strengths of China, you have to adapt to different economic stages in different geographical areas. That is a big challenge."

In addition to differences in spending habits, MNCs grapple with variations in geography and climate, language (through regional dialects), religion and culture, educational background, and international exposure. Philip Murtaugh of General Motors China says his company must meet "different tastes, different customer expectations" across the nation. Not only do cars in the south need air-conditioning, while cars sold in the north may not, but customer preferences vary in other aspects. "There isn't a homogenous market. In Beijing, red is the best-selling color [for GM cars], while in Guangzhou, white is the best-selling color," says Murtaugh. "There are regional differences. And there are differences in income."

Much of the sales strategy for Unilever China also hinges on tracking customer preferences across China. Alan Brown points to skin-care products as an example: "The requirement of consumers in Beijing is moisturizing; while in Guangdong [province], consumers want a smooth finish to the skin, clean and fresh."

Adapting product to fit a dry climate in one area and a tropical climate in another may be fairly straightforward, but Brown says MNCs also must identify and meet more subtle differences in customer tastes. Developing the right marketing campaign often requires a very detailed understanding of the target market's tastes, lifestyle, and purchase motivation. Says Brown: "In our business, you must target your advertising message very specifically to consumers. It is complex because what turns on people in Chengdu is very different from what works in Shanghai."

And because vast cultural gaps have developed between urbanites and rural residents, between northerners and southerners, and between generations, this creates additional layers of difference within the consumer population. For example, while the older generations tend to be quite price conscious and are generally cautious in making purchase decisions, younger generations are often driven by appeals to "face" and prestige. Dr. Bryan Huang of BearingPoint points to mobile phone purchasing as an example, stressing that some young Chinese purchase two or even three mobile phones. "Compared with Western people, they are not thinking in an economical way," Huang says, explaining that these 20-somethings do not *need* three mobile phones; they simply *want* them. "They want to show a new phone to others—it's a question of image. That is part of Chinese culture."

> *"You can see the whole value-chain in China: underdeveloped, developing, developed. ... For a global company to fully tap into the strengths of China, you have to adapt to different economic stages in different geographical areas. That is a big challenge."*
>
> **David Chang**, CEO, Philips China

Challenge #5: Low Brand Loyalty

Another characteristic of the China market is that the concept of brands is still young and undeveloped, meaning that most Chinese consumers simply have not used branded products for long enough to develop an emotional attachment to them. Instead, in China, consumers are still accustomed to unbranded, unlabeled products. "They don't have the 50 to 60 years of brand heritage that you have in the West," says McKinsey & Company's Gordon Orr.

As a result, Chinese customers tend not to place a high priority on branding in purchasing decisions. "You don't see the brand loyalty that you see in the U.S.," says John Wong of The Boston Consulting Group. He points out that while many of the top consumer brands in the U.S. have held leading positions for the past 50 years, this would be impossible in China. "China doesn't have that history."

> *"Every new company that comes in is bombarding the consumer [with product]. And the Chinese consumer is trying everything that is out there."*
>
> **John Wong**, Managing Director Greater China, The Boston Consulting Group

For most branded products, the China market is open territory since nearly all competing brands are starting from zero. What this means, especially in China's urban centers, is that a slew of companies are "bombarding" the consumer, says John Wong. How are consumers responding? "The Chinese consumer is trying everything that is out there."

Unilever China's Alan Brown agrees that Chinese consumers tend to be curious and adventurous. "The good news is that you get a pretty good trial rate—[Chinese] people will try almost anything once," he says. "In Europe, it's harder. People grew up with certain brands and are set in their ways."

The downside to buyer curiosity is that, while you may easily attract consumer interest in a promoted product this week, another brand may attract them next week.

Then, too, one of the main consequences of low brand commitment is high emphasis on price. Says BCG's John Wong: "Because there is much less brand loyalty, there is a lot more shopping around, a lot of price comparison." He also advises MNCs that, because of the relatively low wages in China, domestic consumers tend to consider seriously before purchasing foreign-branded products. International managers targeting China should generally expect local consumers to gather more information and consider purchases more carefully than do shoppers elsewhere. "There is a lot of asking, 'What am I getting, functionally, from this product?'" says Wong.

McKinsey & Company's Gordon Orr sums up how low brand loyalty can either benefit or harm MNCs. "It means you can be a late entrant and swing people to your product. But it also means that a lot of people compete on price, rather than on other characteristics."

There is hope for international companies seeking to build their brands in China, however. Alan Brown stresses that low loyalty is common in developing markets. He points to the transformation Unilever has witnessed in Taiwan. "I think that [low brand loyalty] is specific to the stage of development that China is in now. In Taiwan, we saw pretty much the same things; but if you establish a strong brand, you can create loyalty." Brown points out that Unilever's Dove soap brand "didn't exist in Taiwan 10 years ago" but now is "one of the biggest brands."

BCG's John Wong agrees that branding is gaining a foothold in China, though slowly. He points out that some domestic Chinese companies already enjoy strong brand equity in China. For example, Haier refrigerators have a solid reputation which now influences purchasing decisions. Still, for the near term, Wong warns that MNCs should expect the level of brand commitment in China to remain "much lower than in Western markets."

> "*[Market research requires] frequent refreshing because of the pace of change in the marketplace and the volatility of consumer behavior.*"
>
> **Gordon Orr**, Director, Shanghai office, McKinsey & Company

Challenge #6: Lack of Reliable Consumer Marketing Information

Another constraint mentioned by interviewees is that gathering reliable market research can be difficult in China. Publicly available information sources, such as domestic media or government statistics, have traditionally been either unreliable or difficult to access. Says one consultant: "The market research companies are not very good, and the government agencies don't give good information."

But both consultants and managers agreed that access to reliable information is improving. Gordon Orr of McKinsey says the situation is "a magnitude better than before," adding that his research teams are fully able to conduct market studies in China. A more pressing problem, however, is that market research requires "frequent refreshing because of the pace of change in the marketplace and the volatility of consumer behavior."

Best Practices for Reaching Chinese Consumers

Now that we have introduced the challenges of selling to today's Chinese consumer—on the one hand, increasingly wealthy and worldly; on the other hand, demanding, fickle, and price conscious—the following section covers the best practices shared by our MNC managers. The primary message heard throughout our

TIP While retaining the international image and power of your brand, localize your products to suit local tastes and preferences.

interviews was that winning over Chinese buyers depends on successful localization—localizing products, localizing marketing campaigns, localizing strategy. Ultimately, the path that many MNCs are following has been, first, moving production to China, then moving sales and marketing to China, and now bringing R&D to China.

Strategy #1: Match the Market

Many of our interviewees discussed the delicate balancing act they perform in retaining international standards and guidelines for their products and services, but, when appropriate, adapting some aspects of their products to the China market. At L'Oréal China, Paolo Gasparrini explains that the Lancôme cosmetics line, for example, retains its brand perameters but does emphasize different products in Asia, and even in China, than elsewhere worldwide. "Our star brands are the same worldwide: Lancôme is Lancôme. But inside the brand, you can find that [while there is] the same general positioning, some products are adapted to Chinese skin characteristics." For example, he points out that whitening lotion—which is a top-selling skincare product in Asia—doesn't exist in Europe. In other cases, the same makeup lines are offered, but some shades sell in Asia that don't sell abroad.

Such specialization requires careful tracking of preferences and quick release of new products.

Strategy #2: Localize Marketing

Marketing campaigns must also be localized. Unilever China's Alan Brown explains that the "emotional hooks" that trigger Chinese consumers to buy certain products are often quite different from those in the West. For example, he points out that China's one-child policy creates a different family dynamic for advertisers to tap into. "The one-child policy has a major impact on our marketing. The bond between mothers and only children is not like [the bond] anywhere else in the world," says Brown.

Young Chinese children tend to be doted on by their parents and grandparents in a way that youngsters from multiple-child families are not. China's "little emperors" are referred to as having "six pocket syndrome," meaning that each youngster is served by two parents and four grandparents, each opening his or her pockets to fund the whims of the child.

TIP Given the vast differences in geography, climate, history—and even culture—in China, marketing programs must vary as well.

Brown also warns that the motivations that compel purchasing in one part of China may not work well in another part. Given the vast differences in geography, climate, history, and even culture—in China, marketing programs must vary as well. "There is generally a logic or a history behind the differences, whether it is functional or emotional," says Brown.

TIP Demographics are changing rapidly across parts of China. Many cities are gaining rapidly in wealth and consumerism. Watch the second- and third-tier cities as potential new markets.

Strategy #3: Choose Your Destination

Another critical strategic decision for MNCs to make in China is where to target consumers. Choosing the correct markets within the nation is tricky, as different locations vary widely in terms of economic demographics, tastes, and customs. Many of China's mega-cities—Beijing, Shanghai, Guangzhou, Chengdu—have been focal points for international companies for two decades. While those cities still represent the highest concentration of consumer wealth, many MNCs are targeting up-and-coming cities, places with growth potential and increasing wealth, but a less-crowded playing field. "The market is geographically deepening into second-, third-, and fourth-tier cities. It is happening quickly," says McKinsey's Gordon Orr.

Typically, such cities offer excellent new markets for first-round consumer products such as white goods, electronics, and higher-end foods. "Income levels are passing through the threshold and the market is reaching critical mass in many more cities very quickly. If you're not in those cities, you aren't necessarily aware that it's happening," says Gordon Orr. Which cities? Orr recommends that clients consider the developing regions of the Pearl River Delta, as well as the Sichuan province cities of Jiangzhou or Mianyang as high-potential markets.

Paolo Gasparrini is one China top executive who carefully

researches where to launch specific L'Oréal products. "When we launch a brand, many times we don't go nationally, but we start in one city, then another," he says. The company monitors the China as a collection of different markets, and is constantly updating these profiles as they develop and change. Whenever a city reaches the ability to provide a minimal level of income for L'Oréal, it is added to the radar screen.

Many companies are now finding a balance between rushing to enter new regions without spreading themselves too thin or miscalculating new markets. Siemens is following a two-pronged strategy in China: increasing its presence in high-density, upper-end urban areas, while also pioneering into underdeveloped regions of western China. "You have to spread out. You have to have market presence," says Ernst Behrens. But he stresses that such a plan means marketing in two vastly different markets at once.

At The Boston Consulting Group, John Wong sometimes advises clients to increase their market presence in emerging regions of China as a better strategy than competing via marketing and advertising in more developed areas. "Some [multinational companies in China] have clearly way over-spent on branding their products and media spending," he says. "They would have been better off building their distribution system and getting to the second- and third-tier cities." Wong points out that in the current rush to pioneer into new areas, some companies have grown strong through sheer presence—a strategy that can be more effective than gambling on the returns of an ad campaign.

Strategy #4: R&D in China, for China

As mentioned earlier, many of the companies we profile in this book seem to be following a strategy of moving from manufacturing in China for export markets, to manufacturing in China for the China market. This progression mirrors the general trend of MNCs since domestic markets began opening after WTO accession in late 2001. And since the domestic China market has emerged as a key strategic "win" for international companies, the natural progression for an increasing number of international companies serving the China market is to begin conducting R&D in China, for China. This is the ultimate method for effectively understanding and serving domestic customers.

Spurred by increased interest from MNCs, coupled with increasing support from the Chinese government, the number of foreign-funded R&D centers for international companies grew from 200 nationwide in 2002 to 600 in 2004. These centers represent a total investment of US$4 billion. Shanghai alone had 131 corporate-funded research centers as of late 2004, and many MNCs announced plans to build additional centers in 2005.

Among the 20 international companies we interviewed, the following had set up R&D in China: Alcatel, Bayer, Du Pont, Eli Lilly, General Electric, L'Oréal, Microsoft, Siemens, and Sony. Among these companies, most were conducting product development for the China market, but several were also conducting world-class fundamental research used by their companies' global operations.

Bayer is one example of an MNC shifting research operations into China. The company still conducts most of its R&D in Europe, the U.S., and Japan, but in 2002 it built its first research center, focused on polymers, in China. The facility is "very much customer-related—helping customers to design and develop products," says CEO Elmar Stachels. He adds that Bayer plans to increase its R&D in China and has formed cooperative agreements with Chinese universities, including the Academy of Science in Beijing.

L'Oréal is another good example. The company opened an important R&D center in Shanghai in September 2005. The mission of the center is to conduct and support basic science research to improve understanding of the structure and behavior of Chinese hair and skin. Says Gasparrini: "The knowledge and insights gained through research conducted at the China center will ultimately allow us to develop innovative new products that better service the beauty care needs of the global Asian market."

Sony China opened its US$1 million, 12,000-square-meter Sony Shanghai Technology Center in June 2004 in Zhangjiang High-Tech Industrial Park. As of 2005, it employed 100 researchers focusing on software and electronics components for digital audio and video devices.

Seiichi Kawasaki explains that the company's efficiency of operations depends on conducting product research *for* China, *in* China. "In order to do business in China, we must develop new products; we have to input engineering power, designing power. A key issue for us is how to shorten the development period," he says.

CASE STUDY

MICROSOFT R&D IN CHINA: IF YOU CAN'T BEAT THEM, LEAD THEM

No one knows more clearly the IPR risks in China than Jun Tang, president of Microsoft China, who acknowledges that 90% of products sold under the Microsoft label in China is fake. Even for companies that do not suffer so seriously from IPR infringers, consultants frequently warn their MNC clients in China to take care with the technology and research introduced into this market. Given the country's inadequate enforcement of IPR protections, bringing critical research to China may just be too risky.

But Microsoft has made it a point not to follow this advice. In fact, the software world leader was one of the first MNCs to open a global research lab in China when it established Microsoft Research Asia (MSRA) in Beijing in 1998. Soon after, the company began billing the lab as "one of the best computer science laboratories in the world." By late 2004, the MSRA employed 170 researchers and had published 750 papers in research journals and international conferences such as the prestigious graphics conference, Sieggraft.

Microsoft stresses that the MSRA conducts fundamental research used by the company worldwide, rather than simple product adaptation for Chinese consumers. Far from restricting the level or type of research carried on in China, the company has been expanding the work of the MSRA to include crucial research areas to support global product development. For example, the center supplies most of Microsoft's technology for the Chinese character input used globally. In addition, the lab also develops game software, picture and graphic processing, data mining, and software for flat PC and

Dr. Ernst Behrens explains Siemens China's reasoning behind its investment into R&D in China: "If people want to remain competitive in China and the world market, you have to go on not only to produce in China—you also have to do research and development here. You cannot have your research and development in Europe or in the States alone any more." Behrens points out that, for many MNCs, the China market is large enough to validate the high cost of launching research operations. Siemens began its

mobile phones. "We do export some of the core technology from China," says Tang.

Why would Microsoft risk conducting critical research in China, likely the company's worst offending market for IPR infringement? Simply put, Tang says, the rewards outweigh the risks. First, it is increasingly beneficial financially to locate research in China—the skill level of engineers and researchers in many fields is of an international class, while salaries remain low by Western standards. Second, it makes sense to conduct research within one of Microsoft's largest emerging markets. Much of the research generated at the center is funneled into product enhancement for China. In its first five years, the center achieved 72 "technology transfers" in which MSRA findings were used to enhance or localize products for the China or Asia market. Tang says that half of Microsoft products developed for China are for industrial clients, and half for consumers. An example of MSRA research used for commercial clients is software developed for imbedding into refrigerators made in China for export markets. Examples of hot-selling consumer products using lab technology are Digital Ink, an advanced handwriting recognition software especially useful with handwritten Chinese characters, roaming technology for mobile phones, and digital imaging that can transform photographs into cartoon graphics. The overriding message from Microsoft is that the way to gain market share in China is to continue to lead the software industry, staying several steps ahead of the pirates and building a market among the rising consumer population that is able to afford legitimate products.

China-based research in telecommunications, then expanded into medical products. Eventually, the company will conduct research in China for all of its business groups (including Information and Communications, Automation and Control, Power, Transportation, Medical, Lighting, and Household Appliances).

Alcatel opened a large-scale R&D center in Shanghai in 2002.

CASE STUDY

GE'S CHINA TECHNOLOGY CENTER: "GO WHERE YOUR CUSTOMERS ARE"

Back in 2002, General Electric had one of the largest operations of any MNC in China. The company's China operations brought revenues of US$2 billion and employed 10,200 Chinese and expatriates nationwide and covered nine distinct industries, from aircraft engines to medical systems, from power generation to transportation systems.

But GE China CEO Steve Schneider remembers thinking there was something missing. Although the company was growing fast and gaining market share throughout its major industries, the process wasn't happening as efficiently as it should. GE China was suffering from "product gap issues," Schneider says, caused by trying to serve the China market with products designed in the U.S. or Europe, with Western specifications and performance requirements. "We've got to do new product introductions, and the only way to do that is to locate the capability in the market itself," says Schneider. "If you are trying to get your company to fund product development for China in the U.S. or Europe, it isn't going to happen. There is still parochialism."

At the time, Schneider remembers that new products were needed to meet China's demand for specific types of biomaterials, ceramic magnets, and crystals. This meant offering not only product development, but also fundamental research. And that required funding R&D operations in China.

GE's solution to its R&D needs was unveiled in April 2003 when the 47,000-square-meter General Electric China Technology Center (CTC) opened in the glistening Zhangjiang High-Tech Industrial Park on the eastern outskirts of Shanghai. The center is now one of just four research centers for GE worldwide; the others are located at GE's global headquarters in New York State; Bangalore, India; and Munich, Germany.

By year-end 2004, the CTC boasted 700 researchers and staff and planned to grow

As of 2005 the center employed 2,000 people, and operations had been so successful the company was planning to "bring more and more R&D to China." Says Dominique de Boisseson, "We have to adapt the design to the Chinese requirements." He stresses that the differences in product lines are more complex than simply creating a lower-tech, lower-cost model in China. "In some of

to 1,100 by 2006. All but 30 of the center's employees are Chinese nationals. Center managers say GE's expansion plans for the facility are possible but challenging, given some limitations of China's research talent pool. While China produces a large population of university graduates with research training yearly, there is a limited population of senior R&D personnel with more than 15 years' experience. To compensate, GE China offers more R&D staff training than is necessary in the U.S. or Europe.

Schneider says the concept of "go where your customers are" quickly bore fruit for GE China. After the first year of operation, the CTC began supplying the company with research that was used to improve products for the China market. Two examples: a breakthrough in power electronics led to the development of faster, more powerful MRI (magnetic resonance imaging, used for taking x-rays) machines, while research into advanced manufacturing was raising efficiency on GE factory floors around China. The center also serves as a showroom for GE's China customers, where they can come to commission customized products and systems.

In addition to R&D, the CTC also serves as the main testing ground for GE China's US$5 billion-per-year sourcing operations. Second, the center houses GE's "corporate learning" operations in China. Schneider says the latter helps with GE China's movement toward localization by developing corporate leaders for China, within China.

With the CTC now providing fundamental research, product development, and a customer showcase for GE products, plus improving sourcing and offering leadership training, Schneider feels he has filled the gaps that slowed GE's growth back in 2002. In short, Schneider says, the CTC helps GE to fulfill a simple company credo: "Go where your customers are."

TIP R&D in China, for China, is the ultimate method for effectively understanding and serving domestic customers.

our domains, our latest developments will be launched in China first, as the market is more advanced," he says.

Some of our profiled firms are doing more at their China-based R&D centers than simply adapting products for the China market—some are relocating fundamental, core technology research into China. In other words, multinationals are beginning to move critical strategic research to China. (For two examples of this aggressive approach, see the profiles of GE China's and Microsoft China's research operations in China.) A primary reason for this shift is that China now offers the ingredients necessary for conducting world-class research: a growing talent pool of qualified engineers and specialists, at relatively low cost.

Microsoft China's Jun Tang says China is gaining a reputation as a viable base for regional or even international research. "We are behind India, but China is catching up," he says. Tang points out that as of 2002, China had established 35 software colleges nationwide. He says graduates from these colleges, plus the computer science departments of other schools, were providing China-based companies with a pool of 15,000 educated graduates annually. By 2005, nearly all full-scale universities in China offered a Computer Science major. Tang also predicts that India's current language advantage over China—in terms of the widespread English ability—will diminish because China is increasingly emphasizing English in the mandatory education system. Tang is often asked by the Chinese government to recommend how the nation could become a software giant. He lobbies for expanding education and training in software-related fields, increasing and improving domestic software industrial parks, and making investment capital (mostly foreign sources) accessible to software entrepreneurs. Ultimately, Tang believes the strength and size of China's emerging consumer market will spur the development of the nation's software R&D capabilities. "Our advantage is the market—India doesn't have a market as large as ours," he says. He believes China will be the world's second-largest software producer by 2007—after the U.S., but ahead of India.

Other interviewees stressed that China consumers themselves have created an ideal environment for R&D in other emerging fields.

For instance, the cell-phone industry is in many ways far more advanced in China than it is in Europe or the United States.

Conclusion

China's consumers, while gaining rapidly in wealth (especially in urban areas), have gained a reputation among MNCs as tough customers—sophisticated, demanding, price conscious, and fickle. Many have unreasonable expectations of perfection when purchasing foreign brands. Another serious challenge for MNCs: China represents many markets, not one. Across the nation, consumer groups vary widely in demographics, educational background, and international exposure. China is a mosaic of distinct cultures and languages. MNCs must therefore adapt their offerings and marketing strategies to the diversity they face. In addition, international firms must constantly monitor regulatory changes in their industry, and must battle a number of logistical difficulties in reaching consumers. The best solution to reaching Chinese consumers may be to invest in domestic R&D.

SUMMARY OF TIPS

WINNING OVER CHINESE CONSUMERS

1. Match the Market

While retaining the international image and power of your brand, localize your products to suit local tastes and preferences.

2. Localize Marketing

Given the vast differences in geography, climate, history, and even culture—in China, marketing programs must vary as well.

3. Choose Your Destination

Demographics are changing rapidly across parts of China. Many cities are gaining rapidly in wealth and consumerism. Watch the second- and third-tier cities as potential new markets.

4. R&D in China, for China

R&D in China, for China, is the ultimate method for effectively understanding and serving domestic customers.

Chapter 8
Negotiating With the Chinese Government

"A traditional saying in China is: 'No one man can approve a project, but any one man can veto it.' You have to interface with officials at various levels of government to make sure that they understand what your project is and that they buy into it."

Norman Givant, Shanghai Office Managing Partner, China Practice Group, Freshfields Bruckhaus Deringer

INSIDE CHAPTER 8

Introduction

For newcomers, uncertainty about how best to work with the Chinese government is often the most daunting aspect of transplanting their business operations from their home country to China. Many international businesspeople have heard horror stories of MNCs encountering confusion, frustration, and corruption when working with the Chinese government. In particular, many are concerned about the importance of *guanxi*, or special relationships and connections, in successfully negotiating with officials.

Guanxi Defined: Part II

None of our interviewees claimed that corruption does not exist in China. In fact, most acknowledged working hard to keep their employees from using methods that they may see their competitors (domestic or international) using, such as bribery, kickbacks, or illicit exchanges of business favors for personal favors.

Corruption is a factor to be dealt with for any international manager in China. The nation ranked 71st out of 145 countries included in the 2004 Corruption Perception Index.[1] Making matters worse for many top executives at MNCs, the definitions of what is acceptable and what is corrupt *guanxi* may be different in China than in other countries. For example, gift-giving and client wining and dining are long-running business practices in China, but are restricted under U.S. law. Nepotism and cronyism are also common among domestic companies, and bonds between family members, classmates, or alumnae tend to have more pull in business decisions in China than elsewhere. Because the lines between personal and business relations are often blurred in China, international managers say they must carefully train their domestic employees to adhere to the company's code of conduct and must not assume that employees share the same understanding of acceptable and unacceptable business practices. Well-meaning staff members may unwittingly break corporate policy by using practices that are common at Chinese companies.

In addition, *guanxi* is a tool that competitors or disgruntled business partners (or employees) can use against an MNC. One case that was well-publicized among expatriate businesspeople in late 2005 told of a Danish furniture manufacturer that found this out

1 Transparency International, www.transparency.org.

Our 28 interviewees explain that such impressions can lead outsiders to overly negative views of business-to-government relations in China. (See the box, "*Guanxi* Defined: Part II", below.) In Chapter 8, we separate fact from fiction by laying out detailed advice from our profiled top executives and consultants on working with the government. In years past, it was widely believed that without a specially cultivated relationship with influential officials, business executives (especially foreign management from MNCs) would not receive the official support necessary to grow and develop their business—such as

the hard way after refusing to pay its supplier RMB3 million for inferior-quality leather. Several months after rejecting the order, local officials arrived at the company door with a court order linked to the dispute freezing RMB3 million (US$240,000) in the company's bank account plus more than RMB4 million in other company assets. As this book goes to press, the furniture maker is fighting the case and executives there believe they are the victim of their former supplier's strong *guanxi* with local courts. The lesson: *guanxi* can be used against international companies, especially if your company lacks the connections enjoyed by a rival company.

While guarding against corruption, many international companies in China do look for ways to adopt local practices within their ethical guidelines. For example, companies may be allowed to acknowledge government entities or individuals by practicing the Chinese tradition of gift-giving during the Moon Festival (also known as Mid-Autumn Festival) or Chinese New Year. Some companies set a value limit on gifts given or received. More importantly, companies may look for ways to help a government entity meet its goals in serving its constituency, such as by supporting a local charity, or hosting educational or business training workshops or classes. One example: GE China offers training courses for selected government officials on international business practices for Chinese officials at its China Technology Center.

(For further advice on acceptable business-to-government *guanxi*-building—the kind that does not break Chinese or home-country laws, or bend corporate ethics—see the section "Business-to-government Best Practices" in this chapter.)

receiving licenses or approvals for projects, or clearance to hire key personnel.

Today, our profiled China hands say, the necessity for such special relationships is diminishing. Many of our interviewees said that *guanxi* with officials is now considered less a critical

Father of China's Reform

It is impossible to discuss China's radical cultural, social, and economic transformation over the past 30 years without mentioning the rise, fall, and rise of its chief architect, Deng Xiaoping. It was the bold policies of this early Communist party organizer (who rose to prominence alongside Mao Zedong despite being twice stripped of power) that set China firmly on a path toward adopting a market-based economy.

Deng Xiaoping's story offers a clear insight into the tumultuous political shifts that shook China during his lifetime. After joining the Chinese Communist Party in 1924 at the age of 20, Deng quickly became a party organizer in southwest China. He joined the Long March in 1934–35 and, working under Mao, helped to prosecute intellectuals during the mid-1950s. In 1966, during the Cultural Revolution, Deng himself was purged as a "capitalist roader." He was rehabilitated and became vice-premier in 1973, only to be purged again by the Gang of Four in 1976. The following year, Deng was again reinstated, this time as vice-chairman of the Central Committee and Central Military Committee of the Communist Party of China. He remained a top political leader until his death in 1997.

In 1981, Deng launched a "responsibility system" of farming that allowed farmers to choose which crops they grew as long as they designated a percentage of harvested crops to the government. This system allowed farmers to match crops to market demand. Sales boomed, injecting destitute farm populations with a new prosperity—and a sense of hope. Through these reforms, Deng is credited with lifting 200 million farmers out of dire poverty. An October 1999 tribute to him in *AsiaWeek* magazine stated that "Deng lifted more people out of poverty than any other world leader, anytime, anywhere."

In the mid-1980s, Deng began publicly asserting his belief that the ultimate achievement of socialism is prosperity for all citizens. He focused international attention on China by charting a new course for the nation's economic development. One example statement, made in March 1985: "Our first objective is for our people to necessity and more as a perk or leg-up on the competition. Thus, they report spending a considerable portion of their job time focusing on building and maintaining positive government relations. GE China's Steve Schneider estimates that he spends 65% of his time working with government officials—both bureaucrats and

lead a fairly comfortable life by the end of this century—that is, to reach a level that is neither rich nor poor. Our second objective is to approach the economic level of the developed countries in another three to five decades, so that our people become relatively well-off."

The establishment of China's four Special Economic Zones (SEZs) in 1980, more than any other act, embodied Deng's goal of boosting China's economy through opening its doors to the outside world. The SEZ system, launched in the cities of Shenzhen, Zhuhai, Shantou, and Xiamen, in Guangdong and Fujian provinces, brought the first influx of FDI into China.

Deng characterized the economic reforms as China's second revolution. Under his direction, China began focusing on economic development as the nation's primary goal. In a June 1985 statement, he further clarified: "If the economy develops, we can accomplish anything. What we have to do now is to put all our efforts into developing the economy. That is the most important thing, and everything else must be subordinated to it."

As Deng built support for this economic drive, he faced considerable adversaries calling for a return to Maoist doctrine. By the early 1990s, however, it was clear that Deng had won. In 1992, he took his famous economic tour of southern China, during which he announced, "To get rich is glorious." The establishment and spread of these zones of market-based capitalism brought sudden prosperity to China's mega-cities and along the eastern seaboard and Yangtze River Delta.

Upon his death in 1997, Deng was remembered as the patriarch of economic reform as well as for the ruthless side of his leadership style. (It was Deng who oversaw the suppression of the Tiananmen protesters in 1989.) Whatever his leadership methods and ideological beliefs, none can deny the influence of Deng Xiaoping in stewarding China's economic development.

"*I consider China to be a very complex country because you have to deal with different levels [of government]. When you talk about 'government,' you have the central government, the provincial government, and the local government. According to my experience, we need to have good relationships with at least two levels—the local level and the central level.*"

Jean-Luc Chereau, President, Carrefour China

the appointed heads of state-owned enterprises that are clients of the company. Schneider says that much of this work entails actual deal-making and negotiations, but at least 10% is pure, traditional relationship-building, or developing a foundation of understanding and trust.

In this chapter, our interviewees share their views on business-to-government *guanxi*, discuss positive relationship maintenance versus corruption, and offer advice on building effective business relations while maintaining corporate codes of conduct.

Pendulum Swings: The Government's Changing Mindset

To understand the importance of good government relations in China, it is worth noting that the struggle which international companies face today has been waged for centuries. One glimpse: in 1792, the British Empire commissioned a certain Lord Macartney to negotiate trade relationships with the Middle Kingdom. When Macartney finally succeeded in meeting with Emperor Qianlong, he was abruptly informed that China was self-sufficient and did not need to trade with other nations; the limited trade exchanges China did allow were undertaken "as a favor" to foreign countries.[2]

Clearly, the Middle Kingdom has shifted its stance on foreign trade radically several times over the past 200 years as the pendulum of official position has swung from open to shut and back again. The pendulum has been securely lodged in the "go" zone for international investment since the early 1990s. Utilized foreign direct investment rocketed from US$40 billion in 2000 to US$53.5 billion in 2004.[3] Still, it is worth remembering how drastically the thinking of the Chinese government has changed over the past four decades. Consider that all Chinese officials aged over 50 years

2 Jonathan D. Spence, *The Chan's Great Continent* (New York: Norton Company, Ltd., 1998).

3 *China Statistical Yearbook* (2001 and 2004).

Key Events in China's Economic Reform

1976: September: Mao Zedong dies. October: Gang of Four is arrested.

1977: Third Plenum of the 10th Chinese Communist Party (CCP) restores Deng Xiaoping to his posts as vice-chairman of the Central Committee and the Central Military Committee of the Communist Party of China. August: Cultural Revolution officially ends by decree from the 11th National Party Congress.

1978: Third Plenum of the 11th CCP shifts government policy to focus on economic reform. Economic modernization becomes central to party work. New government operations motto: forget the past; concentrate on the future.

1980: Deng launches the SEZ (Special Economic Zone) system, opening the cities of Shenzhen, Zhuhai, Shantou, and Xiamen to foreign direct investment.

1983: "Responsibility system" for agriculture officially endorsed, allowing households to determine crops on their own. This replaced state-determined crop selection and quickly brought new prosperity to China's rural populations.

1984: Chinese central government adopts the Decision on Reform of Economic Structure, recommending bringing the use of market forces already proven successful in rural areas to the industrial sphere. The goal: to make enterprises more economically responsible. Profit-retention is introduced; tax-for-profit is confirmed.

1987: 13th CCP favors continued economic reform.

1988: April: Enterprise Law is passed, limiting the scope of the Communist Party involvement in state-owned enterprises. The law creates a division of responsibilities between the party and the management of SOEs.

1989: June: Tiananmen Square demonstrations. Deng Xiaoping oversees crackdown on protests.

1990: In part to restore investor interest following Tiananmen, Deng supports the formation of an investment center in Shanghai's Pudong district. Generous investor incentives trigger the rapid development of Shanghai.

1992: Deng tours southern China to kick-start economic reform. Deng states that continued economic reform is vital for the party's legitimacy, and claims that if China's economic reform are reversed, the party will lose the people's support. Fourteenth Party Congress approves renewed economic reform.

1993: Third Plenum of 14th CCP adopts the document "Establishment of a Market Socialist Economic System."

1997: February: Deng Xiaoping, then China's paramount leader, dies. He was the chairman of the Central Committee and the Central Military Committee of the Communist Party of China. Jiang Zemin succeeds him.

1998: Newly installed Premier Zhu Rongji announces major reform measures that cut government subsidies for housing, strengthen the Central Bank with new regulatory functions, allow commercial banks to operate independently, launch a reform program for the national medical system, and reform the tax collection system.

2001: December: China enters the WTO. Under the accession terms, China commits to enacting or revising hundreds of laws to open its markets to foreign investment. Most WTO-entry laws must be implemented by December 2005. Virtually all must be implemented by 2007.

came of age during the Cultural Revolution. For this reason, they come to any negotiating table with a background vastly different from that of most foreign MNC managers. (The man responsible for setting the pendulum in motion is, of course, former Chinese premier Deng Xiaoping. For a brief synopsis of his political life and times, see the box, "Father of China's Reform.")

China's Economic Reform: Groping for Stones

During the past 15 years, China's economic reform has to a significant degree been conducted as a process of trial-and-error, creating a particularly challenging business environment for managers of multinationals. An apt description of the process (which is still under way) is the Chinese idiom "groping for stones to cross the river." For managers of MNCs in China, developing operations in an environment in which the economic system is evolving and changing often creates confusion; newly issued regulations can be vague, inconsistent, or even contradictory. Many complain not only of not understanding the rules of the game, but also of not being sure where the playing field starts and stops.

Philips China's David Chang offers this advice to newcomers to this market: "First, when deciding whether or not to invest in China, you cannot use the normal business plan process. The normal key assumptions for a business plan are: cost, business opportunities, how much investment is necessary. Revenue minus cost equals profit, right? But this is China. Here, there are other factors that are not so obvious." Chang says that managers cannot calculate business opportunity in China by "mathematical exercise," because some factors that will affect your business are not easily foreseen. Why the hidden risks? He explains, "The simple reason is that China is still in a transition period from a planned economy to a market economy. Now, they are in-between. Since they are in-between, there are a lot of gray areas." In other words, standard business decision-making processes will not work in China. Instead, Chang advises incoming MNCs to create and follow a "China-relevant business plan, not an international business plan."

Other executive interviewees echoed this warning of uncertainty and change. As an example of how the environment affects business operations, Airbus China's Guy McLeod summed up his experience in negotiating with the Chinese government to obtain permits and licenses in this way: "It can be a long, laborious, time-consuming process. But other times, it can be very simple. It's never the same."

How can an international manager lead successful business operations under such conditions of uncertainty? Our interviewees had two primary answers to this question: first, go with the flow; second, focus on the long-term objectives.

Attorney Norman Givant best sums up the "go with the flow" message by explaining that China's booming economic development has taken place despite the messy, chaotic, and confusing backdrop of the transformation from a communist to a socialist and market-based system. "The Chinese have no problem at all in living with contradictions. Their question is: Does it work over time?" says Givant. He points to Shanghai's remarkable growth as an example. "Look out the window: you see a prosperous, dynamic city [Shanghai] that has grown tremendously in the last 20 years, and it grew primarily by ignoring the contradictions and focusing largely on the economic development."

David Chang of Philips also stressed that MNCs in China cannot wait for all the gray zones to be cleared away before operating. He says some gray zones involve "opportunities that you need to grab." In other words, foreign companies should follow the regulations as best they can, keep in close contact with the government, but still keep moving as a business despite the fog of uncertainty still clouding certain issues.

The second piece of advice is: think positively and for the long term. If regulations in your industry are currently unclear, it is possible that clarification is under way. Our interviewees point out that many regulations are becoming clearer and more standardized since China's accession to the WTO on December 11, 2001 (after 14 years of negotiation). The act was heralded around the world as a victory for free trade. Within China, entering the WTO served to confirm the current political mindset promoting economic liberalization, globalization, and de facto market capitalism.

"

China is still in a transition period from a planned economy to a market economy. Now, they are in-between. Since they are in-between, there are a lot of gray areas."

David Chang, CEO, Philips China

China's acceptance into the WTO was contingent upon deregulating many industries and opening vast new domestic markets to foreign companies. By 2005, after four years of implementing its WTO commitments, the international business community has acknowledged that China is largely on track for meeting its commitments by passing new regulations that open China's markets and level its playing fields. And even among industries not impacted by WTO entry, our international executives say, China's regulations are being standardized and government is rapidly becoming business-friendly.

The bottom line: working with government remains a challenge to MNCs in China, but the situation is improving. In the *2005 Business Climate Survey* taken of members of the American Chambers of Commerce based in Shanghai and Beijing, the 450 respondents named the following as "Top Challenges to Doing Business in China." Only the top-ranked challenge (lack of management-level human resources) was not directly government-related. The other primary challenges were: (2) bureaucracy, (3) unclear regulations, (4) lack of transparency, (5) inconsistent interpretation of regulations, (6) corruption, (7) difficulty enforcing contract terms, and (8) local protectionism. The good news: reviewing polling results of this annual survey shows that, since 1999, respondents have fairly consistently reported that each of these categories of government-related challenges is "improving" year by year.

The New Chinese Bureaucrat

Many of the challenges international managers face in working with the Chinese government stem from the fact that new laws and policies are being introduced by officials schooled and trained in an entirely different ideology. As mentioned above, Chinese officials aged 50 or older saw their schooling interrupted and began working during the Cultural Revolution and afterward advanced their careers by mastering the ideology espoused during the communist system. Meanwhile, even 40- and 30-something officials were schooled in communist ideology as youngsters. While many Chinese officials today are quite progressive and international, it is inevitable that business and government interactions do still at times suffer from a clashing of ideologies.

"The real problem is that when you find a socialist command economy interfacing with a capitalist market mentality, the potential for misunderstanding from both sides is enormous," says Norman Givant of Freshfields Bruckhaus Deringer. Givant warns that some of the changes that have taken place through economic reform are mainly cosmetic, or "old wine in new bottles." As he explains, "The government still does micro-manage the domestic sector." For example, while many bureaus have been "corporatized" in recent years, and are now ostensibly operated as private companies, the reform is sometimes only skin deep. In some cases, the companies have new names but follow old, established operating models. "The [newly privatized] corporate groups are staffed with bureaucrats from the former bureaus. Thus, the bureau still has effective control of the factories under them, directing their production, interfering in the selection of management personnel, et cetera," says Givant. "What you have are the same factories with the same bureaucrats in charge, reporting to the same government authority. So I would say the form has changed but not the substance." He adds that the problem of ineffective SOE reform is now less prevalent in China's major economic centers. "In Shanghai, the tendency has been to select [factory managers] with technical competency. But in other parts of the country, the choice is still often dictated by political factors rather than professional competence," he says.

One vestige of the planned economic system that remains intact despite economic reform is the multilayered labyrinth of central, provincial, and local governments that MNCs must navigate in seeking approvals. It remains common for a single investment project to need simultaneous interaction with and approval from organizations within the central, provincial, and local government. Dr. Gary Dirks of British Petroleum China explains that agencies at different government levels can operate according to different priorities. Thus, satisfying all governmental requirements can be challenging. "All these different levels will take an interest in the nature of the project, the timing of it, who is involved in it," says Dirks. "That hasn't changed at all."

Ideological clashes can also be caused by the fact that Chinese government officials and managers of multinationals tend to have vastly different attitudes toward business risk. "Our [Western] commercial environment is based on risk-taking—entrepreneurial assessment of risk. The Chinese model, on the other hand, is a system of control," says Givant. Under the communist system, it was considered critical to build in a network of political checks and balances. Risk-taking was impossible, since many approvals were needed for any degree of change. Givant says that while Chinese entrepreneurs tend to be quite willing to take risks, government officials tend to remain distinctly risk averse. "The average bureaucrat is deathly afraid of making a mistake and so is very conservative in any sort of decision-making," he says. "This is a society in which no one gives you kudos for being successful, but your career is on the line if you make a mistake. So, where are the incentives? The incentives are for caution, for conservative behavior, for kicking any decision upstairs because—God forbid—you don't want to take the responsibility for making any decision on your own."

> "*The real problem is that when you find a socialist command economy interfacing with a capitalist market mentality, the potential for misunderstanding from both sides is enormous.*"
>
> **Norman Givant**, Shanghai Office Managing Partner, China Practice Group, Freshfields Bruckhaus Deringer

Other interviewees agreed that there is a kind of acceptance within China that the system is in flux, that the government is still "groping for stones." For example, many business associations and chambers of commerce in China now operate without licenses. In many cases, these high-profile associations have been negotiating for a license for years. In the meantime, they are not only allowed to operate (some on a large scale), but government agencies interact directly with the "illegal" organizations by attending functions and speaking at events. Another example is English-language publishing in China. Any visitor to Shanghai, for example, will find a flourishing business in English-language business and entertainment magazines, none of which are licensed. The government allows them to be produced (most are distributed free at hotels and restaurants or via mailing lists), at least until one of them crosses a line and is then cracked down on and disbanded.

"It is true that you can see many commercial structures being created in the absence of laws, with laws enacted after the fact to give legitimacy to something that has already taken place," says Givant. In other words, officials will allow a business to operate, judge its effectiveness and the impact on the overall business environment, then decide whether it should be legalized or not. "Or you see situations where local regulations are encouraged from the central government but applied locally first to see if they work. Then they are enacted in the national context." Givant stresses that this kind of flexibility has been central to China's remarkable economic progress in recent years.

Mindset Gap Narrowing

Overall, our interviewees generally confirmed that ideological clashes between government and international business are lessening, and that China now enjoys an improving regulatory environment and increasing regulatory stability. "China in the past has attracted investment based mainly on its dynamic growth—investors didn't want to miss the chance to be part of this new story. But now investors are not only attracted by the growth, but even more by the accountability and stability in the country," says Bayer China's Dr. Elmar Stachels. He stresses that economic development has been under way in China for 20 years, and that the country has made great strides toward creating international-standard rules and regulations since WTO accession. Stachels says these changes create "a new basis for foreign investors to be confident."

While the differences between international business thinking and Chinese government thinking had brought some degree of challenge to most managers of MNCs in China, our interviewees agreed that the mindset gap is narrowing. "When I came here, China was still predominately state-planned," says China veteran Philip Murtaugh of General Motors China. "The government controlled almost everything, made all the decisions—how much you needed to produce, how many people you were to employ." But since his arrival in China in 1994, he has seen a "gradual but continuous shift to a more market-oriented economy." Today,

Murtaugh says, China has changed. "By far, most of the government people I meet have a pretty good understanding of macroeconomics, job creation, and the importance of profits," he says. "They realize the importance of the market economy. In the past, people thought that profits were bad, that companies shouldn't be allowed to make profits, and all the wealth should be distributed evenly. That thinking has changed completely toward understanding that what is important is to create jobs and to allow people to improve their standard of living." Murtaugh says many officials now understand that, in order to expand the economy, investors must be allowed to earn a return. "There has been a dramatic shift in government thinking on economics and the importance of investment and profitability. Now the government spends a lot of time talking to you about profitability."

Norman Givant agrees that official thinking is changing. "When you go to the Party School in Beijing, they are no longer teaching you Marxist Leninist economics. They are teaching modern economic modeling. So, even in the sacred halls of communist ideology, they are trying to educate comrades to deal with a changed and changing world." Givant says that such teaching sometimes includes giving elements of market-based economics "a communist label so that it passes muster." Even so, a fundamental shift toward adopting a market-driven system is under way. "As Deng said, 'It doesn't matter whether a cat is black or white as long as it catches mice,'" says Givant. "This is opposed to Mao, who used to say 'Better Red than expert'—meaning that ideological purity is more important than technical competence."

The consensus among our interviewees, although viewpoints differed between industries, was that the government mindset is shifting toward becoming more international and more business-friendly. British Petroleum's Gary Dirks calls the Chinese government "progressive" in tackling economic challenges: "The issues and problems confronting China are quite clear: reform of the banking system, SOE reform, unemployment and pensions, fiscal capacity. These are all problems that the [Chinese] leaders now understand." While Dirks says these are "huge challenges" requiring "every bit of wisdom and innovation" to solve, he is confident that the Chinese government is willing and able to continue economic reform. "What I like about Chinese leadership is that they do their homework quite well. They've got people on the ground, finding out what's going on." As an example, he points to the government practice of inviting foreign experts to educate domestic officials on international best practices, or sending officials abroad for training. When Chinese delegations have visited BP operations for such briefings, Dirks says, the officials are serious about learning. "They actually come well prepared and they ask interesting questions. They know what they are after and they listen closely. Afterward, they shape that experience to China," he says.

> *"There has been a dramatic shift in government thinking on economics and the importance of investment and profitability. Now the government spends a lot of time talking to you about profitability."*
>
> **Philip Murtaugh**, Chairman and CEO, General Motors China

Alcatel's Dominique de Boisseson illustrates the change in government thinking with an example that occurred when Alcatel acquired a majority stake in Shanghai Bell in 2002. The transaction went to the very top of the Chinese government. "We had to wait for Jiang Zemin's approval," de Boisseson remembers. But two years later, when the company established a research center in Chengdu, regulations allowed Alcatel executives to negotiate only with the local government. "Of course, Beijing was informed, but the main partner was the local government, the mayor of Chengdu," says de Boisseson. The governmental attitude was far more business-friendly the second time around.

Another example of the new attitude: government officials tend to actively seek interaction with business leaders today. De Boisseson points out that officials are now often willing to attend and speak at business functions—a significant change over years past. He sums up the new attitude in this way: "In the past, the government focused on making sure you operated under their rules. Now, they try their best to adjust their rules to accommodate the business community's needs—they try to help. It is a different role." He says that much of the change is based on the realization of the benefits of foreign investment to local government. "They've seen the advantage of having foreign investment. They are now very keen to attract you to invest in their location," he says.

One example of the newly progressive and accessible government attitude is the Shanghai Municipal Foreign Economic Relations and Trade Commission (SMERT), the agency that foreign

"*The Chinese government is really trying to make foreign investors comfortable with the environment. ... China is trying to grow its economy. In order to maintain the GDP growth rate at 7% or 8%, the government needs a lot of help from foreign investors.*"

Jun Tang, President, Microsoft China

companies work with in Shanghai to establish operations, receive import–export licenses, or to reach other government agencies. SMERT is generally seen by the international business community as modern and effective. In 2004, the commission launched five special business teams to focus on seeking investment from specific trade partners. The North American Business Team is staffed by well-educated, English-speaking personnel who will visit potential investors' offices to make presentations on investment opportunities. One telling sign of the times: SMERT representatives are required to print their cell-phone numbers on their name-cards, allowing businesspeople to call them directly and so avoiding the dreaded government phone systems.

Seiichi Kawasaki of Sony China says the biggest change in attitude took place after China's WTO entry. "Compared with years past, it's much easier to do business today," he says. "There is a clear understanding that, after entry into WTO, there is one concern [in government]: how to adapt to global standards."

Microsoft China's Jun Tang is decidedly positive in his assessment of current attitudes of officials toward foreign investment. "In general, the Chinese government is very supportive and cooperative when you want to set up an operation here. They are willing to provide as much as they can," he says. "I am very pleased with the experience, not only in Shanghai, but in some other cities like Beijing as well." Tang says investors enjoy "far greater support compared to 10 years ago," and adds that "the Chinese government is really trying to make foreign investors comfortable with the environment." Many recent regulatory changes have been made in order to help investors, he says, rather than to help officials to regulate them. "China is trying to grow its economy. In order to maintain the GDP growth rate at 7% or 8%, the government needs a lot of help from foreign investors," says Tang.

Power Shift: Central to Local

Another change noted by our top executive interviewees is a shift in power from the central to the local governments since WTO accession. Du Pont China Holdings' Charles Browne explains:

"One of the things that has happened since the late 1990s is the decentralization of authority. When we seek permission for a project, previously, the decisions were usually made in Beijing. Now, the rules and regulations are more decentralized to the province level." Today, only the largest of projects still need central government approval, he says. Browne says this is generally a positive change, allowing companies to focus on building government relationships with the same entities that monitor their day-to-day operations.

Another aspect of the power shift toward local governments is that these regional entities are now competing with each other to attract investment—a scenario that benefits investors. Microsoft's Jun Tang says liberalized regulations now allow investors more freely to choose projects and locations. "Now, every city, every district can attract foreign investment. If Shanghai isn't supportive of me investing while another city treats me as a VIP, why do I have to be in Shanghai?" says Tang. "I enjoy the competition."

Unilever China's Alan Brown shares a story illustrating how MNCs can use this competitive atmosphere to their advantage. Several years back, Brown says, Unilever faced a "potential competitive disadvantage" when a local laundry detergent manufacturer achieved very attractive investment terms from a local government. At first, Brown says, Unilever "moaned and groaned" about the competitor's business terms. Later, Unilever switched tactics to negotiate its own attractive investment terms for operations in Anhui province. "We discovered we can get the same level of support through our own relationship with a local government," says Brown. The company later moved its manufacturing to Anhui. "We got really good competitive advantages through this cooperation. The level of support has given us a real competitive asset equal to what local companies can get. It has had a dramatic impact on the profitability of our business."

In fact, Tang and other international managers warn that the pendulum sometimes swings too far toward business-friendliness, to the point where local officials promise more than they can offer in order to win projects. International investors have been burned by accepting terms and perks from local governments that offer more than is legally permissible. In such cases, the MNC loses.

The underlying message from international managers is that the Chinese government is clearly shifting into a pro-business mode—becoming accessible, and even helpful, to international investors. But this new mindset does not mean that problems in working with government no longer exist. Rumors persist of international companies needing to develop and nurture special unofficial government relationships in order to succeed in winning approvals and permits. Newcomers wonder how to go about establishing an unofficial network into key government agencies. In the next section, our interviewees separate government *guanxi* fact from myth.

The Need for Special *Guanxi*

While it remains important to build and nurture relations with key business-related government agencies, our interviewees stressed that the nature of *guanxi* is changing as China evolves into a more international and standardized business environment. Most of them saw the cultivation of relationships with government officials as a benefit for companies, rather than as a "make or break" requirement.

Our interviewees generally agreed with Unilever's Alan Brown, who stressed that relationship-building need not cross over into corrupt practices. "*Guanxi* is more important in China because of the government's heavy involvement in economic matters and the high degree of investment. So, yes, it's very important, but it doesn't require any compromise to one's established business codes of conduct. *Guanxi* has to be interpreted literally, rather than colloquially."

Others also described government *guanxi* as helpful, but not essential, for MNCs. Du Pont China's Charles Browne agrees: "I think [government] relationships are important, but they are not overriding." He adds that "relationships aren't the only way to get things done," but they do help. "If you only rely on the rule of law to solve your problems, you are going to have a difficult time since the laws sometimes are vague and you can interpret them in different ways." Guy McLeod of Airbus China also described *guanxi* mainly as a method for speeding up government procedures. "You do need to maintain a very close contact with the government so they know you well, to speed up approval processes. It's a key element of my responsibility. Whatever we are doing, there are a number of ministries that you need to lobby."

International managers also stressed that government relationship-building in China isn't as different or mysterious as some international businesspeople may fear. As GE China's Steve Schneider says, "Relationships are important everywhere. China is no different from the U.S. Relationships are a critical way to get entry into a discussion—they get you in the door—but ultimately, product performance, services, and people will get the deal done over time."

"*Very often, approvals are subject to official interpretation. So it can slow everything down if you don't have good relationships [with the government] in China.*"

Stanley Wong, CEO, Standard Chartered China

The second point made by our interviewees is that *guanxi* becomes more important whenever regulations or policies are vague or incomplete. Microsoft's Jun Tang explains that one of the main reasons *guanxi* remains important is that China's business laws are often written in opaque terms, leaving interpretation open to individual officials. "Chinese laws don't specify a lot. If [officials] favor you, you get a better judgment. That's the reason *guanxi* in China is super-important," he says. For example, a company without good government relations may spend six months seeking a permit, while another company with good *guanxi* may receive it in two weeks.

Standard Chartered's Stanley Wong agrees that *guanxi* helps when regulations are vague. "Even though the [banking] industry all follows the same guidelines, you still need to maintain a good relationship with the government. It is very important." For example, he says, although China now offers clear rules and regulations on opening bank branches, doing so still requires many types of approval. "Very often, approvals are subject to official interpretation. So it can slow everything down if you don't have good relationships [with the government] in China."

By the same token, relationships become less important when regulations are clarified and standardized. McKinsey & Co.'s Gordon Orr stresses this point to clients. "The issues [of *guanxi*] come up much more when you are a pioneer, the first to do something in a particular place," he says. For example, *guanxi* becomes less important for companies that invest in a science park, where policies and procedures have become standardized for all investors.

(For advice and strategies on building legitimate *guanxi*, see the next two sections of this chapter, "Negotiating With Government," and "Business-to-government Best Practices.")

Negotiating With the Government

While it is becoming easier to form positive working relations with government agencies, the "2005 Top Business Challenges" chart compiled by AmCham Shanghai and AmCham-China (based in Beijing) (see Table 8.1) proves that MNCs still struggle when working with the government.

Our interviewees named similar challenges to those named in the "Top Challenges" chart. To follow are the main difficulties identified by our 28 China experts in working with the Chinese government—lack of enforcement of laws, flawed judicial system, inconsistent interpretation of regulations, and delays—and their expert suggestions for tackling these issues.

TABLE 8.1 *Top Business Challenges, 2005*

Source: From the *2005 Business Climate Survey* of 450 member companies in the American Chamber of Commerce in Shanghai and the American Chamber of Commerce in China (based in Beijing).

TOP BUSINESS CHALLENGES, 2005

		Perceived change 2004	2005
1	Management-level human resources	+	−
2	Bureaucracy	+	+
3	Unclear regulations	+	+
4	Lack of transparency	+	+
5	Inconsistent regulatory interpretation	+	+
6	Corruption	+	+
7	Difficulty enforcing contract terms	+	+
8	Local protectionism	+	−

(+ = improving − = worsening)

Challenge #1: Lack of Enforcement of Laws

The greatest difficulty experienced by our interviewees in working with the government in China is the immaturity of the regulatory and legal system. Across the full spectrum of industries represented, international managers faced challenges related to China's still-developing rule of law. 3M China's Kenneth Yu explains: "China has 5,000 years of history, but the China we know today is a very young country. There are a lot of things the host government is still learning. There is no doubt that they are improving every day. Compared with other governments, they have done an incredible job. The Chinese government has a truly honest, positive attitude in honoring business laws, but sometimes the laws aren't complete enough and things fall through the cracks." In other words, the "will" exists, but the "way" is not yet complete. Yu also stresses that these "cracks" do not prohibit his company from investing, but they do create extra concerns and challenges. In cases of serious legal problems, he says, businesses can generally rely on the Chinese regulatory system. "I don't see [the government] deliberately ignoring business law. As a businessman, I would say that if someone owes us money, yes, we have a way of retrieving it in China. When we enter into a purchase agreement or JV agreement, the laws are quite good."

David Chang of Philips China also describes the regulatory environment as young and undeveloped. "If you look at China from [the standpoint of] a political and economic evolution, they have created their own way; there are no references, no model to follow. They are creating a success story by trial and error," he says. He expects the government to continue making progress and urges international companies to appreciate the difficulties the government is facing. The main problem the government faces now, he says, is the gap between passing and enforcing regulations. "That gap is too big," he says, adding that the government sometimes focuses on the number of laws it has changed in order to comply with WTO commitments, while not facing up to enforcement issues.

Challenge #2: A Flawed Judicial System

One area of weakness mentioned by many of our interviewees is China's judicial system. Several named the courts as the weakest link in the legal system, explaining that China's judicial system is known for a general lack of professional standards and practices. As Norman Givant of Freshfields Bruckhaus Deringer China states, "The courts are not an effective and impartial forum. The promulgation of laws and regulations is progressing in the right direction, but the judiciary is still problematic and has a long way to go." He explains that while improvements are under way, the judicial system suffers from a history of misuse. "1: Deng Xiaoping didn't believe in a separation of powers. 2: When Deng decided to slim down the military, he had to find places for the retired military men, so he put them in the courts. The judiciary in the 1980s was staffed with military people with no legal background who were responsive to local Party direction."

Today, the courts are shedding their unprofessional past, but slowly. Says Givant: "China now has judicial training institutes and they are trying to improve the quality of judges. But again, that is something that will only happen over time." He stresses that the legal system has improved quickly; the judicial system, less so. "The kids graduating from law schools now are bright and have open minds. There is hope for the future. But the judiciary is still problematic. It is still not fully professional; it is definitely not independent of local interests or political influences."

Given the poor reputation of the judicial system, many international managers consider going to court as a last resort. "The law and its observation is, on the whole, good; it tends to be more questionable whether you get it enforced," says BP China's Dr. Gary Dirks. BP generally avoids the Chinese court system as a channel for redress, he says. "We are not a particularly litigious company, so our first reaction is not to go to court. In general, if there are good reasons why you are no longer in alignment with someone, then it's better to negotiate [out of court]." Charles Browne of Du Pont China agrees. "While our experience in local courts has been satisfactory, we prefer to resolve any problems directly with the company rather than resort to going to court.

Through negotiations, you can almost always come out with a result. It may not be the ideal result, but it is still better than going to court."

Our interviewees roundly agreed that the legal system, courts, and enforcement are all improving. "China has made tremendous progress. I think of where we were 24 months ago, and the progress you hear about every single day. I get a legal alert every week from a law firm based here and they continue to talk about the changes," says Steve Schneider of GE China. "The question is, how quickly will the legal changes be disseminated throughout the legal system and throughout China? How will they be perceived? How will they be enforced? Those are the questions many people will be asking next." Schneider says now that the laws are in place, the courts and enforcement systems are the next step. "There are plenty of laws, and they now really design laws that make sense and are in vogue with the times. The court system continues to improve. They continue to focus on that, because that is where the decisions are made. So, the ultimate question comes down to this: once a decision is made, how is it enforced? That's where the questions reside today: the ability to enforce the winning if you win something. There is a big question mark now."

Schneider added that GE's limited experiences in using the court systems have been positive. The company has been taken to court in China, but was treated fairly. "What we've found is that if you are well prepared and you are right—and your processes were sustained and worked well—then the court system [in China] does listen to that," he says.

> "
>
> *There are plenty of laws, and they now really design laws that make sense and are in vogue with the times. ... So, the ultimate question comes down to this: once a decision is made, how is it enforced? That's where the questions reside today: the ability to enforce the winning if you win something."*
>
> **Steve Schneider**, Chairman and CEO, General Electric China

Challenge #3: Inconsistent Interpretation of Regulations

Another oft-named difficulty in working with government is that while a plethora of new business-related laws and regulations have been passed, especially following WTO, many of these are incomplete or confusing. The top executives we interviewed describe welcoming a new law or regulation that liberalizes their industry, but struggling through the details of actually following the new rule.

Executives note some improvements since WTO accession. Du Pont China's Charles Browne says that information on new regulations is more accessible since 2001. "Before, it was difficult to know what the rules and regulations are. Now, they are published; they are on the web."

But if regulations are accessible but unclear, confusion still reigns. John Wong of The Boston Consulting Group still warns clients in China that working with government can be an opaque process. "It is easier to get things done because of liberalization, but it is still as much of a black box as it used to be. It's not a transparent system."

The biggest regulatory difficulty mentioned is that the same regulation is often interpreted differently at different levels of government and in different regional areas. As Dominique de Boisseson of Alcatel puts it, "The law is the same everywhere, but the way of applying it is different."

Christopher Shaw of Eli Lilly China explains that the central government issues "big guidelines," which tend to be open to interpretation. "Each province implements them in a slightly different way. And that slightly different way could have significant impact [when applied to business]." This confusion is multiplied by the number of different jurisdictions a company operates in; each municipality may be interpreting the same regulations differently. Another factor leading to inconsistent implementation of laws, Shaw says, is the "lack of expertise and experience with intellectual property law in China, since this is a new phenomenon." He adds that "many of the Chinese judiciary are not fully trained or qualified to rule on broad aspects of the law."

Adding to the challenge for MNCs is the fact that central and local governments sometimes disagree on regulatory issues. In such cases, Siemens China's Ernst Behrens says, companies can be caught between central and provincial government opinions and directives. "I think, as in other countries, there is a considerable degree of frustration at the central level because the provincial and municipal governments are handling matters their own way, as they consider this to be economically more beneficial to them," he says.

One very serious warning issued by our international interviewees: don't assume that the central government overrides local government opinion when business regulations are vague. In other words, companies that have received assurances from central government agencies with regard to investment projects may still face problems if local government officials disagree. Conversely, assurances from powerful local government agencies do not protect companies from disputes with central government agencies. Carrefour China knows this very well (see "Carrefour: Entanglement in China," to follow).

However, although problems remain, most of our interviewees said the overall business environment is becoming more stable, with increased government support.

"

Each province implements legal guidelines in a slightly different way. And that slightly different way could have significant impact [when applied to business]."

Christopher Shaw, President, Eli Lilly China

Challenge #4: Delays

As is likely true among business executives worldwide, a common complaint among our interviewees is that seeking government approvals in China is a slow and sometimes convoluted process. Du Pont China's Charles Browne reports, "The process of negotiation can take much longer than we expect." He adds that his U.S.-based colleagues tend to become impatient with delays in China. However, he adds that waiting is generally not a serious hindrance to company business plans. "We never run into a situation in which we are barred from something we really want to do," he says.

Patience is often necessary in government negotiations, agrees Paolo Gasparrini of L'Oréal China. He tells of several "challenging" negotiations with Chinese officials. "You need a lot of time. Just when you think you [have] arrived at the conclusion, you can again start from zero. When you get to the last step, the following day, someone again wants to speak about Step One." His advice: "Be patient and play the game." After gaining the trust of key officials, he says, progress will be made. "In negotiations with the government, you cannot go fast. People have to trust you. Then suddenly you will find a solution."

CASE STUDY

CARREFOUR: ENTANGLEMENT IN CHINA

On February 8, 2001, in the midst of the annual Spring Festival holiday, Carrefour China received an unpleasant surprise. Reuters quoted a Chinese official from the State Trade & Economic Commission (STEC) as stating that the French hypermarket giant had disregarded Chinese law by opening stores without permission from the central government. On February 20, the *Financial Times* reported that STEC had demanded that Carrefour China restructure its 27 stores to meet government requirements.

The Carrefour company was founded in 1959 and is now the number 1 chain retailer in Europe and second only to Wal-Mart worldwide. Carrefour entered China in 1995 by establishing hypermarkets in Beijing and Shanghai, the country's two primary consumer markets. Thanks to the explosive growth of China's retail market, average annual sales among the top 100 chain retailers in China jumped from RMB240 million (US$29 million) in 1997 to RMB2.5 billion (US$300 million) in 2002, while the average number of stores among the top retailers increased from 24 to 169. Carrefour successfully took advantage of the rising demand for hypermarket shopping, developing into the largest international general retailer in China by 2000.

Before July 1992, foreign enterprises were largely blocked from entering the retail and wholesale sectors in China. The only exception was that, under the *Law on Chinese–Foreign Equity Joint Ventures* (1983) and the *Law on Foreign-capital Enterprises* (1990), part of the products that foreign manufacturers made in China could also be sold in China.

In July 1992, the State Council of China permitted the establishment of up to two retail Sino-foreign joint ventures in six business centers—Beijing, Shanghai, Tianjin, Guangzhou, Dalian, and Qingdao—and five special economic zones, including Shenzhen, Zhuhai, Shantou, Xiamen, and Hainan. Local governments were required to seek approval for these joint ventures from the central government. In addition, the business scope of these JVs was confined to retail and import/export.

This ruling was not put into practice until October 1995, when the State Council approved the first two pilot foreign–domestic JV chain retailers in Beijing, on the condition that the local partner held at least 51% of equity. In this way, foreign retailers finally entered China.

In order to seize market opportunities and gain first-mover advantage, many foreign retailers establishing in China during the late 1990s began side-stepping the slow central government approval process by working directly with provincial or city governments in making investments. Eager to expand their local economies, many local government officials were generous in promising foreign retailers favorable land-use rights, shareholding ratios, and other enticing terms. Carrefour was among those firms aggressively expanding their networks by forming agreements with local governments throughout China.

Local governments had sound reasons for granting approvals to Carrefour without undertaking the central government approval process. For example, the hypermarket chain fit well with local government goals to boost the local economy and to upgrade the domestic retail business by introducing international retail standards and practices. While Wal-Mart, which had more strictly followed central government approval procedures, was located only in Guangdong province, Carrefour had entered major business centers including Shanghai and Wuhan. By late 1999, Carrefour ranked as the second-largest chain retailer in China, second only to Shanghai Lianhua Supermarkets, with revenue of RMB7.3 billion (US$88 million) in 1999. By 2000, Carrefour China's annual sales reached RMB8.1 billion (US$975 million).

In 2001, the central government realized it had lost control of growth in the foreign-invested retail sector, and Carrefour became a natural target for a crackdown. The government issued the *Circular on Punishments for Carrefour's Deviant Behaviors in Conducting Merchandising Business in China.* The president of Carrefour global rushed to Beijing to apologize. After a negotiation lasting several months between Carrefour and the central government, an agreement was reached. As punishment for not complying with central government procedures, the company had to seek the approval for each of its 27 stores again from the central government. In addition, during the negotiation period, the company was forbidden from expanding its outlets in China.

The negotiation period lasted for six months and was finally lifted in November 2001. As of late 2005, Carrefour operated 65 stores throughout China. Despite the loss of expansion time, the hypermarket chain is now the nation's fifth-largest.

Business-to-government Best Practices

If *guanxi* with officials remains important for an international company's success in China, how exactly can an upstanding corporate leader build relationships while avoiding corruption? This question sparked rich responses from our interviewees.

First, our profiled executives stressed that they take care to ensure that they and their employees obey the laws of China and those of their home country. (For example, U.S. companies must abide by the U.S. *Anti-Corrupt Practices Law*.) On top of that, they must obey global corporate codes of conduct. However, many stressed that they look for ways within these guidelines to build trust and goodwill with government entities, and even with individual officials. This section of the chapter shares the advice of our 28 interviewees on building strong government *guanxi* through legitimate means.

Strategy #1: Involve the Top Executive

The first point made by managers of MNCs in China is that often it is best if the very top executive handles government relations and negotiations—often spending far more time on government interaction than is common elsewhere. Requiring the president or CEO to attend government meetings or events sends a message of goodwill, and gives "face" to officials. Stanley Wong, CEO for Standard Chartered China, estimates that most top executives of international companies in China spend 30% to 40% of their time dealing with regulators and government administrations. "In China, the CEO is seen as the legal representative. Therefore, [officials] look to the legal representative in every aspect of the business," he says. Making a comparison to his previous work for Standard Chartered in Hong Kong, Wong points out that Hong Kong officials tend to be willing to work with mid-level company representatives, but officials elsewhere in China tend to expect to work directly with the top executive.

At the far end of the spectrum is GE China's Steve Schneider; as stated in the introduction to this chapter, Schneider spends roughly 65% of his time working with government, since the company's largest customers in China are SOEs with close government links. "I'm spending a lot of my time with either customers or government agencies. You *have* to," he says.

TIP Chinese authorities prefer to deal directly with the top executive of the organization, for "face" reasons. Be ready to dedicate a significant part of your time to dealing with them.

But while his responsibilities in China revolve around government relations, he stresses that his interaction with government is vastly different from that of his predecessor. "The person I replaced probably was spending 65% to 70% of his time on visiting government officials. I probably spend 20% to 25% of my time doing this," he says. Making traditional "courtesy calls" for the sole purpose of showing respect and building a personal connection with officials is less and less necessary, he says. Schneider says the investment boom in China has left many officials today simply too busy to spend time on straight relationship-building.

L'Oréal's Paolo Gasparrini explains his involvement with Chinese government entities in this way: "I handle the relationship with the government myself. I believe this is the right way. If you try to do things through a lawyer or intermediary, the Chinese don't like it very much. Things only move if you arrive. You have to go yourself. They want to see your face."

Bertelsmann Direct Group Asia's Ekkehard Rathgeber says the effort that top executives make in working with government is generally well worth it. He says since taking up his position as president in 1994, "most of my time is spent in building government relationships—PR work. If you don't pay attention to that, you might face an enormous amount of difficulty that could impact your operations."

Strategy #2: Hire a Local With Government Expertise

But sending the top executive—especially a non-Chinese CEO—into negotiations with the government is not enough to ensure success, our interviewees warned. Many stressed that hiring Chinese nationals with expertise (and often direct experience) in government relationship-building is crucial to the success of any international company's China operations.

> *It's very simple: get a great local to do the work for you. The Chinese have been working with the bureaucracy forever. The only way to function is through the right people."*
>
> **Alan Brown**, Chairman, Unilever China

The methods MNCs use for incorporating government relations expertise into their operations vary widely. At one end of the spectrum is the option of hiring the services of special consultants who promise to supply good government access and relations, for a high price. The Boston Consulting Group's John Wong explains: "There are certain consultants who say, 'If you want to meet the head of the Ministry of Information Industries, I know him well. If you give me US$75,000 as a consulting fee, I'll set up a meeting with him.' There are a lot of these guys in Beijing. They have a set menu: for this level [of official], it's US$10,000; for this level, it's more." Wong says the fact that there is still some demand for such services "shows that access still isn't easy." However, he adds that government officials are generally far more accessible now than they were in the late 1990s, stressing that multinationals today can eventually make contact with any agency they need to reach. The upshot: access isn't impossible without *guanxi*; it just takes longer and the end-result may not be as positive.

None of our international manager interviewees reported making use of such "hired gun" consultants. Instead, nearly all of them recommended hiring experienced in-house staff to handle government relations. Who to hire for this function? Many international companies recruit personnel with a government background, such as retired bureaucrats, or seek to recruit government specialists from other firms. "You need to have very good local teams, because they have good networks in various levels of [government]," says David Chang of Philips China. Government specialists know how to work through the full range of options for the company concerning any specific regulation, he says. "You have to talk to the right decision-makers to really find out the best choice for you, because the deviation between what different government officials say is huge. If you don't do this, you'll miss opportunities." Unilever China's Alan Brown echoes Chang's advice: "It's very simple: get a great local to do the work for you. The Chinese have been working with the bureaucracy forever. The only way to function is through the right people."

The way our profiled companies organized their government relations personnel varied depending on the size of their China operations, and the scope of their business areas and range of geographic locations. Some have established a central Government Relations Department in Beijing. For example, Sony China relies on experts in its Beijing office to negotiate with central government. Says Seiichi Kawasaki: "The relationship with the government is handled by our Beijing office. All the policies are made by the Beijing side [of Sony]."

Other companies set up smaller offices in each of their main operational locations. A third strategy is to establish specific teams focusing on specific industries—such as a team of transportation experts to negotiate with officials monitoring the transport industry, or a team of energy experts to handle interactions with government entities regulating electric power. GE China employs such a method, since the company's areas of focus in China vary from power generation to home appliances to medical equipment.

TIP **Hiring Chinese nationals with connections and expertise in government relationship-building is crucial for the success of your company.**

Strategy #3: Understand the Government Mindset

Successful negotiations with Chinese government entities also depend upon acquiring a full understanding of the government mindset. Knowledge and appreciation of the pressures and challenges faced by government agencies, or even specific individual officials, will go a long way toward alleviating potential trouble spots.

First, our international managers stressed the importance of appreciating the difficulties the Chinese government is experiencing in driving the transition to a market-based economy. Gary Dirks of British Petroleum advises fellow top executives at MNCs to present corporate proposals in light of how the project matches government goals for economic development. "Make sure that, on any strategic move, you think through the implications for the city or the province, and how it would be perceived on the national government level, especially from the point of view of the national interest."

Alcatel China's Dominique de Boisseson explains that international companies should appreciate that while China is "making progress" in establishing the rule of law, the regulatory system will take time to mature. "We must show respect to the people who are leading the change at quite a fast pace," he says, adding that many Western nations went through similar transition periods, but measured in decades instead of years. "We don't complain but adapt," he urges, adding that MNCs should generally assume a positive, compliant attitude. "Meet your commitments, pay your taxes, obey the laws, localize when needed. Comply with the rules and you will form a very deep and lasting partnership with the Chinese government."

> "*This isn't one government; it's a hundred governments. You need to make sure all the potential stakeholders are well informed about your intentions, make them feel they are respected. This will help your process later on a lot.*"
>
> **David Chang**, CEO, Philips China

Another key to winning over the Chinese government is to regard your investment as most officials do: from a big-picture, long-term point of view. Eli Lilly's Christopher Shaw explains the message he sends to government: "Our attitude is that we produce products that help [Chinese] hospitals, help the government, and help patients. And we are going to be here for the long term. This is very important, because if you have a mindset of 'get the money and go,' that isn't the right way. People need to see that you care about the future of China."

Cooperation, rather than negotiation, is the methodology that GE China strives for in government interaction, says Steve Schneider. "In China, the key is working *with* the government. You can't assume that your approach is going to be better than their approach. In fact, they will be influencing you. There has to be a lot of give and take."

Schneider has overseen hundreds of negotiations with Chinese officials since he began heading up GE's China operations in 1998. He says that while GE has at times faced delays and setbacks in China, the company has benefited from trying to see the situation from the government's side. "Sometimes we sat down at the table and reached some decisions, but six months later, [the government officials] changed their minds and decided something else was better," he says. "We, of course, got very frustrated, but you must understand their intention. They are trying to improve the life of the people and the city. I don't think governments are out to hurt business, but they have different priorities."

At Bayer, Dr. Elmar Stachels explains his philosophy in approaching the Chinese government: "It's very important that you not only lobby, but really work from the bottom up to convince everybody that your project is a win-win project, good for the country and for yourself. This is the most important thing. If it isn't a win-win, it's not good for the country, and you shouldn't do it. If it is good, then you should be able to convince everybody about the project." He advises MNCs to use a "down-to-earth" style that covers all the important concerns of the relevant government authorities. "You have to present all the aspects of your project to convince [officials] that it is worthwhile, that it benefits the specific industry. You have to address the environmental issues and the social issues."

Convincing officials of a win-win situation is also a strategy recommended by British Petroleum's Dr. Gary Dirks. "The most important thing is to be sure that what you are trying to do is perceived to be in the interest of some important political entity," he says. "If no particular government entity is excited about the project, if no significant Chinese partner thinks it's a good idea, then you can be sure that it's not going to be easy. Nobody is going to be there helping you, and your project is going to be at the bottom of the pile. If some political entity is interested, usually things keep moving along—not fast, but they keep moving along."

"

The most important thing is to be sure that what you are trying to do is perceived to be in the interest of some important political entity. If no particular government entity is excited about the project, if no significant Chinese partner thinks it's a good idea, then you can be sure that it's not going to be easy."

Dr. Gary Dirks,
President and CEO,
British Petroleum China

Norman Givant of Freshfields Bruckhaus Deringer advises his international clients in China to adopt a tone that government officials will find palatable. "No one likes to hear problems. But at the same time, local officials do want their city to be successful. Therefore, if the message can be couched in a way that does not put [officials] on the defensive, they will be willing to listen." He also advises clients to choose their battles, recognizing that there are limits to what specific individuals or agencies can do. He further reminds them that local governments are ultimately overseen by the central government, and there is a limit to the scope and scale of decisions that can be made without involving Beijing. "Shanghai cannot get too far ahead of central government policy," says Givant. "Shanghai may have a looser leash than many cities, but it's still on a leash."

At McKinsey & Company, Gordon Orr also advises his clients to consider the importance of their project from the government's

TIP Be appreciative of the government's efforts in driving the transition. It's better to project a cooperative attitude than a confrontational one.

point of view. One key to successful negotiations, especially with local government officials, he says, is to "recognize your role in the community." He points out that if your company is "the biggest investor in town," you can expect more government support. "If you are the number 100 company in the Suzhou Science Park, then, frankly, probably no one is going to pay much attention to what you are doing." Again, MNCs can benefit from viewing their project through government eyes.

(For more on the benefits of understanding the government mindset, see "Strategies for Battling IPR Pirates" in Chapter 6.)

Strategy #4: Win Support at All Levels of Government

One clear piece of advice from our interviewees is to build relationships with government entities at all levels, from central to local. Bayer China's Dr. Elmar Stachels explains: "You need to deliver all the arguments to all the levels and get the support from the top-down and the bottom-up combined." He says the key to successful government negotiations is widespread support: "You need to convince everybody, step by step."

Steve Schneider of GE China agrees: "You have to have relationships at all levels in the government—from the State Development and Reform Commission to the Foreign Minister to the deputy directors who are really leading the [decisions]."

David Chang of Philips China adds that it is critical for companies to develop an understanding of all the key officials who influence decisions that concern them. "To help you to get government approvals, you have to talk with all the responsible—and the not-responsible-but-still-connected—authorities," he says. While these officials may not help you, he says, they could block you. Chang adds that such work is too complex and too China-specific for non-Chinese to undertake. "This isn't one government; it's a hundred governments," he says. "You need to make sure all the potential stakeholders are well informed about your intentions, make them feel they are respected. This will help your process later on a lot."

Several interviewees warned those managing MNCs in China that receiving an approval from one government level isn't enough to go forward. Says Carrefour China's Jean-Luc Chereau: "In Taiwan, we learned that the local level [government] is as important as the central level. People coming from Europe into China consider the central level is enough, but this isn't true. You need to establish a good relationship with both the central and the local level." In fact, Carrefour is well known among MNCs in China for having learned a tough lesson on the importance of seeking approval at all levels of government (see earlier box).

TIP **Ensure that you show respect to all the different levels of the administration by keeping them well informed of your plans.**

Another piece of advice from our interviewees: do not rely on any one relationship too heavily. Says GE's Steve Schneider: "People [place all their bets] on one person in one government agency. But things change; you have to have relationships throughout the organization."

Strategy #5: Do Your Homework, and Follow the Rules

All our interviewees stressed that MNCs should prepare fully for any government negotiation. Many agreed that significant delays can be avoided simply by making the effort to fully research and comply with procedures before seeking an approval from the government. "We hear people complaining about the difficulties they have. That's because they don't know exactly what the procedure is," says Du Pont China's Charles Browne. "The greatest difficulty is that the [approvals] process is less understood in China than in the U.S., partly because the process is still evolving." Some companies make the mistake of applying for approval before they fully understand the process required, Browne says. "You can't do it in the reverse order. I think people are more frustrated by the process than by the end-result."

Gary Dirks of British Petroleum advises his fellow executives at international companies to take the following steps: "Be very clear about what the actual approval process is. You need to find the right person in the right department at the right time." After an approval process is under way, companies should keep

TIP Be clear about the actual administrative process. Identify the right person in the right department at the right time. Your team of experts is critical for this task.

tracking their case, he advises. "Find out who has got it now, [and] have [your staff] work with them. Find out what kinds of questions they might have and what additional information they might need. Understand the individual [officials] and be sure to keep things moving along."

Another key piece of advice from our interviewees is to be sure to adhere to all government rules and regulations. "First of all, never cheat," says Dominique de Boisseson of Alcatel China. Second, he advises MNCs to follow through with promises. "When you commit to do something, you do it. That way, you earn their respect. After you gain their respect, you still may not get their 'yes' every time but you have a much better chance of doing business because they know you won't take advantage of them. They know they can trust you."

Strategy #6: Stand Your Ground in Negotiations

Despite advising international managers first to understand and appreciate the viewpoint of the Chinese government, then to do your homework, and to take the time to win support and build trust, many of our interviewees also advised standing your ground in negotiations. Although maintaining good relationships is important, MNCs should not feel they need to bend over backwards or tippy-toe around government officials when trying to negotiate in China.

Bertelsmann Direct Group's Ekkehard Rathgeber says MNCs can—and should—take a tough line on demands. He says expatriate managers should expect the government to take a hard stance in negotiation, and that MNCs should be prepared to hit back. Brinkmanship is a common tactic in Chinese negotiations. Most frustrating for non-Chinese managers is that officials may use indirect methods of influence—so that rather than stating their disapproval of some aspect of a project, the company will face delays and difficulties until that aspect of the project is changed to their liking. "What is clear is that the Chinese have a very tough way of negotiating. It's not a brutal way of openly confronting you, but they have a way of being indirect, of being extremely manipulative and extremely tough," says Rathgeber.

How should an international manager respond to such tactics? "It's important that people also be really tough and not afraid of stating what they want," advises Rathgeber. "Be clear and specific. Do it at an early point of time." And he warns managers to be prepared for a dramatic ending to some negotiations, during which the Chinese side may be testing the MNC to find out exactly where their breaking point is. Says Rathgeber: "Don't be afraid of playing the chicken game. The Chinese will always test you up to the limits. That's part of the process. Don't be afraid of playing to the end."

TIP **Don't be afraid of stating what you want, clearly and specifically.**

Rathgeber adds that China's increasingly open and transparent legal system helps MNCs to take a tough line, at least when the law favors them. He stresses that international companies can now request clear information, then use this in defense of their projects. "You have to insist on seeing the law, getting the facts on the table. There is a lot written down. You don't have to wait three months for an answer. If you ask, you can get the facts," he says. "Very often, if you talk to authorities, they want to make things more transparent. They are frustrated, too."

GE China's Steve Schneider agrees that in today's China, if companies have done their homework and established good government *guanxi*, they can insist on receiving their legal rights. "I have always been very direct. If [the government] suggests things that I don't think are correct, I will let them know. I tell them what I can do and ask them to do what I think is the right thing." He adds that the divide between China's bureaucrats and its entrepreneurs is narrowing. Says Schneider: "With the government people, I do the same thing as with businesspeople."

Conclusion

The ability to negotiate successfully with the government remains a critical factor for any MNC in China. Because China's legal system is still young and shallowly rooted, companies are well advised to form close and positive relationships with the many government entities that monitor their operations. China's complex administrative system requires companies to maneuver through a maze of central, provincial, and local government entities, sometimes with clashing or contradictory interests.

In building good *guanxi* at all levels of government, managers and other company personnel must also avoid corrupt practices and maintain the corporate code of conduct. Working with older-generation officials schooled in the state-run system can be particularly difficult. Other challenges include the lack of enforcement of new laws and regulations, the ineffective court system, inconsistent interpretation of laws, and delays in government procedures.

SUMMARY OF TIPS

NEGOTIATING WITH THE CHINESE GOVERNMENT

1. Involve the Top Executive

Chinese authorities prefer to deal directly with the top executive of the organization, for "face" reasons. Be ready to dedicate a significant part of your time to dealing with them.

2. Hire a Local With Government Expertise

Hiring Chinese nationals with connections and expertise in government relationship-building is crucial for the success of your company.

3. Understand the Government Mindset

Be appreciative of the government's effort in driving the transition. It's better to project a cooperative attitude, than a confrontational one.

4. Win Support at All Levels of Government

Ensure that you show respect to all the different levels of the administration by keeping them well informed of your plans.

5. Do Your Homework, and Follow the Rules

Be clear about the actual administrative process. Identify the right person in the right department at the right time. Your team of experts is critical for this task.

6. Stand Your Ground in Negotiations

Don't be afraid of stating what you want, clearly and specifically.

Chapter 9
Living in China

"Expatriates don't want to leave China because this is the greatest potential market in the universe. Who wants to go to the U.S. right now? Who wants to go to Europe? Even the Chinese managers at this point, they don't want to go abroad either; they want to be in China."

Helen Tantau, Senior Client Partner, Korn/Ferry International China

"For the husband, his life doesn't change much [after moving to China]. He is in contact with the same people, doing the same job, and dealing with highly educated, English-speaking Chinese people. Meanwhile, the wife may be dealing with very different people—the crowds in the supermarket, the uneducated maid and driver, strangers who don't speak English and who may not be used to foreigners."

Victoria Hine, Founding Director, LifeLine expatriate support hotline in Shanghai

INSIDE CHAPTER 9

Introduction

The contrast between the two quotes set out above is the main theme of this chapter: when it comes to non-work life, China can offer either the best or the worst of living environments. Importantly, whether one loves or hates the experience of living in China will depend largely on the personality, attitudes, and mindset of the expatriate manager and his or her family, as we will see in this chapter.

Several problems commonly occur when expatriates are adapting to life in China. Interviewees for this book stressed that some executives who are otherwise excellent in their work may simply not be suited to an overseas assignment. In fact, learning to live happily in China requires certain qualities in a person that may differ from or even conflict with the qualities that make them an expert at their job: traits such as flexibility, adaptability, humility.

A frequent problem for transported executives is that some family members adapt well to China, while others do not. A sobering statistic for companies to consider when sending executives to China: a common industry rule of thumb is that 15–25% of expatriate assignments are aborted early, and the failure rate can run to 70% in developing countries.[1] According to a major study of 270 companies employing a total of 65,000 expatriates conducted in 1999 by PricewaterhouseCoopers (PWC),[2] more than 80% of the companies surveyed reported that employees had turned down assignments "primarily because of dual career problems or family issues." In addition, half of the polled companies reported that when overseas postings fail, the expatriate employee's partner was "a major factor" in the failure. Clearly, companies relocating executives to China must consider the suitability of the executive to overseas life; *but they must also consider the suitability of the family for such an assignment.*

This chapter outlines the advice given by our 20 expatriate managers and eight consultants on living happily in China. We

---

1 "Are You Taking Your Expatriate Seriously?" *McKinsey Quarterly* (McKinsey & Co., 1999).

2 *International Assignments European Policy and Practice: Key Trends 1999/2000* (PricewaterhouseCoopers, 1999).

then outline the most common problems faced by the families of international executives. The chapter ends with suggested best practices for companies preparing to send managers—and their families—on assignment in China.

Life in China for the Expatriate Manager

The first point to be made concerning quality of life in China among the 20 international managers we interviewed was that the overwhelming consensus was positive. Nearly all of those interviewed reported finding China a fascinating and rewarding place in which not only to work, but also to live. While many did report missing certain aspects of life in their home country, none reported being outright unhappy in, or even dissatisfied with, their non-working life in China.

In fact, one of the biggest surprises in researching this book came from asking our expatriate managers when they planned to return to their home country. Among the 20 country managers and China directors interviewed, not one had set a date for returning home. Even more surprisingly, no one—from the head of GE China to the heads of Unilever and Sony—said they hoped to leave China in the near future. In fact, many stated that they would prefer to remain in China for the long term, while one said that, if asked to repatriate, he would likely leave his current employer to seek another position in China.

Many of our China managers identified with the response given by Carrefour China's Jean-Luc Chereau, who had extended his original assignment in China. "I accepted the position for no more than three years in Asia. Now, I have been here for 13 years. My wife and I are very happy in this place. I am willing to stay here for a long time."

For the most part, they described China as offering a distinctly positive living environment, both for themselves and for their fellow expatriate friends and peers. The viewpoint of Airbus

"*I accepted the position for no more than three years in Asia. Now, I have been here for 13 years. My wife and I are very happy in this place. I am willing to stay here for a long time.*"

Jean-Luc Chereau, President, Carrefour China

China's Guy McLeod is common. He says many businesspeople he knows find China better than they expected. "A great number of people who left the job [in China] have returned or say that they would love to come back."

In reviewing the responses of our interviewees, it became clear that there were two primary aspects to their satisfaction with living in China: challenging and rewarding work, and a largely enjoyable—though not perfect—lifestyle. (None of the China managers interviewed reported that their families were experiencing difficulties in adjusting, although the consultants we interviewed identified family adaptation as a common problem—as explained in the section "Life in China for the Expatriate Family".)

High Job Satisfaction

When pressed to describe which aspects of life in China they enjoy, many of our international manager interviewees first mentioned the rewards of their work. Most described the job of heading up China operations as extremely interesting and satisfying. Christopher Shaw of Eli Lilly China explains the allure of his position: "When I first graduated from university, I thought it would be great to run my own company. Running a country [for an MNC] is like running a company. CEO is the best job in the company. You've got all decision-making, operational focus."

Shaw adds that the job of managing operations in China is very satisfying: "I enjoy the operational side [in China]. I enjoy the fast pace." He says that while high-level executives working back home in the head office make decisions that "have influence around the world," his work tends to be focused narrowly on managing operations within China. The flatter, leaner structure of operations in China allows him to enjoy more autonomy, creating a job that is fast-moving and rewarding.

In general, international managers in China shared the belief that they are performing more interesting work, and enjoying more independence, than would be possible in many other work environments. As Unilever China's Alan Brown commented, "What do you do after China? I think I have the best job in

Unilever." Asked about leaving China, he says: "My emotional reaction is that it would be very difficult. [My work in China] has been an exhausting, but phenomenal experience. I don't find China a compelling place to live, but it is a compelling place to work." For Brown, the quality of the work experience makes up for a less-than-ideal quality of life.

Such a viewpoint—that China offers an exciting work experience that is difficult to match elsewhere—is fairly common among the high-level executives placed by Helen Tantau of Korn/Ferry Shanghai. "Anywhere else, you've got layer upon layer upon layer of people above you. But in China, you have the decision-making power—much of what you do is within your control. Managers grow a lot here, because they have to deal with everything, with the business, the government, the ambiguity, the rules, the regulations—absolutely everything you can think of." The result is that job responsibilities are greater and more varied, and while the position may be more challenging, it is also more rewarding. Says Tantau, "You can have a much bigger impact [in China] than in any other economy. The job satisfaction is huge."

She mentions other factors as well. For one thing, international managers in China tend to travel more than do managers elsewhere, as China is such a large country with multiple markets. Frequent travel may be considered by executives to be either a hardship or a perk, but it does make one's job more interesting. In addition, the overall economic boom in China often benefits business operations, while the overall economic performance of the United States, Europe, or Japan may impact corporate operations in those locations less positively by comparison.

The upshot is that once in China, many international executives want to stay. Says Tantau: "Expatriates don't want to leave China because this is the highest-potential market in the universe. Who wants to go to the U.S. right now? Who wants to go to Europe? Even the Chinese managers at this point, they don't want to go abroad either; they want to be in China." Such a strongly positive assessment of China means that many companies face difficulties when repatriating China managers back home.

Another view commonly expressed by international managers is that they have invested time and effort in learning how to

"*Among the 20 country managers and China directors interviewed, not one had set a date for returning home. Even more surprisingly, no one—from the head of GE China to the heads of Unilever and Sony—said they hoped to leave China in the near future.*"

The authors, *China CEO*

succeed in China—experience they don't want to lose by moving back home. Paolo Gasparrini of L'Oréal China had this to say about the prospect of being relocated back to Europe: "You are a pioneer here, because you are in a growing market. From one side, [by going home] you will gain something in terms of quality of life, but you will also lose something." After 10 years in China, he says he no longer finds life in Europe compelling. "When I go back to Europe, by the fourth day, I start to want to come back to China."

Carrefour China's Jean-Luc Chereau expresses a similar sentiment, but attributes his attitude to seniority. "Going back to Paris headquarters may be difficult for somebody who had been CEO of a region. It depends on the age. ... I wouldn't like to go back to Paris—I am so happy to be far away. When you are 35 or 40 years old, you have to work back and forth. Maybe at that age you want to go back."

But even our youngest China manager expressed a strong desire to remain in China. Bertelsmann Direct China's Ekkehard Rathgeber, born in 1965, explains: "For me it would be very difficult [to leave China]. After 10 years here, I have 'China' stamped on my forehead. I came here as project manager, made my career move, and developed quite well. So, for me it would be really difficult to go back, emotionally difficult. I would have an enormous culture shock." In fact, Rathgeber says, he would be unwilling to return to Europe, and would only consider leaving China for another international posting—and then only for one that would prove equally as "interesting."

(Mostly) Enjoyable Lifestyle

Most of our manager interviewees described their after-work life as enjoyable, if imperfect and sometimes challenging. Much of this assessment is likely due to the fact that all 20 of our China managers live in either Shanghai or Beijing—cities that are modern and international by any standard. (Both cities offer world-class shopping, five-star dining, modern telecommunications, and accessible transportation via roadways or subway. In Shanghai, amenities for expatriates include dozens of international elementary schools, international-standard hospitals and clinics, Christian and Catholic churches, sports facilities and Western-owned health clubs, and even a fast-growing number of international MBA and EMBA programs offered in English.)

Eli Lilly China's Christopher Shaw explains why he and his wife enjoy life in China. "My wife has adapted well here. It was easy," he says. Shaw compliments Shanghai on its international-standard housing, restaurants, and widespread availability of goods. He also points out that major travel destinations in China are just a short flight from Shanghai. "We have been to a number of places in China, and there is still a lot to see," he says. "Even if your Chinese isn't good, you can still go very easily."

> ***"When I go back to Europe, by the fourth day, I start to want to come back to China."***
>
> **Paolo Gasparrini**, President, L'Oréal China

In fact, human resources specialists such as Korn/Ferry and Hewitt Associates stress that China's major cities are generally no longer considered "hardship postings" by most multinational companies.

Seiichi Kawasaki of Sony China explains: "In the past, living in China wasn't so comfortable for foreigners, even in Shanghai. But nowadays, I don't think there are any difficulties. Compared with the past, life in China is very much changed." Kawasaki says that it was relatively easy for him and his wife to adapt to living in Shanghai, compared with his earlier international postings. "In Saudi Arabia, I couldn't drink alcohol or eat pork. My wife had to wear a black robe. For her, China is much more comfortable. In China, I don't see any problem; she is enjoying life here."

Some of our interviewees even voiced nostalgia for the "good old days" when day-to-day life in China was an adventure. Airbus China's Guy McLeod says, "When I arrived in 1995, finding a good place to stay was almost impossible, but today there is so much availability. When I first arrived, there were only five bars that weren't in hotels, but now there are a lot more. [Back then], you had the thrill of doing something new, the pioneer spirit."

... Still, There's No Place Like Home

Despite the positive assessment of life in Chinese urban centers, our interviewees did report missing certain aspects of life in their home countries. The language barrier was one of the most commonly cited hardships encountered. Paolo Gasparrini of L'Oréal explains: "This is a big challenge—living in a country where you don't understand what people are saying or writing." He says the language gap affects his everyday life. "I'm used to having a good chat with my neighbors, people in the local stores, or with taxi drivers. But here it's hard." Overall, however, Gasparrini stresses that these hardships have a relatively minor impact on his daily life. "I miss small things, not big things," he says. "I want to go to the cinema and understand 100% of the film, or go for a cappuccino in a café."

Another common complaint is the crowds in China and the difficulty in slipping away to find peace and quiet. "If you want a European weekend—going to the lake or the mountains—here, you don't have this," says Gasparrini. "I like to drive, but here I cannot drive a car. Even if I could drive, where can I go? Shanghai isn't structured for this." Because of the difficulty in driving on China's crowded roads, and the lack of nearby getaways, Gasparrini says he ends up staying in Shanghai more than he would like. "I lose the sense of nature. I like to stay in a place where there is greenery, but here, there are a million people around. It's difficult to find a place where you can sit in nature and read a book."

Fighting the crowds, especially on weekends and holidays, was the top complaint from Du Pont China's Charles Browne as well: "If you go on holiday to a famous place, you have to be prepared for a sea of people. Some people want a little bit of peace and solitude, but in China you can't find it in many places during holidays."

The gist from among the international managers interviewed is that while they were sacrificing some aspects of the lifestyle that were possible in their home country, these sacrifices were generally outweighed by other rewards of living in China. Jean-Luc Chereau of Carrefour explains it this way: "China is a fascinating country. It's not the best in terms of quality of life—if I had to choose, I would say that Spain is number 1, France is number 2—but China is special. I have spent 10 years already in Asia, but I discover new things every day, new challenges. It's a fascinating country."

Unilever China's Alan Brown sums up his life in China with this tongue-in-cheek assessment based on Shanghai's infamous traffic: "I think Shanghai must be the most exciting city in the world. It's exciting just trying to cross the road."

The reputation of China as an interesting, rewarding posting has spread internationally, our interviewees said. Several reported that China assignments are increasingly sought-after within their company. Says Gary Dirks of British Petroleum China: "So many people want to come to China that usually you don't have any trouble [recruiting expatriates]. I can find all I want."

> *"So many people want to come to China that usually you don't have any trouble [recruiting expatriates]. I can find all I want."*
>
> **Dr. Gary Dirks**, President and CEO, British Petroleum China

When Expatriate Managers Don't Adapt ...

But some expatriates simply don't adapt well to China, a fact that the top executives profiled in this book addressed even while stressing their own personal successful adaptation. Our interviewee managers and consultants offered clear assessments of why some expatriates struggle culturally and socially in the Middle Kingdom.

The first point raised was that, assuming the company sends an executive who is technically well-suited to the position open in China, the main reasons for failing tend to be "soft" qualities such as a lack of patience, flexibility, and adaptability. Alcatel China's Dominique de Boisseson explains the qualities he looks for before sending an executive from Europe to China. "Besides technical knowledge, we also look for other qualities such as openness and international experience," he says. Not everyone with the right technical expertise can succeed in China. Those who have never lived overseas or are set in their lifestyle are particularly ill-suited to adapting to China. "Most young people have been to many places and have been exposed to other cultures. It is more difficult for older people—for someone who has always lived close to Paris and has a house with a garden and roses." He sums up his philosophy in this way: "People with closed minds and small ambitions have problems [in China]."

Seiichi Kawasaki of Sony China agrees that it is often the soft skills that make or break an executive attempting to adapt to China

> "
> ***Globally, the failure rate [of expatriate assignments] tends to be much higher than companies expect. ... I think companies are now paying more attention to the soft skills, like patience and not tending to blame China for everything."***
>
> **Simon Keeley**, Head of the Hewitt Asia Leadership Center (HALC), Hewitt Associates China

life. "We have infrastructure such as Japanese schools in Shanghai," he says. "This is an important part, but it's not everything. I think [adaptation] is very much related to personal character."

Philip Murtaugh of General Motors China agrees that personality type and background are the primary keys to adjusting to life in China. "During the seven years I've spent here, there were only two expats who didn't work out [in GM China]. One of them had grown up in one city, met his spouse in that city, and had never left that city before. They didn't have broad horizons, so moving to Shanghai was very tough for them."

Because the ability to adapt to China depends largely on personality type and background, expat executives tend either to adapt quickly or to experience problems within a short time of arriving. Jun Tang of Microsoft China describes this phenomenon: "I have seen many expatriates living in China. One kind of expatriate loves China very much, and says: 'China is great. I love China. I want to live here forever.' The other type thinks China is bad. It depends on attitude." Tang describes one Microsoft executive from the United States who returned early from China: "He hated Chinese food. He hated crowds. He came over, and after three months he quit."

3M China's Kenneth Yu has also seen relocated expatriates fall into two camps, based largely on their personality and mindset. "I have seen Westerners live [in China] very happily; they fell in love with the country and the city. But I have also seen people who landed here, spent one or two years and every time I met them they were talking about, 'When can I leave?' There are two extremes."

Many managers stressed that failure to adapt can occur with overseas assignments anywhere, not only in China. Seiichi Kawasaki has seen Japanese executives fail to adapt to life in the United States and Europe, for example. Du Pont's Charles Browne adds: "I also have had experience with people who didn't adjust to Chile, or even Texas."

HR specialist Simon Keeley of Hewitt Associates says that MNCs today are paying attention to these softer skills when making China assignments. "Globally, the failure rate tends to be much higher than companies expect," he says. But he adds that companies are wising up. "I think companies are now paying more attention to the soft skills, like patience—and not tending to blame China for everything."

Life in China for the Expatriate Family

Among the 20 international top executives interviewed for this book, most had met with few problems in relocating their own or other expat families to China.

The first key to adapting, the interviewees stressed, is that the "hardware" for families is in place—at least in China's major cities. In Beijing, Shanghai, Guangzhou, and other mega-cities, expatriates now find excellent international schooling, top-end housing, and rapidly improving health care. The primary urban centers also offer world-class shopping, dining, health clubs, nightclubs, and entertainment. In addition, families can easily find perks not available in their home country, such as very affordable live-in nannies, maids, cooks, drivers, and tutors. In addition, spouses interested in doing volunteer work can find charitable organizations, churches, or schools to support.

"The quality of life is good even if you don't speak Chinese," assures 3M China's Kenneth Yu. Yu has seen many Westerners come to love living in China. The only challenge, he notes, is when expatriates with school-age children are relocated to cities without international schools. While the number of international schools is growing rapidly, there are still many cities without such facilities.

A word about schooling in China: although international schools are generally considered to be of excellent quality in the major cities, they are also among those in the very top price range worldwide. Average tuition at an international school in Shanghai or Beijing is around US$20,000, and up to US$22,000 for high school. These rates are generally above the cost of international schools in Hong Kong, Tokyo, or Singapore. This makes

"

We have infrastructure such as Japanese schools in Shanghai. This is an important part, but it's not everything. I think [adaptation] is very much related to personal character."

Seiichi Kawasaki, Director and President, Sony China

the cost of schooling a consideration for companies contemplating relocating a family to China, and it is a serious hardship for those who must cover school expenses themselves.

Relocation Mindset

But while the hardware for international families is generally in place in the major business centers, these amenities alone don't ensure that an expatriate manager's family will adapt well to China. Even more important is the mindset of the spouse and children.

Happily, our interviewees reported that most of their companies' relocated families adapt well to China. Philip Murtaugh of General Motors says the family members of expats at GM tend to be pleased with life in China. "Most of our families really enjoy their stay here. We have never had serious problems," he says. In fact, 95% of GM expat personnel "want to extend their assignment."

Ironically, one aspect that helps to ensure a positive and flexible attitude among GE's Western families relocating to China, Murtaugh says, is that China is vastly different culturally from the West. "Moving away from home is always difficult. But with moving to China, [Western] people expect big differences," he explains. Thus, the preconceived ideas which incoming families have of China help prepare them for the differences. In fact, many international families moving to Shanghai or Beijing tend to expect life to be more challenging and less international than it is. When they arrive and find modern housing and schools and amenities, many are "really very impressed" and "satisfied," says Murtaugh.

Murtaugh comments that culture shock is often more severe when families move to a new country that they expect not to be so different from their home country. When Americans move to England, for example, he says, they tend to expect life to be very similar to home. "There is a huge shock in finding that England is a completely different country," he says.

During his nine years as president and managing director of

L'Oréal China, Paolo Gasparrini says he has had no problems with expat families failing to adapt. In his previous posting in Brazil, by contrast, he experienced more challenges because security concerns were more pressing.

One of the key deciding factors for spouses who adapt well to China is their willingness to take the initiative in finding interests and a role for themselves in China. Just as with expat managers, family members who adapt well to relocation are those who come to China with an open mind and a willingness to adapt. Du Pont China's Charles Browne describes his wife's satisfaction with life in China. "I am here with my wife. Both of us adapted equally well. Most of my career has been spent outside the U.S., so she has the flexibility, adaptability, and openness necessary for a successful transition. For us, living in China is enormous fun, a great opportunity to learn. We enjoy it a lot."

When Ekkehard Rathgeber of Bertelsmann Direct Group Asia first arrived in China, the prospects of his wife adapting to life in China seemed slim. "In the beginning, we both saw a problem emerging. The day I arrived, for me it was work 12 to 14 hours a day. For her, she had left her job and her friends, and we were living in a remote place, a huge cold house. It was really, basically, a nightmare." Rathgeber recalls having a discussion with his wife early on. "We realized this could be an extremely serious problem. For me, [my job] was fulfilling; but for her, being in China was a waste of time." The solution, Rathgeber says, came when his wife began treating the China stint as an opportunity for her. "She said, 'Do I take back something after four years, or do I take back nothing?'" Soon after, his wife began studying Chinese. After two years, she also began studying Chinese medicine. "She is now enrolled in a university program and is working in a hospital already." Rathgeber says his wife is now happy and satisfied in China. "She's extremely proud of what she has done."

Dominique de Boisseson of Alcatel says that his wife has similarly found interests to explore in China. "Initially, it was difficult to convince my wife to come [to China], but after three months she was totally taken by this place. She now speaks Chinese and knows all about Shanghai."

"

In the beginning, we both saw a problem emerging. The day I arrived, for me it was work 12 to 14 hours a day. For [my wife], she had left her job and her friends, and we were living in a remote place, a huge cold house. It was really, basically, a nightmare."

Ekkehard Rathgeber, President, Bertelsmann Direct Group China

One final point: many of our international managers stressed that when expat families invest the time and energy in adapting well to China, many may end up preferring to stay on in China rather than move back home. Ernst Behrens of Siemens has experienced wives not wanting to leave China after their husbands' postings had ended. "It's difficult to motivate the wives of expatriates to move from a place like Germany to a place like China, because their understanding about China isn't there," he says. "But once they make the decision and come along, it is often even more difficult to move the wives away from China." Behrens says many wives enjoy exploring China. "This is totally a new world open to them, a different culture. They take trips here while their husbands are working. Some of them are learning the language. In principle, we don't have a problem in settling expatriates here."

When Families *Don't* Adapt

While the assessment of life in China among our 20 top managers was largely positive, all acknowledged that some families don't adapt well—and when they don't, the result often is that the expatriate manager leaves his posting early. Victoria Hine, founding director in Shanghai of the counseling hotline LifeLine, is a specialist in addressing the problems expatriates experience in adapting to life in China (see the box opposite). She explains that one of the most common problems is that while the executives tend to enjoy their new work and living environment, the spouses and children may not. Says Hine: "For the husband, his life doesn't change much [after moving to China]. He is in contact with the same people, doing the same job, and dealing with highly educated, English-speaking Chinese people. Meanwhile, the wife may be dealing with very different people—the crowds in the supermarket, the uneducated maid and driver, strangers who don't speak English and who may not be used to foreigners."

Hine explains that when husband and wife live in very different circumstances, a division can occur. She points out that, before

LifeLine Shanghai

Long working hours, frequent travel, high-pressure–high-stakes jobs, culture clash, language barrier, homesickness. Nearly every expatriate executive and his or her family face these common sources of stress when living in China, at least to some degree. But although many expats suffer from similar problems, there are few places to turn to for help in coping with them.

It was with this need in mind that LifeLine Shanghai was launched in March 2004. The purpose was to offer the city's growing international community a free, confidential, and anonymous hotline providing easy access to emotional support and crisis intervention.

LifeLine Shanghai is accredited by LifeLine International, a not-for-profit organization (funded in part by the World Health Organization) which operates in 22 countries using 30,000 volunteers. In Shanghai, LifeLine operates through an Executive Committee of expatriates with expertise in counseling who oversee the training and screening of a corps of dozens of English-speaking telephone volunteers. Volunteers work in shifts to keep the hotline open from 10 AM to 10 PM daily.

Volunteer telephone operators are trained in "active listening" and are taught to "ask the right questions to help callers come up with their own solutions or work out their options," says LifeLine Shanghai Founding Director Victoria Hine. In some cases, operators refer callers to professional counselors or psychologists. The top three reasons for calling LifeLine Shanghai are:

1. *Work-related stress, including related problems such as alcoholism*
2. *Relationship problems*
3. *Intercultural issues, especially concerning intercultural marriages*

Who calls LifeLine? Callers cover a wide range of ages, from teenagers to seniors, and roughly half the callers are men, which surprised Hine and other hotline founders. Another surprise is that a growing number of calls (roughly 15%) come from English-speaking Chinese citizens, often seeking assistance in coping with cross-cultural relationships.

> "
> ***Executives may not understand the dissatisfaction of their spouses. He sees only that the spouse need not work, and has the support of the maid and driver. He may feel resentful, since he is working extremely long hours; the spouse may feel resentful, since she cannot work, while her partner's career is flourishing. The upshot is that postings in China can be hard on marriages."***
>
> **The authors,** *China CEO*

leaving the home country, the executive may have undergone a personality test to assess suitability for the job change; however, it is rare for a spouse and children to be assessed to determine whether they are suited to an overseas posting. Also, while the expat executive might face some new work stresses, most face relatively small changes in their lifestyle compared with their families. For the expat manager, Hine says, moving to China is often "not really a big deal." However, the wife and children will face a major change. "They have lost their whole lives, and they might not have had a say in the decision to move to China."

Hine points out that many spouses and children leave their support networks behind when they move to China. "Back home, you have your churches, your neighbors, schoolteachers—all that support network," she says. "But you move here and suddenly your closest friend is a person you met for five minutes at an AmCham [American Chamber of Commerce] coffee morning. The depth of relationships is very different."

Moving to China is often particularly difficult for dual income couples, because many "trailing spouses" cannot legally work in China. Thus, one partner—usually, the wife—suddenly finds herself in a strange country and culture, and without employment. As compensation for her losing her job, her husband's company may "throw a little money her way." But the extra income often doesn't make up for the change in lifestyle that occurs when she loses her career. Hine describes the mindset of many trailing spouses: "She was this busy woman, working full-time, and she gave up everything to come here." Such drastic changes in lifestyle often lead to dissatisfaction with life in China and general unhappiness. Says Hine, "Her self-esteem and confidence go down."

Making matters worse, the expatriate executive is likely to be far busier at work than he was back home. Suddenly, his responsibilities are greater, his hours are longer, and he travels more. One of our top executive interviewees explains how his social life has diminished during his years in China. "I almost don't have a private life," he says. "There's no work–life balance in [my company] in China because we are growing so fast. It is extremely demanding. I work very long hours. I have a negligible social life in China. I just don't have time. I don't take anything approaching the full amount of vacation time; in fact, I hardly take vacations."

The consultants we interviewed said that many spouses become lonely and resentful when faced with their partners' long working habits in China. This can cause a rift between the expat manager and his family, especially when he is enjoying working and living in China but his wife and children are not. In such a scenario, spouses can feel isolated and trapped.

Making matters worse, executives may not understand the dissatisfaction of their spouses. The executive (most often the husband) sees only that the spouse (most often the wife) need not work, and has the support of the maid and driver. He may feel resentful, since he is working extremely long hours; the spouse may feel resentful, since she cannot work, while her partner's career is flourishing. The upshot is that postings in China can be hard on marriages. LifeLine's Hine acknowledges that many marriages do suffer in China, and some dissolve, when the "drift" between the executive and the trailing spouse becomes too great.

Hine describes a typical scenario: "In her new home, the wife may suddenly find herself spending her day doing mundane domestic tasks that used to be simple and easy back in her home country. Job opportunities for the wives are very limited. So after trying to fill her day with meaningful activities, she may want and expect her husband to come home early and talk with her," she says. Also, wives typically struggle with the language barrier more in handling domestic tasks and problems. "These experiences can make her think China is a difficult place to settle in, while her husband thinks China is very interesting. So, whenever the wife complains, he wonders why. 'You have a maid to take care of the home, you have a guy who drives you anywhere you want, and you have a nice apartment. How can you not be happy?'" This difference in perception of China, if not addressed, can create a serious rift in a marriage.

A further added strain on expat marriages is the pressure for some executives to entertain clients in the evenings. Says Hine, "The expatriate may have to spend long hours drinking with

"

She was this busy woman, working full-time, and she gave up everything to come here. Her self-esteem and confidence go down."

Victoria Hine,
Founding Director,
LifeLine, Shanghai

"

[Teenagers] call and say, 'Dad travels a lot. Mom isn't dealing with it well. I feel bad for her. I'm having trouble with homework, but I don't want to burden Mom—she's already under pressure.'"

Victoria Hine,
Founding Director,
LifeLine, Shanghai

clients and sometimes has to go to KTV [karaoke bars], which is so popular in China. Their wives are not happy about this." Such practices keep executives away from home more than would be the case in the West, says Hine, and create added risk of affairs and divorce.

Transplanting Children to China

Relocating to China poses special challenges for children and teenagers. Victoria Hine says roughly 10% of calls to the LifeLine counseling hotline come from teenagers. One of the main reasons teenagers call is to seek advice on behalf of their parents. "They call and say, 'Dad travels a lot. Mom isn't dealing with it well. I feel bad for her. I'm having trouble with homework, but I don't want to burden Mom—she's already under pressure.'"

Another hardship for transplanted teenagers and children is the lack of stability and continuity that is common in expat communities where families may be relocated often. "Children make friends fast, but there isn't a lot of continuity," says Hine, adding that children can be devastated when friends, teachers, or coaches move away. "At home, they have a stable community. Here, they don't have that community." Then, too, for youngsters who have adapted to China, moving away if Dad or Mom is relocated can be deeply distressing.

Best Practices for Helping Expatriate Families Adapt to Living in China

Based on her work at LifeLine, Victoria Hine names five factors she considers critical if spouses are to relocate successfully to China: ability to make new friends, good communication with one's partner, good pre-move preparation, language learning, and involvement in social causes.

While employers can do little to assist with the first two qualities, they can—and should, says Hine—help with the last three. The good news for employers is that, in many cases, relatively simple efforts from the company, such as training classes or information guide-sheets, can go a long way toward helping spouses and children to adapt. Hine believes that international companies in China can reduce the failure rate of expat postings by taking proactive steps to better prepare executives and their families before relocating them to China. It is also important, Hine stresses, for companies to follow up with expat managers and their families after they settle in.

TIP **Assess candidates before sending them to China. Check their "soft" skills, such as their openness to, and ease of dealing with and trusting, people from a different culture, and their ability to change in order to adapt to a different environment.**

Hine's recommendations are borne out by Pricewaterhouse-Coopers research. In a recent 270-company global poll,[3] PWC urged companies to pay closer attention to the well-being of families when sending expats overseas. In the survey, employers were asked to rate the importance of different factors in a candidate's suitability for an international assignment. The five factors rated "least important" by companies were the most common reasons for assignment failure: inter-culture adaptability of the spouse/partner, children's educational needs, emotional resilience, partner/spouse career, and lifestyle suitability.

To follow are the strategies our 28 China hands advise companies to use to ensure that executives and their families adapt to life in China.

Strategy #1: Psychological Screenings for Expat Managers

The first tip from our interviewees is to screen carefully anyone being considered for an overseas assignment. Many of the companies we have profiled have established screening processes. For example, Du Pont conducts psychological screening for those under consideration for overseas postings. General Motors also began conducting psychological assessments prior to overseas assignments in the mid-1990s. GM China's Philip Murtaugh says the assessments help to determine if there is any danger of

3 Ibid.

TIP Interview the expatriate's family members before sending them to China. Ensure the spouse is equally open and flexible.

mis-adaptation. "I've found this very effective and I am encouraging our HR department to continue this," he says.

Murtaugh says the assessment tries to show whether a person is really prepared to accept a different culture, seeking to uncover any problem attitudes, such as a general distrust of people from other cultures or an inability to change in order to adapt to a different environment. "If [the applicant for overseas posting] has a strong bias against Chinese culture, why would you send him here?" says Murtaugh. He also stresses that companies should take seriously the results of such assessments; if conducted correctly, the tests can offer important warnings—a lesson he has learned first-hand. Murtaugh says that when the company reviewed the assessment results of two families who had failed to adjust to living in China, "there were a lot of danger signs appearing in the results."

Strategy #2: Assess the Families, Too

Another strategy suggested by the consultants interviewed, but still uncommon among the multinational companies we profiled, is to assess not only the expat manager being sent to China but also his or her spouse and children. LifeLine's Victoria Hine says companies rarely interview or assess the family members before sending them to China, an oversight she calls "silly."

Charles Browne of Du Pont China considers interviewing the spouse to be a critical step before sending an executive overseas. "One of the most important things is to ensure the spouse is equally open and flexible," he says. "If one is open and flexible and the other one isn't, the home situation will cause the posting to fail. I have seen many cases in which the family situation forces the expatriates to return home."

Strategy #3: Offer a Pre-move "Look-see"

Another method that international managers recommended before posting an executive to China is to send the family on a "look-see" visit. The trip can include visiting housing complexes, international schools, hospitals, recreation areas, and the China offices where the expat will work. Such a visit should help prepare the family for relocation, or confirm before the move if they aren't suited to life in China. Gary Dirks of British Petroleum China says, "We are pretty careful about whom to bring in in the first place. We ask them to come and look around first." L'Oréal's Paolo Gasparrini says it is especially helpful during the visit to have the executive and spouse meet other China-based expats, peers who can answer their "burning questions."

TIP Send the family on a "look-see" visit. The trip can include visiting housing complexes, international schools, hospitals, recreation areas, and the offices where the expat will work.

3M China also makes pre-move visits a standard step before moving a top-ranked expatriate. "When we bring over an expat from the U.S., I always make one point to them: 'Don't accept [the posting] so quickly. Come to China for a look-see for a week and bring your spouse," says Kenneth Yu, the company's China managing director. "Sometimes we underestimate the impact on the family when a family moves to a country like China. For the employee [the work environment isn't so different;] they switch on their PC, they are doing the same work. But you forget the spouse and children; they are living in a totally different environment, especially the spouse." Yu stresses the importance of giving spouses a vote in the decision to move. "If the spouse didn't have a say in the move, she or he could become very negative and that is the beginning of the end," Yu says. "If I can offer some advice to fellow CEOs in China: when you bring people to China, allow the employee and the spouse—especially the spouse—to participate in the decision-making about housing, schools. Don't make it a done deal."

TIP Provide China briefings or cultural training for both the managers and their families.

Strategy #4: Pre-move Preparation and Training

After screening applicants, many companies also provide China briefings or cultural training for both the manager being sent on assignment and his or her family. Victoria Hine of LifeLine considers pre-move training for families as critical to adaptation. She urges companies to help families prepare for life in China by providing useful, relevant information on the issues most critical

TIP Encourage expatriate families to participate in language training. Although they will rarely acquire fluency in Chinese, some knowledge of the language will give them a better understanding of China.

to them: choosing international schools, sourcing healthcare providers, finding community organizations to join or social causes to support, or investigating employment options.

Du Pont, General Motors, Bayer, and Sony, for example, offer such pre-move informational sessions before sending managers on assignment to China. GM's Philip Murtaugh says the training sessions allow those going on assignment to China to meet with GM employees who have recently returned from the country. They cover many aspects of living in China, from traffic conditions to practice in using chopsticks. He stresses that the training sessions are offered for the entire expat family.

Strategy #5: Language Classes

While international managers differed on whether language classes for expatriate executives and their families were essential, all agreed that knowledge of Chinese does help in adapting to China. Bayer China was among those recommending mandatory classes for those being relocated to China. "I strongly encourage anybody coming to China to participate in language courses. I think it is the key to understanding the characteristics of China," says the company's Elmar Stachels. "You can learn a lot through the language. It is the key to the culture and door-opener to personal relationships. ... We put [expats being sent to China] into inter-culture seminars and also language courses. I strongly recommend this as a requirement for the assignment."

Strategy #6: Offer Flexible Support and Customized Benefits

Recognizing both that every family is different and that many companies are under pressure to downsize expatriate packages, several of our interviewees recommended offering expatriate hires customized benefits where they (and their families) choose those perks that are of most benefit to them. In some cases, for example, companies give new hires a choice between company-paid annual trips home and fully funded tuition for children.

In addition, companies could ask relocating executives to choose what services will be of most use to them. If it is critically important that the spouse find employment during the assignment, for example, the MNC can focus its efforts there. If children have special needs, such as a strong interest in sports, the company can assist in sourcing schools with matching athletic facilities. If a spouse is interested in seeking a professional degree, for instance, the company can look into education programs in China or distance learning programs. The PWC report showed interest among expat families in job-finding for spouses/partners and in distance learning.

TIP **Customize benefits and allow expats and their families to choose those perks that are of most benefit to them.**

Strategy #7: Provide Ongoing Support for the Family

In her own study of 13 trailing spouses in Shanghai, Victoria Hine found that one of the key sources of unhappiness was a perceived lack of a support network. The spouses felt that while their husbands' needs were being carefully monitored and met by the company, their needs were forgotten. "A lot of times, it's just that the women want to feel they are considered in the equation. They want to be supported," she says. Hine found that simple actions on the part of companies could make spouses feel supported. "Many said that all they would have wanted was a phone call [from the company management] asking, 'How are you going?'" Others mentioned wishing for small personal perks that would have made the transition easier, such as subscriptions to magazines from home.

TIP **Pay attention to the spouses of expats living in China. Even simple actions will help to make them feel supported.**

Hine urges companies to set up a network for expat families to tap into, such as a company hotline. "Companies shouldn't just leave the family [to cope] alone," she says. "It's good if companies can call the family and ask what they could do to make their relocation better. For the family, they would appreciate someone calling to see that they are okay. They want to have the feeling that the company cares. People need the psychological support, even if it's only a telephone number."

Conclusion

When asked to assess their quality of life in China, our 20 top executive interviewees were overwhelmingly positive. Not one of them wished to leave China in the near future. Many said the quality of their work experience was the primary reason. Although most listed some difficulties in adjusting to life in China outside of work, for the most part they missed only minor aspects of life back home.

The expatriate counseling expert we interviewed cautioned that while many expatriate managers enjoy life in China, the situation can be more difficult for their families. Typically, the "trailing spouse," or partner, of an expat has given up her (or his) work and social network in order to move to China. The spouses and children may feel lonely and isolated, and often lack the support system that is available to the expatriate to help them bridge the cultural and language barriers. Dissatisfaction among family members is the primary reason for expatriate assignments failing or ending early.

Companies can take steps to ensure that both the expatriate professional and his or her family members adjust well to life in China.

SUMMARY OF TIPS

LIVING IN CHINA

1. Psychological Screenings for Expat Managers

Assess candidates before sending them to China. Check their "soft" skills, such as their openness to, and ease in dealing with and trusting, people from a different culture, and their ability to change in order to adapt to a different environment.

2. Assess the Families, Too

Interview the expatriate's family members before sending them to China. Ensure the spouse is equally open and flexible.

3. Offer a Pre-move "Look-see"

Send the family on a "look-see" visit. The trip can include visiting housing complexes, international schools, hospitals, recreation areas, and the offices where the expat will work.

4. Pre-move Preparation and Training

Provide China briefings or cultural training for both the managers and their families.

5. Language Classes

Encourage expatriate families to participate in language training. Although they will rarely acquire fluency in Chinese, some knowledge of the language will give them a better understanding of China.

6. Offer Flexible Support and Customized Benefits

Customize benefits and allow expats and their families to choose those perks that are of most benefit to them.

7. Provide Ongoing Support for the Family

Pay attention to the spouses of expats living in China. Even simple actions will help to make them feel supported.

Chapter 10
Conclusion

There is a saying among expatriate writers in China: "After you have been in China for a week, you can write a book. After you have been in China for a month, you can write a short article. After you have been in China for a year, you keep silent." The point is, the more you learn about China, the more you realize there is simply too much to learn.

Having gone through the long process of researching, writing, checking, revising, and editing *China CEO: Voices of Experience from 20 International Business Leaders*, we certainly understand the reasoning behind that saying. China is an extremely complex, fast-moving, confusing, and often-contradictory environment for international business executives. Happily for us, however, our task did not require that we become experts on succeeding in the China market; we set out only to interview experts and share their insights, anecdotes, and advice—a far more manageable goal.

The writing of *China CEO: Voices of Experience from 20 International Business Leaders* has been a long and arduous, but ultimately extremely rewarding, journey. Our task was to boil down a vast collection of professional and personal information shared by our expert sources on the ground in China—most of it fascinating, some of it surprising—and to present it fairly, accurately, and succinctly. It is our hope that the book will deliver to readers all of the rewards we derived from writing it.

Another challenge in completing the book was grappling with the full-throttle pace of change in China's business environment. In some cases, the operating environment changed between the time of the interview and our publication date. All the information had to be painstakingly updated and reviewed with each interviewee before the book went to press. Then, too, some of our group of high-powered CEOs were promoted or changed companies between the time of the interview and the publication date. Such is the whirlwind environment among MNCs in today's China.

The underlying message: the China story is only just beginning, and many fascinating twists in the plotline lie ahead. As one of our interviewees expressed it, his company's headquarters has "a laser light focused on China." We expect that laser light to continue shining on China in the coming decade. With its dual allure as the factory of the world and the world's largest consumer market, China must play a central part in the global strategies of the majority of MNCs. In the coming years, the world's most ambitious companies and most promising entrepreneurs will be growing in China, with China.

In this conclusion, we recap the key points uncovered in the book by reviewing the questions we set out to answer in our interviews with top executives at successful multinational companies in China, and with specialist consultants based in China who have focused their careers on advising MNCs and expatriate clients. In the pages that follow, we present the main findings as our interviewees answered:

- What skills do I need to manage business operations in China today?
- Should I adapt my management style to China?

- How can I recruit and retain top-grade professional personnel in China's highly competitive market?
- What is the secret to forming successful JV or business partnerships?
- How should I establish effective communication with corporate headquarters?
- How can my company attract China's newly demanding and fickle consumers?
- How should I prepare to fight China's rising domestic competitors in my field?
- What is the best strategy for safeguarding intellectual property rights?
- How can my company form good relations with the Chinese government?
- How can I ensure that I—and my spouse or partner and children—lead a satisfying life in China?

Our goal in this concluding chapter is to offer a reference for readers by boiling down the primary "take-aways" from each of the chapters of the book. To follow is a synopsis of the main themes covered, a listing of the selected quotes from CEOs and consultants, and a recap of the tips presented in each chapter.

Key Points From Chapter 1 **Qualities of a Successful International Manager in China**

Chapter 1 introduces the key professional and personal qualities that our China experts named as necessary for managing operations for an international company in China. After analyzing the rich descriptions shared by our interviewees, we organized their responses into three levels of critical success qualities—namely, professional qualities, personal global qualities, and personal

China-specific qualities. The concept of levels implies certain career progression in which solid professional qualities form the foundation. From that foundation, a candidate manager for any overseas assignment must also show certain personal qualities, including a "multicultural mindset" and a commitment to learn. Finally, interviewees described China-specific personal qualities, such as humility and strength, patience and speed, and *guanxi*-building, or Chinese-style networking.

Chapter 1: **Selected Quotes**

"If I had to focus on any one message [for incoming managers], I would emphasize that relationships are very important. ... It is really about people—relationships between people and the confidence they have in each other. China is even more that way than in Europe or in the States."

Dr. Gary Dirks, President and CEO, British Petroleum China

"When expatriates come to China, local people expect them to bring something—in terms of knowledge or skill—that they need but that is not available here. There is a strong expectation that the expatriate will do that."

Simon Keeley, Head, Hewitt Asia Leadership Center (HALC), Hewitt Associates

"We have very few first-time expats in China. ... Our expats almost always have at least 10 years' experience."

Alan Brown, Chairman, Unilever China

"The first international posting cannot be in China. You must choose someone who already has the skills to run this position. It must be someone with the necessary calm and balance to face all kinds of different things."

Paolo Gasparrini, President and Managing Director, L'Oréal China

"My belief is: if you pick the wrong person, no matter how much training you give, it won't work. You need to find a person who is very determined and can handle the ambiguity you find every day [in China]. ... You must be very open to new things, excited by new things—not someone who wants to preserve his own culture and identity."

Ekkehard Rathgeber, President, Bertelsmann Direct Group Asia

"You should try to understand the [foreign] culture and the language. Sometimes you get so tied up by the numbers and the projects that you lose sight of that. It is your understanding of customers and employees that really matters. Don't ignore that."

Charles Browne, President, Du Pont China

"Leadership in China means not forcing your point of view—not saying, 'I am the expert, I know everything. We do it this way worldwide.'"

Dr. Elmar Stachels, CEO, Bayer China

"If you simply adapt yourself to the local habits, then you lose a lot of advantages. You end up with something you didn't want."

Ekkehard Rathgeber, President, Bertelsmann Direct Group Asia

"When people have just arrived, they want to change things. But making quick moves in the wrong way isn't the right thing to do. You need to have patience, patience, patience. It is one of the clichés you hear in China, but it is true. You need to make a long-term strategy and stick to it."

Guy McLeod, President, Airbus China

"The pace of change is so fast [in China] relative to a lot of other places that, unless it is well articulated as an evolution, the corporate headquarters often find it hard to understand why the company had Strategy A in China and now has Strategy B."

Gordon Orr, Director, Shanghai offices, McKinsey & Company

Chapter 1: **Summary of Tips**

LEVEL 1: PROFESSIONAL QUALITIES

1. Technical and Corporate Expertise

Select people with a rock-solid professional background and an excellent knowledge of the company. Send your best personnel to China.

2. International Experience

A posting in China becomes vastly more manageable after an assignment in either another Asian location or another developing market, or both.

LEVEL 2: PERSONAL GLOBAL QUALITIES

1. Multicultural Mindset

When selecting an executive for an overseas posting, look for a person with an adventurous spirit, a sense of humor, and an open mind.

2. Commitment to Learn

Learn from those around you. Listen to your employees, JV partners, clients, and customers.

LEVEL 3: PERSONAL CHINA-SPECIFIC QUALITIES

1. Humility

Be humble and avoid using an authoritarian style. Influencing and coaching is the way to get the best out of your Chinese employees.

2. Strength

Be unyielding in defending core corporate values and culture.

3. Patience

Be patient; use a step-by-step approach in China, not a Big Bang approach.

4. Speed

Be flexible and quick. Stay well informed; the business environment in China is in constant and rapid flux.

5. *Guanxi*-building

Build your *guanxi* not only internally (with subordinates, peers, and superiors) but also externally (with clients, suppliers, and government officials). A strong *guanxi* network is a fundamental element in your success in China.

Key Points From Chapter 2 **Managing Chinese Employees**

The biggest single problem experienced by our interviewees across a wide spectrum of industries was lack of white-collar employees. On the one hand, China is seeing fast growth and high demand for professional staff among both international and domestic firms. On the other hand, the workforce suffers from a gap in mid-level managers because the 45-and-older generation suffered from a disrupted education and work experience during the Cultural Revolution. In addition, China's professionals today hold extremely high expectations for a fast-track career. All this adds up to difficulties for international managers in recruiting and retaining managers and technical specialists.

The central message from our interviewees in regards to addressing workforce shortages is: good *guanxi* between employers and employees can be an extremely useful tool in slowing the high turnover rate and creating a positive, effective work environment.

Chapter 2: **Selected Quotes**

"The Chinese—and Asians generally—enter into employment with a different understanding than we have in Europe. For us, the company certainly is important, but mainly as an employment base. To the Chinese, the company is more like a family. The idea is, 'I am giving myself to Siemens. Now you have to take care of me.'"

Dr. Ernst Behrens, President, Siemens China

"There is an incredibly capable workforce here. ... The key is being able to delegate. You have to be able to trust your subordinates. Local Chinese can do the job a lot better than anyone coming in. Let them do their job."

Guy McLeod, President, Airbus China

"We MNCs [in China] all kind of laugh because we have become the target not only of other MNCs but also of Chinese companies. There's such a need for great talent. Executive recruiters are very popular right now."

Steve Schneider, Chairman and CEO, General Electric China

"There are huge numbers of graduates each year, but there is a middle management level that you need."

John Wong, Managing Director Greater China, The Boston Consulting Group

"One of my frustrations is that when you hire smart people who graduated from Tsinghua University or Jiaotong University, they come to your desk and say, 'In three years, I want your job.' It took me 25 years to get here. There is such a thing as learning the business, and you don't do that in three years."

Philip Murtaugh, Chairman and CEO, General Motors China

"This [company-sponsored language class] is something our employees value and something we value. ... When they join my company, they say, 'Eli Lilly is looking out for my future.'"

Christopher Shaw, President, Eli Lilly China

"[Chinese professionals] come to foreign companies with very different expectations from what they expect at Chinese companies. They expect to be trained and developed. If you cannot help them to grow, you are going to lose them."

Helen Tantau, Senior Client Partner, Korn/Ferry

"Part of retention begins on Day 1 with managing expectations. A lot of folks [in China] have the desire to move to the president level in a short time."

Steve Schneider, Chairman and CEO, General Electric China

"People [in China] will work hard for the company because they like working for [their supervisor], because of their personal relationship with that person. This requires a very different management style. You need not only to care about the employees' work, but also care about their families and other personal issues."

Bryan Huang, Senior Vice President and China President, BearingPoint

"[Chinese] employees like to have a good relationship with the boss. You need to make sure you are not only a boss, but also a friend and a teacher."

Dominique de Boisseson, Chairman and CEO, Alcatel China

Chapter 2: **Summary of Tips**

1. The Right Compensation

- Performance-based pay may initially be a hard sell, but is often welcomed by young and ambitious Chinese professionals.
- While retaining people is not just a matter of money, managers in China must constantly track fast-rising salary standards in order to stay competitive.

2. Recruit Smart

Lack of competent staff can hinder growth. Smart companies hire and train in advance more people than they currently need, in order to build a reserve.

3. To Retain, Train

- Companies unable to recruit professional staff hire young staff and develop extra training programs. Offer new employees a "mini MBA" to get them up to speed with international standards and practices.
- Chinese employees tend to place a higher value on company-sponsored training than do counterparts elsewhere, making training programs a key retention "weapon."
- MNCs can use the promise of sending Chinese professionals on overseas work assignment or training sessions as an extremely valuable perk.

4. Offer a Fast Track

Career opportunities are the first motivation for Chinese employees to stay. You may need to promote people faster in China than you would elsewhere.

5. Promotion Problems: Loss of Face

- Be aware of loss of face if one team member is promoted but another is not. Objective promotion rules, and personal attention to them, will ease the problem.
- The hardest thing to manage is Chinese employees' high career expectations. Focus on your top talent and high potentials. Show them a clear career path with no glass ceiling for Chinese professionals. Remember that job titles are extremely important.

6. Building Employer–Employee *Guanxi*

- Chinese employees have to feel that their supervisor supports and looks after them. They must feel that their workplace is a second family.
- In China, people work for a person, not for a company. Thus, when a manager leaves a company, their staff members will sometimes quit as well, either to stay with their previous supervisor or to avoid working with a new supervisor.

Key Points From Chapter 3 **Working With Business Partners**

Managing a joint venture or business partnership is like managing a marriage. The first decision for MNCs in China is to decide whether to form a JV or operate as a wholly foreign-owned enterprise. Regulations now allow international companies to invest as WFOEs in more sectors. Thus, the first step is to be clear on current regulations. While most of our interviewees recommend forming a WFOE if legally possible, all acknowledged that JVs can offer significant benefits, especially in providing expertise in negotiating with government, detailed market knowledge, and established operations.

Chapter 3: **Selected Quotes**

"In choosing a JV partner, some people may want [first] to make sure the partner has business experience. But if I am the person choosing, trust is very important. This basically means that we can share the same vision. Character is very important—more than business experience. A JV is like a marriage."
Seiichi Kawasaki, Director and President, Sony China

"If you are working in a highly regulated industry, then JV partners are almost essential. If you are working in a highly de*regulated industry, they can be a damn nuisance."*
Alan Brown, Chairman, Unilever China

"If you team with a JV company with distribution and an existing operations base, you get started right away. [On the other hand], in a WFOE, you call the shots. In a JV, it takes longer to get things done."
Kenneth Yu, Managing Director, 3M China

"If we were doing it now from scratch, we would still take local partners. The Coke business is a local business. We need a local partner. ... They smooth the way to getting things done with the local government. They get rid of some of the red tape."
Paul Etchells, President, Coca-Cola China

"In China, when we establish a new JV, we share the investment but never the management. You cannot have two bosses."
Jean-Luc Chereau, President, Carrefour China

"The key to success for partnerships is the alignment of your strategic interests, your ability to maintain the alignment over a significant period of time, and making sure your partner can contribute to those strategic interests."
Dr. Gary Dirks, President and CEO, British Petroleum China

"You have to be sensitive to cultural mores of the country you are working in. Some managers take a bark-and-bite approach to management, but that method doesn't go down very well here. … People who work with you have to understand that you mean what you say, but you have to say it with a smile."
Norman Givant, Shanghai Office Managing Partner, China Practice Group, Freshfields Bruckhaus Deringer law offices

"This country is built on the idea of: 'Don't do anything on your own.' If you look back 15 years, thinking was detrimental to your health."
Volkmar Ruebel, General Manager, Hilton Shanghai

Chapter 3: **Summary of Tips**

TO JV, OR NOT TO JV?

1. **Know the Regulations**
   The first task for any newcomer is to fully investigate how the regulations pertain to your sector, your company, and the region of China you seek to enter. What was true six months ago may no longer be valid today.

2. **The Case Against JVs**
   Avoid JVs unless you are required to form one or are certain of the benefits. WFOEs are generally simpler, faster, and more efficient to operate.

3. The Case For JVs

Use JVs when the local partner offers connections with authorities and market knowledge that a WFOE would be unable to achieve on its own.

PARTNER SELECTION, PARTNERSHIP TERMS

1. Choose a Weak, Silent Partner

When regulations force you to form a JV in which the partnership adds limited value to the business, choose a weak partner that you can easily control.

2. Choose an Active, Value-added Partner

Companies that choose to form a JV today can look for Chinese partners that can contribute toward the company goals by bringing insight into the local business environment, established operations, a strong client base, and skill at negotiating with government.

3. Know Your Partner

Assess a potential JV partner by making on-site visits, requesting detailed financial and operating records, and gathering input from industry insiders.

4. Align Your Goals

It is critical that you and your partner agree on goals and priorities. The problem of "same bed, different dreams" has led many JV partners to divorce.

5. Set the Correct "Marriage" Terms

When forming a JV, it is best to create the organization from scratch to avoid bringing old mindsets to the new entity. Steer clear of 50–50 partnerships. Consider JV alternatives such as a merger or acquisition.

MANAGING THE PARTNER-TO-PARTNER RELATIONSHIP

1. Mutual Trust

Build a sense of trust within the JV by stressing your

long-term commitment to China, and by acknowledging the value which each side brings to the partnership.

2. Good Communications

When communicating with your Chinese partner, remember to preserve their "face." Sometimes indirect communication is more effective.

3. Effective Decision-making

Encourage Chinese colleagues to voice their opinions. Create an environment in which honest mistakes are accepted.

4. Shared Ethics and Standards

While you must adapt to Chinese business practices, don't compromise your corporate culture, values, and ethical standards.

Key Points From Chapter 4 **Communicating With Headquarters**

One of the critical challenges for the head of the China operations is communicating with their headquarters in the home country. Not only are China managers geographically distant from their supervisors (out of sight, out of mind), but those at corporate headquarters may have little understanding of the China business environment and little appreciation of the challenges and the pace of activity. These gaps can lead to slow decision-making processes and lost business opportunities. For these reasons, the goal of many top executives we interviewed is to increase autonomy for the China operations, thus improving efficiency of operations.

At the China operations of the 20 MNCs we profiled, many

have passed through (or are passing through) development stages similar to the development of a human being: infancy, adolescence, and adulthood. The final stage is reached when the local China operations achieve the status of strategic partner to the headquarters.

Chapter 4: **Selected Quotes**

"Our CEO and the whole corporate leadership have had a laser light focused on China during the last 24 months. It's one of the few countries nowadays whose economy doesn't show signs of slowing down."
Charles Browne, President, Du Pont China

"Our headquarters realize that China is a very big market. Because of this, the expectation tends to be built very high. But China is going to be a very long-term play. China is about potential, potential, and potential."
Stanley Wong, Chief Executive, China, Standard Chartered

"Problems that seem urgent to an international manager in China can seem unimportant to the upper management in Pittsburg or Paris."
The authors, *China CEO*

"[Westerners] think of China as being still in the bicycle [era]."
Jun Tang, President, Microsoft China

"The current 'China fancy' in the West has not translated into a deep understanding of market conditions, business culture, or economic development."
The authors, *China CEO*

"In Europe or the States, 'yes' means 'yes,' so we can work together toward a common goal. Here, 'yes' doesn't always mean 'yes,' and 'no' doesn't always mean 'no.' ... One piece of advice I give people about China: everything is difficult, but everything is possible."
Guy McLeod, President, Airbus China

"In our current environment—the market-oriented economy—you have to react fast. But the time needed for communications [with headquarters] can be very long."

Dr. Bryan Huang, Senior Vice President and President Greater China, BearingPoint

"You cannot say 'yes' all the time. Sometimes you have to discuss and sometimes you have to say 'no.' It is my job; I am paid for this. I have to be listened to. You cannot escape from the fact that the [China leader] is important."

Paolo Gasparrini, President and Managing Director, L'Oréal China

Chapter 4: **Summary of Tips**

1. Head-office Commitment to China

Try to establish support for China operations among the top management at corporate headquarters. Having two or three top decision-makers take an interest in your operations will make things much easier for you.

2. Corporate Clout for the China Head

Appoint a China top executive who is well-respected and well-connected at headquarters. Improve efficiency by giving autonomy to the China operations wherever possible.

3. Bring China to the Headquarters

Bring people from headquarters to China regularly. This will further their understanding of business conditions and your operations.

4. Shift Power to China

It is essential that corporations give those on the ground in China strategic capability, not only operational capability. Corporate headquarters must recognize the fast growth and rising importance of their China operations.

Key Points From Chapter 5 **Facing Competitors**

As one of our interviewees explained, China is a "dog fight." Another described China as the "most competitive" market in the world. MNCs find all of their familiar global rivals in China and some may have been there for up to 20 years. Meanwhile, domestic competitors are leaping ahead in quality, sophistication, and speed. Many international companies are now squeezed by local players adept at replicating their best product features while slashing selling prices. Survival skills for China now are innovation, speed, flexibility, marketing, and careful tracking of consumer preferences.

Chapter 5: **Selected Quotes**

"China is full of contradictions. Here we are in a socialist country, but it's one of the most competitive societies on earth."
Simon Keeley, Head of the Hewitt Asia Leadership Center (HALC), Hewitt Associates China

"All the big guys are [in China], right down the list. For the international players, this is a dog fight."
Dr. Gary Dirks, President and CEO, British Petroleum China

"I can say this is the most competitive market in the world. There are a lot of international companies here—Japanese companies, European companies—plus local companies. They all try to compete in China."
Seiichi Kawasaki, Director and President, Sony China

"Here, we have the combination of local companies that are globalizing more and more, and global players that are localizing in China."
Dr. Elmar Stachels, CEO, Bayer China

"Prices have moved down for foreign products and up for local products—so they are coming closer to each other. There has been an extremely painful period of readjustment."
Alan Brown, Chairman, Unilever China

"These are the new Chinese companies—with advanced products and global competitiveness."
Dominique de Boisseson, Chairman and CEO, Alcatel

Chinese companies are trying as fast as they can to be like MNCs. So, the distinctions are going to blur."
John Wong, Managing Director Greater China, The Boston Consulting Group

Chapter 5: **Summary of Tips**

1. Pick Winnable Battles
For MNCs targeting the China market, there are some battles not worth fighting. Avoid competing against domestic cost-based products.

2. Innovate
The best survival strategy is to keep moving: continually upgrade to stay ahead of competitors.

3. But Beware of Over-innovation
Avoid over-engineered products. Offer quality and functionality that matches demand, but don't lose sight of cost.

4. Don't Fight, Merge
If you can't beat 'em, join 'em (or buy 'em).

Key Points From Chapter 6 **Battling Intellectual Property Rights Infringers**

IPR infringement is a huge industry in China with a long history. While China has recently improved its intellectual property rights protection laws, especially since joining the WTO in 2001, enforcement remains weak. Nearly all MNCs in China experience piracy of their products. (Among our profiled companies, only Airbus was exempt.) Of particular concern is piracy of pharmaceutical and chemical products. Enforcement suffers partly because the rule of law remains shallowly rooted in China and because piracy is a key source of economic activity in many parts of the nation. Challenges faced by MNCs include: lack of government support (especially at the local level); the rewards outweigh the risks for many infringers; and the growing sophistication and internationalization of many piracy operations. China's IPR infringement industries will likely die down with economic development (as has been the case in other developing countries). The true key to improving enforcement will likely come when more Chinese businesses begin fighting to protect their own intellectual property rights.

Chapter 6: **Selected Quotes**

"The more successful you are [in China], the more IPR issues you will suffer from."
David Chang, CEO, Philips China

"Each of the 20 multinational companies profiled in this book, with the exception of Airbus, has suffered directly from at least some degree of IPR infringement in China."
The authors, *China CEO*

"During the past 20 years of economic development in China, the rule of thumb seems to be: anything that can be copied has been, and anything that cannot be copied, has been attempted."
The authors, *China CEO*

"In the period of 1949 to 1979, the Chinese Communist Party wasn't terribly interested in the law and courts. What they were interested in was the exercise of government policy and power."
Norman Givant, Shanghai Office Managing Partner,
China Practice Group, Freshfields Bruckhaus Deringer

"The problem is that a police officer has to execute the court decisions. The [police and IPR infringers] still have their network; they rely on one another."

David Chang, CEO, Philips China

"We take action whenever we are aware of [IP infringement]. But shortly afterward, it all starts up again. These manufacturing operations are very small, and are located in all sorts of obscure places in this huge country."

Paul Etchells, President, Coca-Cola Beverages China

"You see DVDs and VCDs anywhere, everywhere. You can buy them by the hundreds and thousands."

Ekkehard Rathgeber, President, Bertelsmann Direct Group Asia

"My people are poor; people in western China are making RMB200 (US$24) per month. Now a bunch of foreigners want me to protect their Gucci handbags? I couldn't care less."

Ekkehard Rathgeber (explaining the mindset of many rural police officers), President, Bertelsmann Direct Group Asia

"You cut off one counterfeiter and two spring up in his place. Sometimes, they are the same persons with a different name. And sometimes, they may close their factory, give the equipment to their brothers-in-law, and open a new facility in the village down the road."

Norman Givant, Office Managing Partner, China Practice Group, Freshfields Bruckhaus Deringer

"When we became cooperative and patient, [the government] listened to us. Gradually, they became cooperative as well. Now they have even become proactive, approaching QBPC members to see if we can help with difficult cases."

Jack Chang, Chairman, Quality Brand Protection Committee, China Association of Enterprises with Foreign Investment

Chapter 6: **Summary of Tips**

EXTERNAL MEASURES

1. Work With the Government

When approaching the Chinese government for support in protecting IPR, avoid taking a confrontational stance; seek to help the government in its work to fight infringement.

2. Join Forces With Others

Join forces with other businesses and associations in the IPR battle to share best practices and present a common front to the government.

INTERNAL MEASURES

1. Dedicate Resources

Dedicate resources and personnel to protecting IPR in-house. Build awareness and support for IP protection throughout the company.

2. Focus on Prevention

Top executives should personally convey the importance of IP protection to employees and to the government. Conduct company-wide IP audits to detect vulnerable areas.

3. Use Contractual Safeguards

Be extremely selective in giving employees or business partners access to core technologies. Be clear on the regulatory tools available to employers in protecting against employee misuse of critical IP information.

4. Protect Sensitive Technologies

Create safety mechanisms to limit employee or partner access to core technologies. In some cases, companies may not want to bring critical technology to China.

Key Points From Chapter 7 **Winning Over Chinese Consumers**

China's consumers, while gaining rapidly in wealth, especially in urban areas, have gained a reputation among MNCs as tough customers—sophisticated, demanding, price-conscious, and fickle. Many have unreasonable expectations of perfection when purchasing foreign brands. Another serious challenge for MNCs: China represents many markets, not one. Across the nation, consumer groups vary widely in demographics, educational background, and international exposure. China is a mosaic of distinct cultures and languages. MNCs must therefore adapt their offerings and marketing strategies to the diversity they face. In addition, international firms must constantly monitor regulatory changes in their industry, and must battle a number of logistical difficulties in reaching consumers. The best solution to reaching Chinese consumers may be to invest in domestic R&D.

Chapter 7: **Selected Quotes**

"It is impossible to sell second-rate technology in China. Chinese want the best. China is often the first place we introduce a new technology. Chinese are very demanding customers."
Dominique de Boisseson, Chairman and CEO, Alcatel China

"A lot of people come to China assuming that Chinese customers' expectations are low. What I've found out is that consumer expectations are much higher in China than in other countries, such as Japan. My impression is that Chinese consumers are among the most sophisticated in the world."
Philip Murtaugh, General Manager and CEO, General Motors China

"The world's most populous nation now offers a consumer base that is not only vast but also wealthy, worldly, and willing to spend."
The authors, *China CEO*

"Right now, and for the next 20 years, China is probably going to be one of our largest customer bases. China is a very important part of our strategy."

Steve Schneider, Chairman and CEO, General Electric China

"The rate at which modern [retail] trade is developing in China is without parallel. It has never happened before, not even in Europe."

Alan Brown, Chairman, Unilever China

"The expectation of the picture quality of the color TV is very high in China. It may not even be so high in Japan. And for product design, [Chinese consumers] expect much more. The Chinese consumer is very demanding. We have to listen to them carefully."

Seiichi Kawasaki, Director and President, Sony China

"Chinese customers have very high expectations. They are very demanding on quality. ... They are also superb negotiators on price."

Charles Browne, President, Du Pont China

"Sometimes products are over-engineered [for the China market]. People won't pay for things they don't need."

Kenneth Yu, Managing Director, 3M China

"You can see the whole value-chain in China: underdeveloped, developing, developed. ... For a global company to fully tap into the strengths of China, you have to adapt to different economic stages in different geographical areas. That is a big challenge."

David Chang, CEO, Philips China

"Every new company that comes in is bombarding the consumer [with product]. And the Chinese consumer is trying everything that is out there."

John Wong, Managing Director Greater China, The Boston Consulting Group

"[Market research requires] frequent refreshing because of the pace of change in the marketplace and the volatility of consumer behavior."

Gordon Orr, Director, Shanghai office, McKinsey & Company

Chapter 7: **Summary of Tips**

1. Localize Smart
While retaining the international image and power of your brand, localize your products to suit local tastes and preferences.

2. Localize Marketing
Given the vast differences in geography, climate, history, and even culture—in China, marketing programs must vary as well.

3. Choose Your Destination
Demographics are changing rapidly across parts of China. Many cities are gaining rapidly in wealth and consumerism. Watch the second- and third-tier cities as potential new markets.

4. R&D in China, for China
R&D in China, for China, is the ultimate method for effectively understanding and serving domestic customers.

Key Points From Chapter 8 **Negotiating With the Chinese Government**

The ability to negotiate successfully with the government remains a critical success factor for any MNC in China. Because China's legal system remains young and shallowly rooted, companies must form close and positive relationships with many government entities monitoring their operations. China's complex administrative system requires companies to maneuver through a maze of central, provincial, and local government entities, sometimes with clashing or contradictory interests.

In building good *guanxi* at all levels of government, managers (and company personnel) must also avoid corrupt practices and must maintain the corporate code of conduct. Working with older-generation officials schooled in the state-run system is particularly difficult. Other challenges include lack of enforcement of new laws and regulations, an ineffective court system, inconsistent interpretation of laws, and delays in government procedures.

Chapter 8: **Selected Quotes**

"A traditional saying in China is: 'No one man can approve a project, but any one man can veto it.' You have to interface with officials at various levels of government to make sure that they understand what your project is and that they buy into it."

Norman Givant, Shanghai Office Managing Partner, China Practice Group, Freshfields Bruckhaus Deringer

"I consider China to be a very complex country because you have to deal with different levels [of government]. When you talk about government, you have the central government, the provincial government, and the local government. According to my experience, we need to have good relationships with at least two levels—the local level and the central level."

Jean-Luc Chereau, President, Carrefour China

"China is still in a transition period from a planned economy to a market economy. Now, they are in-between. Since they are in-between, there are a lot of gray areas."

David Chang, CEO, Philips China

"The real problem is that when you find a socialist command economy interfacing with a capitalist market mentality, the potential for misunderstanding from both sides is enormous."

Norman Givant, Shanghai Office Managing Partner, China Practice Group, Freshfields Bruckhaus Deringer

"There has been a dramatic shift in government thinking on economics and the importance of investment and profitability. Now the

government spends a lot of time talking to you about profitability."
Philip Murtaugh, Chairman and CEO, General Motors China

"The Chinese government is really trying to make foreign investors comfortable with the environment. ... China is trying to grow its economy. In order to maintain the GDP growth rate at 7% or 8%, the government needs a lot of help from foreign investors."
Jun Tang, President, Microsoft China

"Very often, approvals are subject to official interpretation. So it can slow everything down if you don't have good relationships [with the government] in China."
Stanley Wong, CEO, Standard Chartered China

"There are plenty of laws, and they now really design laws that make sense and are in vogue with the times. ... So, the ultimate question comes down to this: once a decision is made, how is it enforced? That's where the questions reside today: the ability to enforce the winning if you win something."
Steve Schneider, Chairman and CEO, General Electric China

"Each province implements legal guidelines in a slightly different way. And that slightly different way could have significant impact."
Christopher Shaw, President, Eli Lilly China

"It's very simple: get a great local to do the work for you. The Chinese have been working with the bureaucracy forever. The only way to function is through the right people."
Alan Brown, Chairman, Unilever China

"This isn't one government; it's a hundred governments. You need to make sure all the potential stakeholders are well informed about your intentions, make them feel they are respected. This will help your process later on a lot."
David Chang, CEO, Philips China

"The most important thing is to be sure that what you are trying to do is perceived to be in the interest of some important political entity.

If no particular government entity is excited about the project, if no significant Chinese partner thinks it's a good idea, then you can be sure that it's not going to be easy."
Dr. Gary Dirks, President and CEO, British Petroleum China

Chapter 8: **Summary of Tips**

1. Involve the Top Executive
Chinese authorities prefer to deal directly with the top executive of the organization, for "face" reasons. Be ready to dedicate a significant part of your time to dealing with them.

2. Hire a Local With Government Expertise
Hiring Chinese nationals with connections and expertise in government relationship-building is crucial for the success of your company.

3. Understand the Government Mindset
Be appreciative of the government's effort in driving the transition. It's better to project a cooperative attitude, than a confrontational one.

4. Win Support at All Levels of Government
Ensure that you show respect to all the different levels of the administration by keeping them well informed of your plans.

5. Do Your Homework, and Follow the Rules
Be clear about the actual administrative process. Identify the right person in the right department at the right time. Your team of experts is critical for this task.

6. Stand Your Ground in Negotiations
Don't be afraid of stating what you want, clearly and specifically.

Key Points From Chapter 9 **Living in China**

When asked to assess their quality of life in China, our 20 top executive interviewees were overwhelmingly positive. Not one of them wished to leave China in the near future. Many said the quality of their work experience was the primary reason. Although most listed some difficulties in adjusting to life outside of work in China, for the most part they missed only minor aspects of their life back home.

The expatriate counseling expert we interviewed cautioned that while many expatriate managers enjoy life in China, the situation can be more difficult for their families. Typically, the "trailing spouse" or partner of an expat has given up her (or his) work and social network in order to move to China. The wives and children may feel lonely and isolated, and often lack the support system given to the expatriate to help them bridge cultural and language barriers. Dissatisfaction among family members is the primary reason for expatriate assignments failing or ending early.

Companies can take steps to ensure that both the expatriate professional and his or her family members adjust well to life in China.

Chapter 9: **Selected Quotes**

"Expatriates don't want to leave China, because this is the greatest potential market in the universe. Who wants to go to the U.S. right now? Who wants to go to Europe? Even the Chinese managers at this point, they don't want to go abroad either; they want to be in China."
Helen Tantau, Senior Client Partner, Korn/Ferry International China

"For the husband, his life doesn't change much [after moving to China]. He is in contact with the same people, doing the same job, and dealing with highly educated, English-speaking Chinese people. Meanwhile, the wife may be dealing with very different people—the

crowds in the supermarket, the uneducated maid and driver, strangers who don't speak English and who may not be used to foreigners."
Victoria Hine, Founding Director, LifeLine expatriate support hotline in Shanghai

"I accepted the position for no more than three years in Asia. Now, I have been here for 13 years. My wife and I are very happy in this place. I am willing to stay here for a long time."
Jean-Luc Chereau, President, Carrefour China

"Among the 20 country managers and China directors interviewed, not one had set a date for returning home. Even more surprisingly, no one—from the head of GE China to the heads of Unilever and Sony—said they hoped to leave China in the near future."
The authors, *China CEO*

"When I go back to Europe, by the fourth day, I start to want to come back to China."
Paolo Gasparrini, President, L'Oréal China

"So many people want to come to China that usually you don't have any trouble [recruiting expatriates]. I can find all I want."
Dr. Gary Dirks, President and CEO, British Petroleum China

"Globally, the failure rate [of expatriate assignments] tends to be much higher than companies expect. ... I think companies are now paying more attention to the soft skills, like patience and not tending to blame China for everything."
Simon Keeley, Head of the Hewitt Asia Leadership Center (HALC), Hewitt Associates China

"We have infrastructure such as Japanese schools in Shanghai. This is an important part, but it's not everything. I think [adaptation] is very much related to personal character."
Seiichi Kawasaki, Director and President, Sony China

"In the beginning, we both saw a problem emerging. The day I arrived, for me it was work 12 to 14 hours a day. For [my wife], she had left her job and her friends, and we were living in a remote place, a huge cold

house. It was really, basically, a nightmare."
Ekkehard Rathgeber, President, Bertelsmann Direct Group China

"Executives may not understand the dissatisfaction of their spouses. He sees only that the spouse need not work, and has the support of the maid and driver. He may feel resentful, since he is working extremely long hours; the spouse may feel resentful, since she cannot work, while her partner's career is flourishing. The upshot is that postings in China can be hard on marriages."
The authors, *China CEO*

"She was this busy woman, working full-time, and she gave up everything to come here. Her self-esteem and confidence go down."
Victoria Hine, Founding Director, LifeLine, Shanghai

"[Teenagers] call and say, 'Dad travels a lot. Mom isn't dealing with it well. I feel bad for her. I'm having trouble with homework, but I don't want to burden Mom—she's already under pressure.'"
Victoria Hine, Founding Director, LifeLine, Shanghai

Chapter 9: **Summary of Tips**

1. **Psychological Screenings for Expat Managers**
   Assess candidates before sending them to China. Check their "soft" skills, such as their openness to, and ease in dealing with and trusting, people from a different culture, and their ability to change in order to adapt to a different environment.

2. **Assess the Families, Too**
   Interview the expatriate's family members before sending them to China. Ensure the spouse is equally open and flexible.

3. **Offer a Pre-move "Look-see"**
   Send the family on a "look-see" visit. The trip can include

visiting housing complexes, international schools, hospitals, recreation areas, and the offices where the expat will work.

4. Pre-move Preparation and Training

Provide China briefings or cultural training for both the managers and their families.

5. Language Classes

Encourage expatriate families to participate in language training. Although they will rarely acquire fluency in Chinese, some knowledge of the language will give them a better understanding of China.

6. Offer Flexible Support and Customized Benefits

Customize benefits and allow expats and their families to choose those perks that are of most benefit to them.

7. Provide Ongoing Support for the Family

Pay attention to the spouses of expats living in China. Even simple actions will help to make them feel supported.

Appendix
Research Methodology

The purpose of this book is to identify and address the primary challenges facing the presidents and managing directors of multinational companies operating in today's China. Our research method was to go directly to the source, by interviewing 20 international top executives from Fortune 500 corporations operating successfully in China. We chose interviewees from a wide range of fields, from cars to cosmetics, software to supermarkets. (See the Introduction for a full listing of interviewees, with titles.)

We balanced these 20 first-hand, industry-specific interviews with a second series of discussions, this time with eight business consultants. These experts have made it their profession to guide foreign executives through the Chinese business environment. The interviewees came from a variety of disciplines—law, human resources, business development strategy. The firms and organizations represented were (in alphabetical order): BearingPoint; The Boston Consulting Group; Freshfields Bruckhaus Deringer; Hewitt Associates Consulting; Korn/Ferry International; LifeLine

Shanghai; McKinsey & Company; and Quality Brands Protection Committee of the China Association of Enterprises with Foreign Investment.

Information, impressions, and specific quotes from these interviews form the basis for this book. The interviews guided us in creating a structure—the "bones" of the book, chapter by chapter—as well as providing the "meat" of each specific chapter.

An interview is only as good as the questions asked. Therefore, a great deal of thought and effort went into the drafting of our questions. While there was room for flexibility in each interview, and the discussion inevitably touched on specific issues special to particular companies, we followed a fairly structured format with each international manager profiled. In drafting the questions, we called upon our own extensive experience in the Chinese business environment, drawing upon our skills as a professor of management and a business journalist, respectively.

In interviewing international managers, our questions covered six main categories:

- Personal background, career history
- Setting up operations in China
- Adapting one's management style to China
- Adapting the business to China
- Tackling the Chinese market
- Living in China

For the eight professional consultants interviewed, our questions were by necessity tailored to their specific areas of specialization. Since these experts make it their business to advise clients on how to succeed in China, we asked them to share their battle-tested advice with us, and to offer their objective opinions on the concerns expressed and recommendations made by the international managers interviewed. The consultant interviews were composed of three blocks of questions:

- Scope of their work in China
- Primary concerns of their MNC clients and their specific advice on these issues
- Predictions as to how the concerns of MNCs in China will change in the future

The final step in the writing process for each chapter was to analyze the messages relayed by our interviewees, then organize the key points into a useful model. Our goal is that each chapter provides a practical "roadmap" to guide managers who need to address specific issues in China, from motivating local employees, to negotiating with the government, to winning-over Chinese consumers.

Sample Interview Questions

We developed the following interview questions based both on our experiences as a China-based professor of management and a China-based business journalist, and on the simple desire to hear answers to the questions we expected to be most interesting and pressing for readers. Although specific questions were added depending on the interviewee's industry or personal areas of expertise, all interviews included the basic questions listed below.

1. Managing in China

- Please briefly explain your international career track so far.
- What are your main responsibilities as President of XXX China?
- Have you changed your management style in China? If so, why?
- What are the 3 or 4 most important qualities of a successful CEO of an MNC in China?
- Suppose you are promoted out of China. What "do's" and "don'ts" would you tell your successor?

2. Setting up operations in China

- What is your advice in developing relationships with the government, successfully obtaining licenses and approvals?
- Has your company had difficulties with contracts being honored, laws being enforced?
- Has your company had trouble with intellectual property rights protection in China?
- Do you recommend setting up a wholly owned company or a JV? Why?

3. Adapting the business to China

- Briefly explain the relationship between your China operations and your regional and worldwide headquarters.
- How do you reconcile country culture with the corporate culture of your company?
- What challenges do you face in human resources? Are you localizing in China?

4. Tackling the Chinese market

- Are your competitors in China local or global companies? Is the mix changing?
- What is your current business strategy in China? What are the biggest challenges to meeting your goals?
- How important is China to your company's overall global corporate strategy?

5. Living in China

- How has your family adapted to life in China? What challenges have they faced? What is your advice on helping spouses and children to adapt?
- How does your after-work life in China differ from that back home?
- Does your company provide support for foreign managers and their families in adapting to China? What would you do differently in hindsight?
- What are your plans after China? Do you anticipate any difficulty adapting to returning home or to your next assignment?

Index